THE CELL BLOCK PRESENTS...

JAILHOUSE PUBLISHING
FOR MONEY, POWER, AND FAME!

Published by: THE CELL BLOCK™

THE CELL BLOCK
P.O. Box 1025
Rancho Cordova, CA 95741

Corrinks: info@thecellblock.net
Instagram: @mikeenemigo
Facebook.com/thecellblockofficial

Copyright© 2020 MIKE ENEMIGO

Cover design by Mike Enemigo

Send comments, reviews, or other business inquiries:
info@thecellblock.net
Visit our website: thecellblock.net

All rights reserved. No part of this publication may be reproduced, stored in retrieval system, or transmitted, in any form or by any means, electronic, mechanical, photocopying, recording or otherwise, without the prior permission of the publisher; exceptions are made for brief excerpts used in published reviews.

PRAISE FOR MIKE ENEMIGO & THE CELL BLOCK

"This author has a unique voice and his versatile pen is refreshing. Mike has my stamp of approval." – JaQuavis Coleman, *New York Times* Best Selling Author

"Mike Enemigo is the truth. An emerging writer who plies his trade inside the belly of the beast. A convict author of epic proportions, reaching out to the world with his pen as he fights an unjust system." – Seth Ferranti, writer/producer of *White Boy* (STARZ)

"My man Mike represents the west coast like a literary OG! I respect his grind and pen game! Look out for The Cell Block!" – Dutch

"Mike Enemigo's work is raw, authentic, and powerful. It's made all the more remarkable by the fact that Mike's books are written from inside a California prison. His work gives hope to incarcerated writers everywhere struggling to get their voices heard." – Kevin Deutsch, Award-winning True Crime Writer, Author of *Pill City: How Two Honor Roll Students Foiled the Feds and Built a Drug Empire*

"Mike [Enemigo] and I have corresponded for several years; he is intelligent and offers a unique perspective into prison life. Despite his restrained circumstances, he has managed to produce more helpful advice than anyone Outside. Quite an Achievement! People can use any of his reference books with confidence because he does his homework. He has developed into a fine writer; one any reader can follow and understand. He is committed to rehabilitation for himself and those he is helping." – Dr. Terri LeClercq, *School of Law, University of Texas*

"[Mike Enemigo is] proof that success is still possible after incarceration." – *The Huffington Post*.

"Mike has taken his negative situation [prison] and turned it into a positive by writing about his experiences and publishing over twenty books from his prison cell. A perfect example of the hustle we represent at *Street Money Magazine.*" – i Hustle, *Street Money Magazine*

"Mike is the only one nailing down this street lit authentically. Salute to brudda brudda." – Snubbz Zilla, CA Mozzy

"Mike Enemigo's books are tremendously popular and among our most requested titles." – Pietro Bartoli, Books Beyond Bars

"Thank you for using your platform to help dudes get their stories heard, and help others, especially young niggas, learn how to stay out of trouble and not end up a loser. I first got your info out of a *Phat Puffs* magazine. I was tryna learn how I could get money and really stumbled upon a way to really get money! I appreciate what you do. Don't stop for nothin', man, we need you!" – Zaire Smith, New Jersey Prisoner

"I would like to write this letter to thank your team for the books you have published. I'm currently serving a 10-year sentence, so motivation and confidence is key to one's spirit. Reading books like *The Money Manual*, *The CEO Manual*, etc., help me to motivate the ones that believe in me as well as themselves. A free mind with an incarcerated body is better than a free body with an incarcerated mind. I'm thankful for what I've learned from Mike Enemigo and Sav Hustle. When I spread the knowledge to the ignorant, it makes me look like a genius. I'm a product of a fallen race, and it's going to take me uplifting and bettering myself in order to do the same for my fellow man. So again, thanks." – R. Taylor, North Carolina Prisoner

"I was given a book by The Cell block to read by one of my peers. To make a long story short, I fell in love. I like what I read, and also the knowledge and wisdom you guys put out. Thank you guys." – Samuel Lewis, California Prisoner

"First I wanted to congratulate you on your book *How to Hustle & Win: SMM Edition*. The three words appealed to me, so I was compelled to give the book and your movement a chance. The book was definitely a must-read, and it came right on time. I really like the examples of different scenarios. The psychological chapter that explains how people think is one thing that really stand out." – James Vaughn, Delaware Prisoner

"I received my books from your company, and since I got them, I've not been able to put them down. Everything I've been looking for, everything I've been talking about to my celly, you had it in these books. From day one, when I saw your ads in *PLN* [*Prison Legal News*] and *Straight Stuntin*, I knew you had been through some shit, and overcame it through your books! Your [*How to Write Urban Books for*] *Money and Fame* book got me out my writing slump and I've been back on my shit. It just motivated me and inspired me, man.... The book *Hood Millionaire* is good, too.... I chase that knowledge! I have three of your books, and ordered another three. I will be getting more as soon as I get the three I'm waiting on. I'm definitely gonna keep spending with you. Once again, thanks for motivatin' me. Your books is what I've been lookin' for the whole time. Straight to da oils, no cut! Keep 'em coming, you and your team, and I will keep chasin' the knowledge and spreadin' the word." – Heem, Florida Prisoner

"I have bought every book that you've published and I encourage you to keep serving it like you're doing. Much love and respect." – Ethan McKinney, Prisoner

"It's a great privilege to become a customer of The Cell Block. I have to say, I've been incarcerated for 20+ years, and this is the first time I've invested money into something that's profitable." – Jorge Cabrera, Oregon Prisoner

"Mike Enemigo is the Big Meech of Street Lit." – PaperBoy, Leader of The MOB

"Read Mike Enemigo. He lays courses of words down like a master mason lays bricks: tight and bold. It's no wonder he's one of America's most published prisoners." – George Kayer; Author, Editor, and Founder of *Inmate Shopper*

"Mike Enemigo is the blueprint – a great motivation for guys like me with a lot of time." – Big Chris, Author of *East Side or Die Chronicles*

"I've read three books [by Mike Enemigo and The Cell Block]. Very well written with a true interpretation of what prison and street life is like. [I'm] certainly going to buy more books. *How to Hustle and Win: Sex, Money, Murder Edition* is very interesting." – NASA, *thizzler.com*

"I'm in prison in Tennessee. I'm a huge fan and receive knowledge and wisdom from your teachings. Upon receiving my order, I'll be spending more!" – J. Johnson, Prisoner

"Thank you for all you do to help make life easier for us prisoners. Your books and reports are money well spent!" – F. Hendricks, CA Prisoner

"I purchased your Resource book about a year ago and sent out for many of the resources listed. Thank you! Btw, I've gotten a lot of help!" – J. Coffman, Coffee Creek Prisoner

"CEO Mike Enemigo and associates of The Cell Block are killing it. Both fiction and nonfiction, you are sure to find something to feed your brain. Love your books, bro!" – Lucas DeYoung, Oregon Prisoner

"I would like to thank you for changing my life behind the wall. Your company and books inspire me to build my own empire from prison. Its real men like you that give me hope." – Michael Suarez, Virginia Prisoner

"Your book *Get Out, Get Rich: How to Get Paid LEGALLY When You Get Out of Prison* has given me my fire back. I now have a blueprint and a plan. I thank you big time and I want to know if you would be my mentor. You're raw, pure, honest, real, and I can go on. I see a lot of quality in how you write. Lack of knowledge was my biggest obstacle. My plan was to get my DL's [driver's license] and keep driving, but this book gives me real options without being on the road, yet still be able to live the glamorous life.... Keep doing what you're doing. Salute. You have a friend for life." – Jamaine Mackell, Maryland Prisoner

"I am a true fan of Mike Enemigo and have been inspired to write because of him." – Garland Coleman, Delaware Prisoner

"Can you tell Mike and King Guru I just got *How to Hustle & Win* [*Sex, Money, Murder Edition*] and that book changes my life every time I read it? That shit is fire and I'm not disappointed at all.... Mike, hold your head up, big brah. Real recognize real. Keep doin' what you doin'. From my turf to yours." – Davontiere Hollinshed, Ohio Prisoner

"I am a fan of Mike Enemigo as he is an inspiration and role model on how one can hustle legit from prison." – Nahshan Williams, California Prisoner

CONTENT

Foreword By Seth Ferranti
Chapter 1: Why I'm Writing This Book
Chapter 2: Why Your Should Write A Book
Chapter 3. A Guide To Creative Writing
Chapter 4: A Quick Guide to Journalism
Chapter 5: Writing Well From Inside Prison
Chapter 6: 12 Secrets To Improve Your Writing Style
Chapter 7: The Write Secret
Chapter 8: My Writing Process
Chapter 9: Great Ways To Generate Ideas On What To Write About
Chapter 10: Write To Market
Chapter 11: 80/20 Publishing
Chapter 12: Simplify, & Concentrate Your Forces
Chapter 13: Tips To Simplifying & Concentrating Your Forces
Chapter 14: Platform
Chapter 15: Book Cover
Chapter 16: Publicity Stunt
Chapter 17: The Secrets & Strategies To Publishing Short Stories & Reports For Promo & Profit
Chapter 18: Writing For Online Publications
Chapter 19: Your Amazon Author Page
Chapter 20: Metadata: The Strategies
Chapter 21: Additional Online Opportunities
Chapter 22: Website
Chapter 23: Blog
Chapter 24: Social Media
Chapter 25: Promotional Videos
Chapter 26: E-Books
Chapter 27: Distribution
Chapter 28: Audio Books
Chapter 29: Urban Books
Chapter 30: Legal Books
Chapter 31: Mixbooks
Chapter 32: Magazine Money
Chapter 33: How To Start Your Own Newsletter
Chapter 34: Where To Get Free Material For Your Books

Chapter 35: How To Write Low-Budget Horror
Chapter 36: The Mike Enemigo Story
Chapter 37: Seth Ferranti: The Gorilla Convict
Chapter 38: Michael Santos: The Write To Freedom
Chapter 39: Shaka Senghor: Writing My Wrongs
Chapter 40: Tookie Williams: The Write To Redemption
Chapter 41: Donald Goines: The Black Gangster
Chapter 42: Paul Wright: Prison Legal News
Chapter 43: Alaric Hunt: Cuts Through Bone
Chapter 44: Curtis Dawkins: The Graybar Hotel
Chapter 45: Vickie Stringer: How I Did It
Chapter 46: Interview With Wahida Clark
Chapter 47: Interview With Seth Ferranti
Chapter 48: Interview With Dutch
Chapter 49: Lessons From Rick Ross
Chapter 50: Lessons From Catch & Kill
Chapter 51: Lessons From Ethic
Chapter 52: A Lesson From Best-Selling Author & Financial Guru
Chapter 53: Sample Magazine Query Letter
Chapter 54: Sample Magazine Cover Letter
Chapter 55: Sample Financial Assistance Letter
Chapter 56: Sample Foreword
Writer/Author Resources

FOREWORD

When I got locked up by the feds in 1993 and sentenced to 25 years for a first-time, nonviolent Cannabis and LSD Conspiracy, I had no idea what life had in store for me. I was angry as fuck and didn't have any direction. Buried inside the belly of the beast and stuck in the criminal justice machinery that the War on Drugs era had built into a monstrosity, I wanted the world to know about what I was experiencing and the price I was paying for smoking weed and tripping on acid.

I needed a platform. I needed a network of support. I needed some guidance. I knew I wanted to get an education. There were books on that. I got three degrees, eventually earning my Masters degree from California State University. But I wanted to write. I wanted to express myself from the cell block. I wanted my voice to be heard. I accomplished my goals through trial and error. It wasn't easy. I was left frustrated and angry many times as I figured out how to become a content creator from the cell block.

I didn't have a book, or a guide, or directions on how to break into the writing and entertainment worlds when I was in prison. I did it through sheer will and luck, I guess. I refused to lose and kept grinding until someone was receptive to what I was trying to say. But fast forward three decades, and now there is a how-to book for prisoners who want to be heard and have their voice recognized from prison.

Mike Enemigo's *Jailhouse Publishing for Money, Power, and Fame* is the book that prisoners need to read if they want to break into the publishing and multi-media world. If I would've had this book, I could've accomplished my goals in half the time. Mike Enemigo has taken what others like myself have done behind the fences and not only used it as inspiration for his own success in
the publishing world, but he's turned it into a step-by-step guide. A blueprint for success. From the penitentiary to the streets.

If you are locked up and have artistic and creative ideas, or are just an entrepreneur that wants to jump in the content creation game, you need to read this book. It will show you what Mike and others like me have tried and what has worked and what hasn't worked. We have failed many times and learned from our failures. This book contains all the wisdom and know-how you need to become a success from behind bars.

- Seth Ferranti, writer and filmmaker

"Is the pen mightier than a sword? Can words have so much power? Consider the Bible, the Koran, Das Kapital, The Wealth of Nations.
Only words, and yet they have moved nations and destroyed empires. Words are powerful beasts, and the ability to control them makes
the writer a potent foe. If you are a writer, you are a dangerous entity. If you are a good writer, you are a positive menace." – Unknown

WHY I'M WRITING THIS BOOK

I've had the idea to write this book for a minute now. Actually, my first idea was to write a how-to-write-urban-books book, but I felt like I needed to touch on more than just the urban genre, especially since I consider myself primarily a nonfiction and how-to writer. So, I got with my guy King Guru, and had him put together a book on the jewels of writing urban books.

I began to think about this book some, but I was in no real hurry to write it. I didn't want to write it based only on info I learned by reading books on the business of writing and publishing. I wanted to write it based on experience – what I personally went through; the ups, and especially the downs. See, publishing from prison is vastly different than publishing from the free world – what the other self-publishing books teach you – where you have access to things like the Internet, and you don't have to rely on someone to do most of the work for you. Jailhouse publishing is done with the barest of resources, and to do this successfully is something I had to learn the hard way, the expensive way, through trial and error, as I had no mentors on publishing from prison, and no books existed on the subject.

Another reason I was in no real hurry to write this book is because I was focused on writing and publishing other books for my team and I. In doing this, however, I had to write my team many letters about everything I was learning, so they knew what direction to go, and how best to move. I would write long, detailed letters to one person, then I'd have to write virtually the same letter to someone else. Then someone else. Then a fan and upcoming author would write me with questions, and wanting to be helpful, I'd write him or her a similar letter. Then someone on the yard would read my books, become inspired and ask questions, and I'd respond with yet another letter – or kite, as they're usually called in prison. I started to think, 'Man, I've already written the book a few times via letters. I'd make much better use of my time just going ahead and writing the actual book. That way, I could just write everything once, then send the book to those in my cypher.' Simply put; I wasn't using my own Hustler's Mathematics and simplifying, something I often preach, as it's one of the major keys to being successful. And that is why I'm writing this book now. Because it's time.

This book you are holding is a collection of what I've learned over the last 10 years – again, often the hard way. Some of the info I collected over the years from books, magazines, and newspapers (wherever I could find it!) that inspired me in some way or taught me something valuable, that I adjusted so it's relevant to Jailhouse Publishing. This book you are holding is full of my personal secrets and strategies, the ones I used to become America's #1 incarcerated author. This book is what I send to my team – it is our company manual. It's the book I wish I had before I started, before spending 10 years and 10-20 thousand dollars to learn. I now offer all of it, to you, in one book.

Let's get to it.

Truly,

Mike
#TrueStory
#JewlsOfTheGame
#Americas#1IncarceratedAuthor

WHY YOU SHOULD WRITE (AND PUBLISH!) A BOOK

If you've read my book *The Art & Power of Letter Writing for Prisoners*, you will know that I am a strong advocate of prisoners learning how to write well. As a prisoner, being able to write well is one of the most, if not *the* most, powerful skills you can have. And this doesn't only go for letter writing, but writing of any kind, including books. Some of the most famous and powerful men in the history of the world have written books from prison. So, should you, as a prisoner, write a book, or books? Ab-so-fuckin-lutely. And not just for the reasons above. There are many reasons why writing (and publishing!) a book is beneficial as a prisoner. Here are a few more of them...

> *"Once you become a published author, your life will change."* – Dan Poynter

1. An enormous amount of power can be gained by writing a book and publishing it. As a voiceless people, this gives you a voice! If you learn to write well, and compellingly, you can also bring people to your side of thought in a given subject! They say the pen is mightier than the sword, and it's true. You can do a tremendous amount of damage with the written word, and you could spread the truth. I'm notorious for destroying my enemies by writing long, detailed letters and books, exposing them for the snakes, rats, suckas, and dick-in-da-booties they really are, then distributing them all around the prison system.

> *"I'm all in favor of keeping dangerous weapons out of the hands of fools. Let's start with typewriters."* – Frank Lloyd Wright

And if you need to get out your personal story, perhaps to bring attention to your legal situation, writing a book is a great way to do it! Rubin "Hurricane" Carter wrote a book titled *The Sixteenth Round*. Lesra Martin bought the book at a book sale for 25 cents, then wrote Carter a letter. They became friends and Lesra became a strong advocate for Carter, assembling a team to comb over his case, which eventually lead to his release from prison. And he's not the only one. Jack Henry Abbott, who wrote *The Belly of the Beast*, was lobbied for release by Pulitzer Prize winner Normal Mailer, and it worked! Writing is how Mumia Abu-Jamal has brought an enormous amount of attention to his case, as well.

2. You can make a lot of money from writing and publishing a book, or books, including by what I love most, and that's turning your negative into a positive. I will show you in this book how several prisoners have taken their street, crime, or prison experiences (negatives), and used their knowledge to write fascinating books that have made them a ton of money (positive).

3. Unlike other products you as a prisoner with flowing entrepreneurial ideas may have, books can be written right inside your prison cell with nothing more than a pen, some paper, and your thoughts. You don't need any special equipment (like I did when I was recording my raps). Everything you need, you are allowed to have. And no matter where you are in America, though some rules may differ as to how you have to do it, writing a book is perfectly legal – a key element in our quest for true wealth. And when you're done writing your book, you can send it to whoever's publishing it, right through the mail – legally!

4. A book can bring you passive income for many, many years to come. You can publish a book today, and as long as you have it set up and promoted properly, you will be getting checks for it in 10, 20 years from now, long after the pain of the hard work is gone. This is one of my favorite parts about this business. I love getting checks today from something I haven't touched in five years. It feels like getting free money, and who doesn't like that?

5. If you want to be famous, publishing a book is a great way to do it. In fact, it is easier to gain fame from writing a book than it is to make money from it. It's much easier to get people to read your book for free, where they will then know about you and your book and talk about you and your book than it is to get people to part with their money. If you are trying to impress your family, friends, other prisoners, bitches, staff, whatever, writing a book is one of the best ways to do it.

6. Writing a book can help to establish you as an expert in some other, non-book related area you wish to make money in. For example, let's say you want to start your own prison consulting business when you get out. If you write books about surviving prison – how to navigate the prison system successfully, how to use the prison system to help you grow, and rehabilitate – it would help establish you as an expert. You can then charge soon-to-be prisoners – including rich, white-collar folks, like Madolf and Weinstein – and attorneys big, big bucks to teach them what you know. And it doesn't have to be something prison-based. Maybe you want to get out, flip houses and brand yourself as a go-to real estate guy so you can also give seminars. If you know what you're doing and write a book about flipping houses, it will help establish you as a real-estate expert. People don't have to know you wrote and published the book from prison. Although, these days, it doesn't really hurt. People love a redemption story.

A few literary works penned by prisoners

- *Prison Epistles* (St. Paul): In 62 AD, St. Paul the Apostle was arrested in Jerusalem for his passionate sermons on behalf of Christianity that enraged the local Jewish population. He was taken to the nearby town of Caesarea and imprisoned there for two years. During this time, St. Paul wrote four of the famous Epistles that appear in the Bible's New Testament: Ephesians, Philippians, Colossians and Philemon.

- *Le Morte d'Arthur* (Sir Thomas Malory): Many Arthurian scholars consider "Le Morte d'Arthur" the definitive work in the cycle of legends surrounding the semi-mythical King Arthur and his chivalric Round Table. All the more surprising, then, that it was written by Sir Thomas Malory, a convicted thug, thief, kidnapper and rapist. Malory wrote the cycle of romantic legends while sitting in London's Marshalsea prison, awaiting trial on charges that he had masterminded a string of over 100 violent robberies. Malory never did end up being brought to trial. Instead, he was sprung from prison in 1461 when Edward IV ascended to the throne.

- *Don Quixote* (Miguel de Cervantes): An even greater novel conceived in debtor's prison is "Don Quixote", a book that many critics consider the first modern European novel as well as one of the finest novels ever written. Its author Miguel de Cervantes had found work as a purchasing agent for the Spanish Armada after an adventurous life that included five years as a slave on the Barbary Coast. Unfortunately, authorities detected financial irregularities in his accounts and he was imprisoned. However, after the first part of "Don Quixote" was published in 1605, it proved so popular that Cervantes never suffered from money troubles again.

- *The Travels of Marco Polo* (Rustichello da Pisa): The Venetian merchant Marco Polo did not actually write the famous book that describes his adventures along the fabled Silk Road. Instead he dictated the story of his travels to Rustichello da Pisa while both men were prisoners of Venice's rival, the Genova Republic. Released from captivity in 1299, Polo fled straight back to Venice and never left his beloved city again. The memoir based upon his adventures is widely credited with launching "The Age of Exploration."

- *The Prince* (Niccolò Machiavelli): Niccolò Machiavelli was a well-respected diplomat in the short-lived Florentine republic when in 1512, Florence's one-time ruling family, the Medicis, regained power. Viewed as an enemy of the state by the Medicis, Machiavelli was accused of conspiracy, arrested, tortured and imprisoned. After his release, he was banished from Florence, and it was during his exile that he wrote "The Prince." The treatise has been a touchstone of political strategy ever since, revered by power brokers as diverse as England's Henry VII, America's Benjamin Franklin and Thomas Jefferson, France's Napoleon and Mafia leader John Gotti.

- *To Althea from Prison* (Richard Lovedlace): "Stone walls does not a prison make," wrote Richard Lovelace in 1642, "nor iron bars a cage." The poet wrote these words while locked up in Westminster's Gatehouse Prison on charges related to his passionate support of King Charles I in Puritan England. Although Lovelace was finally released from prison, King Charles was eventually executed and Lovelace's fiancée – the "Althea" of the poem's title – married someone else.

- *Memoirs of Napoleon Bonaparte* (Napoleon Bonaparte): Napoleon's prison was larger than most. In 1815, France's most famous general was exiled to the small island of St. Helena off the coast of West Africa. He spent his time there until his death in 1821 dictating his "Memoirs."

- *Short Stories by O. Henry* (William Sydney Porter): William Sydney Porter was a Texas bank teller. In 1896, federal auditors found irregularities in his accounts, and Porter was brought up on charges of embezzlement. Porter fled to the Honduras where he holed up in a hotel and began writing short stories. The phrase "banana republic" first originated in one of these short stories. One year later his wife lay dying of tuberculosis, and Porter went back to the United States to be with her. He was promptly arrested, convicted of the embezzlement charges and incarcerated in a federal prison in Ohio. In prison, he continued writing short stories and began sending them out for publication, acquiring quite a reputation as a writer with his finger on the pulse of the popular imagination. Today, Porter is better known as O'Henry, the pen name he chose to conceal his identity as a felon.

- *Mein Kampf* (Adolph Hitler): On November 8, 1923, Adolph Hitler and 2,000 Nazis marched through the streets of Munich to take over a political meeting being held at a beer hall there. Hitler was charged with treason for his role in this abortive revolt and sent to Landsberg Prison in Bavaria. He used his incarceration to write an autobiography entitled "Mein Kampf."

- *The Story of My Experiments with Truth* (Mohandas Karamchand Gandhi): Throughout the long struggle for Indian independence, the great statesman Mohandas Gandhi was imprisoned many times both in South Africa and in India. He used his imprisonments as a time to reflect and hone his theories on civil disobedience. Gandhi wrote his autobiography "The Story of My Experiments with Truth" in 1932 while serving time in Maharashtra's Yerwada Jail.

- *One Day in the Life of Ivan Denisovich* (Alexander I. Solzhenitsyn): In 1945, a Red Army soldier named Alexander I. Solzhenitsyn was arrested for writing critically of Joseph Stalin in a private letter to a friend. Solzhenitsyn was sentenced to eight years of forced labor in a Siberian camp. Despite the harshness of the camp's conditions, he began to take notes on his prison camp experience on whatever scraps of paper he managed to find. He was released from prison following Stalin's death in 1953, and nine years later, following the cultural thaw under Nikita Khrushchev, these notes were published as a novel entitled "One Day in the Life of Ivan Denisovich." In 1970, Solzhenitsyn was awarded the Nobel Prize for Literature.

- *Letters from Birmingham Jail* (Dr. Martin Luther King Jr.): In April 1963, Dr. Martin Luther King, Jr. was the president of the Southern Christian Leadership Conference, a civil rights organization that was deeply involved with coordinating marches and sit-ins against racial segregation in Birmingham, Alabama. On April 12, 1963, Dr. King was arrested for ignoring a ruling prohibiting such public demonstrations. While incarcerated in the Birmingham jail, Dr. King read a public statement issued by eight white Alabama clergymen condemning his civil disobedience methods. "Letters from Birmingham Jail" is a spirited defense of civil disobedience that makes a strong argument that people have a moral responsibility to break unjust laws.

- *On the Yard* (Malcolm Braly): By the time Malcolm Braly was 40, he'd spent nearly half his life in prison, serving time in such notorious penal institutions as Nevada State Prison, San Quentin, and Folsom State Prison. While behind bars, he'd written three novels. Braly's big literary break, though, came with his fourth novel "On the Yard," which he began writing when he was paroled in 1965. When prison authorities found out that he was writing the book, they threatened to revoke his parole so Braly had to complete the novel in secret. "On the Yard" was a huge critical success, and after its publication, Braly never returned to prison again.

- *Soul on Ice* (Eldridge Cleaver): In 1958, Eldridge Cleaver was convicted of rape and assault with intention to murder. During his subsequent incarcerations in Folsom State Prison and San Quentin, Cleaver began writing a series of political essays that were first published in the magazine "Ramparts" and later collected into a book called "Soul on Ice." These essays argued that the rape of a white woman by a black man was essentially an insurrectionist act of political rebellion. After his release from prison in 1966, Cleaver joined the Black Panthers, and ran for President on the Peace and

Freedom Party ticket. Eventually, however, Cleaver renounced his radical past and became a Born-Again Christian. At the time of his death in 1998, Cleaver was a member in good standing of the Church of the Latter-Day Saints.

- *The Belly of the Beast* (Jack Abbott): In 1977, Norman Mailer won the Pulitzer Prize by writing a novel entitled "The Executioner's Song," based on the execution of Gary Gilmore. Among the many fan letters, he received was one from an inmate in a Utah prison called Jack Abbott. Gilmore, Abbott told Mailer, had not been truthful with Mailer in describing the details of his prison life. Abbott offered to write Mailer a more factual depiction of life behind bars, and Mailer took him up on it. Mailer became so impressed by Abbott's literary talent that he helped Abbott publish a book based on Abbott's experiences behind bars entitled "The Belly of the Beast." Mailer also lobbied hard for Abbott to be released on parole in 1981 over the objections of prison officials. Six weeks after his release on parole, Abbott fatally stabbed a man in a bar fight. Abbott was subsequently returned to prison where he committed suicide in 2002.

- *Conversations with Myself* (Nelson Mandela): In the eyes of the white apartheid South African government, lawyer and anti-apartheid activist Nelson Mandela was a seasoned terrorist. Mandela was arrested in 1962 and convicted of conspiracy to overthrow the government. He was sentenced to life imprisonment and spent 27 years in prison. During this time, he wrote his autobiography, "Conversations With Myself." In 1990, amidst civil strife and increasing international pressure on his behalf, Mandela was finally released. Shortly thereafter, South Africa's apartheid government was toppled. In 1994, in the first multiracial elections ever held in South Africa, Nelson Mandela was elected that nation's President.

- *Sleeping With the Enemy* (Wahida Clark): Wahida Clark is a pioneer and one of the best known practitioners of a literary genre known as street lit, which uses the inner city underworld as a setting for gritty tales of sex, drugs and violence. She began writing while serving a prison sentence at a women's federal prison camp in Lexington, Kentucky for mail and wire fraud, and money laundering.

While she wrote "Sleeping With the Enemy" well after her release, the novel draws heavily on her experiences behind bars.

- *Orange Is The New Black: My Year in a Woman's Prison* (Piper Kerman): In 1993, upscale Smith College graduate Piper Kernan did a favor for her lover, which involved laundering the monetary proceeds of an international heroin smuggling operation. Kernan quickly grew disillusioned with the operation and moved on with her life, so she was not at all prepared for a subsequent indictment on those charges in 1998. Legal maneuvering kept Kernan out of prison until 2004. "Orange Is the New Black" is the memoir Kernan wrote about the 11 months she spent in the Danbury Federal Correctional Institution. The book became an instant bestseller and was adapted as a miniseries by the on-demand streaming video provider Netflix.

"I persevered because I recognized that writing was my sole choice of creating something, of climbing from the dark pit, fulfilling the dream, and resting in the sun." – Edward Bunker

A GUIDE TO CREATIVE WRITING!

Before you try and write a book that you plan to sell, or try to sell, you have to learn how to write. Too many inmates try to skip this part of the process. This is not a part of the process that can be skipped! You have to know how to write. And just because you know how to write letters and words on a piece of paper, and just because you have an idea for a story (probably one about yourself), doesn't mean you know how to write. When I say "write," I mean write well – at least well enough that people will buy what you write and be satisfied with it.

And this applies to submitting to publishers, too. You'd be surprised how many submissions I get where the person doesn't even know how to use basic punctuation – like commas, quotation marks, and sometimes even periods! You'd be surprised how many people don't know how to write a complete sentence, or know where to stop a sentence so that it doesn't become a run-on sentence. When I first started accepting material, I didn't mind as much because I was inexperienced and naive and I didn't know all that goes into publishing a book. *Loyalty and Betrayal* was one long run-on sentence. But I will never accept anything like that again. Now, not understanding the basics will get you an immediate denial from me as a publisher, and a reader – I won't even read what you send. And I usually know where one is at with their craft (and their dedication to writing) just by reading their introduction letter. If your letter isn't written properly, odds are your book isn't either.

Listen: Writing is your power. Your ammo. You must get it down. Trying to skip this part of the process is like a basketball player trying to skip learning how to dribble. You have to do the work if you want to be great!

With that said, here's a basic guide to writing. Study it, learn it.

Now, without further ado, let's get to it so we can get through it.

Types of Creative Writing

Creative writing doesn't always mean fiction; creative non-fiction and personal essay are two types of creative writing that are gaining more popularity.

Creative non-fiction is exactly what it sounds like, non-fiction stories told in a creative way. Typically, what this means is that the story is based on a real event or situation, but may be exaggerated in parts to make the story more interesting and compelling to readers. Personal essay is usually one story or a collection of vignettes that are based on a real event or situation. Personal essays are more telling than showing, meaning you are telling a story rather than recanting an event, using characters and dialogue.

Memoir v. Autobiography

There is a very fine line between what a memoir is and what is an autobiography, and as writers it is important to know the difference. An autobiography follows chronology (arrangement of events or dates in order of occurrence) of the writer's entire life whereas a memoir covers only a specific time period of the writer's life. It doesn't have to be just one time period, either, it can be various time periods within a person's life, and it doesn't have to be in any particular order. Think "memories." It doesn't have to be just one time period, either; it can be various time periods within a person's life, and it doesn't have to be in any particular order. Think "memories."

Exercises & Rules in Mechanics

Every writer is different. Some writers edit their own work as they write, whereas some writers choose to get all their ideas out on paper, and once finished, they edit the entire piece. Either way is perfectly fine, it's always best to do what you feel comfortable doing. As a writer, I typically write everything down and edit later. Sometimes this means even ignoring the basic grammar, punctuation and even spelling mistakes. For me, it's more important to write down my story, develop characters, scenes and situations before paying attention to mechanics. But, in the end, mechanics are important. Having incorrect grammar and spelling will make even the most brilliant story less desirable to readers and publishers.

Grammar Terms

Abstract nouns: names, ideas, characteristics, or qualities, such as courage, pride, goodness, and success.

Action verbs: Verbs that show action.

Active Voice: When the verb of a sentence is in the active voice, the subject is doing the acting, as in the sentence "Kevin hit the ball." Kevin (the subject of the sentence) acts in relation to the ball.

Adjectives: modify and affect the meaning of nouns and pronouns and tell us which, whose, what kind, and how many about the nouns or pronouns they modify. They generally come before the noun or pronoun they modify.

Adverbs: modify verbs, adjectives, and other adverbs. They tell how (manner), when (time), where (place), how much (degree), and why (cause). Why is a common one-word adverb that tells why.

Antecedent: the word for which the pronoun stands. An example would be: The boy threw the football. He threw it over the fence. Boy is the antecedent for he, and football is the antecedent for it.

Appositive: A word, or group of words, that identifies or renames the noun or pronoun that it follows. Commas set off an appositive, unless it is closely tied so that it identifies or renames. Examples: My son Carl is a medical technician (no commas). Badger, our dog with a missing leg, has a love for cats (commas needed).

Articles: are the adjectives a, an, and the.

Case: means that a different form of pronoun is used for different parts of the sentence.

Clause: A group of words having a subject and a verb.

Complex sentence: A complete sentence made up of an independent clause and a dependent clause.

Compound sentence: A combination of two or more independent clauses. Commas separate the clauses of a compound sentence.

Compound verb: When two or more verbs are in a sentence. A compound verb is joined by either a coordinate conjunction or a correlative conjunction. Example: The bell rang and rang.

Concrete nouns: name things that exist physically as sidewalk, bird, toy, hair, and raid.

Conjunction: A word that joins other words, phases (group of words), or clauses (group of words with a subject and verb).

Conjunctions: are the following: and, but, or, nor, for, yet, either-or, neither-nor, both-and, not only-but also, and whether-or.

Dependent clause: An adjective, adverb, or noun that cannot stand alone as a sentence.

First person pronouns: are when a pronoun refers to the speaker or speakers. First person pronouns include I, my, mine, me, myself, we, our, ours, us, ourselves.

Helping verbs: are verbs used to make verb phrases. They are usually grouped in the following five groups:

    Group 1: is, am, are, was, were, be, being, been
    Group 2: has, have, had
    Group 3: do, does, did
    Group 4: shall, will, should, would
    Group 5: may, might, must, can, could

Independent clause: A clause that cannot stand alone as a sentence.

Linking verbs: (state of being verbs) show that something exists; they do not show action. Some common linking verbs include is, am, are, was, were, be, being, been, seem, look, feel, and become.

Noun: A word that names a person, place, or thing. Examples of nouns include man, city, book, and courage. Nouns often follow words like a, an, and the.

Passive Voice: A verb is in the passive voice when the subject of the sentence is acted on by the verb. For example, in "The ball was thrown by the pitcher," the ball (the subject) receives the action of the verb, and was thrown in the passive voice. Stephen King says to never use this.

Possessive pronouns: are personal pronouns that show whose something is. Possessive pronouns include my, mine, your, yours, his, her, hers, its, our, ours, their, and theirs.

Possessives: are the adjectives my, our, your, and their.

Preposition: A word that indicates location (in, near, beside) or some other relationship (about, after, besides) between a noun and pronoun and other parts of the sentence.

Pronoun: A word that replaces a noun, or a group of words used as nouns – it, her, his, they, etc.

Proper nouns: name a special person, place, or thing and begin with capital letters – United States of America, President Barack Obama.

Qualifiers: are verbs that strengthen or weaken the words they modify.

Sentence: A group of words expressing a complete thought, and it must have a subject and a verb.

Subject: A word that tells who or what about the verb. When finding the subject and the verb in a sentence, always find the verb first and then say who or what followed the verb. Example: The bell rang. Find the verb – rang. Now say who or what rang? The bell rang. Bell is the subject.

Transitive verbs: are verbs that have subjects or objects that receive an action.

Verbs: show action or state of being. Most verbs are action words, but a few verbs indicate state of being or existence.

Punctuation

Commas and **periods** are the most frequently used punctuation marks. Commas customarily indicate a brief pause; they're not as final as periods. Use commas to...

- Separate words and word groups in a simple series of three or more items.
- Separate two adjectives when the adjectives are interchangeable.
- When two independent clauses are joined by connectors such as and, or, but, etc., put a comma at the end of the first clause.

The **apostrophe** is a punctuation mark! It serves two purposes:

- The marking of the omission of one or more letters (as in the contraction of do not to don't).
- The marking of a possessive case (as in the eagle's feathers, or in one month's time).

It's no accident that a **semicolon** is a period atop a comma. Like commas, semicolons indicate an audible pause – slightly longer than a comma's, but short of a period's full stop. A semicolon can...
Replace a period if the writer wishes to narrow the gap between two closely linked sentences.
Before such words and terms as namely, however, therefore, that is, i.e., for example, e.g., for instance, etc., when they introduce a complete sentence.

A **colon** means "that is to say" or "here's what I mean." Colons and semicolons should never be used interchangeably. A colon may be used to...
- Introduce a long quotation.
- Between independent clauses when the second sentence explains, illustrates, paraphrases, or expands on the first sentence and to introduce a series of items.

Note: Do not capitalize the first item after the colon in a list of things. For example: You may be required to bring many things: sleeping bags, pans, utensils and warm clothing.

Use **double quotation marks** to set off a direct (word-for-word) quotation and use single quotation marks for quotations within quotations. Periods and commas always go inside quotation marks.

Example: He said, "Dan cried, 'Do not treat me that way.'"

Dashes, like commas, semicolons, colons, ellipses, and parentheses, indicate added emphasis, an interruption, or an abrupt change of thought. Experienced writers know that these marks are not interchangeable.

Words and phrases between dashes are not generally part of the subject. For example: Joe – and his trusty mutt – was always welcome.

An **ellipsis** (plural: ellipses) is a punctuation mark consisting of three dots. Use an ellipsis when...
- Omitting a word, phrase, line, paragraph, or more from a quoted passage.
- To save space or remove material that is less relevant.
- They are useful in getting right to the point without delay or distraction.

For example...

Full quotation: "Today, after hours of careful thought, we vetoed the bill." With ellipsis: "Today...we vetoed the bill."

Underlining & Italicizing Titles of Books, Plays, Articles, etc.

Prior to computers, people were taught to underline titles of books and plays and to surround chapters, articles, songs, and other shorter works in quotation marks, so all of these titles should still be underlined in WRITTEN works.

- However, if you are TYPING, there is a new set of rules:
- When quoted in text or listed in a bibliography, titles of books, journals, plays, and other freestanding works are italicized.
- Titles of articles, chapters, and other shorter works are enclosed in quotation marks.

Sentence Structure: Run-ons, Fragments & Eliminating Wordiness

Run-on sentences, sometimes called "fused sentences," are terms describing two independent clauses that are joined together with no connecting word or punctuation to separate the clauses.

A **sentence fragment** fails to be a sentence in the sense that it cannot stand by itself. It does not contain even one independent clause.

Wordiness in the use of too many words to express an idea. Wordiness can sometimes create run-on sentences or detract from the idea you're trying to express.

Subject-Verb Agreement

Subjects and verbs must AGREE with one another in number (singular or plural). Thus, if a subject is singular, its verb must also be singular; if a subject is plural, its verb must also be plural.

Articles & Prepositions

An **article** is an adjective. Like adjectives, articles modify nouns. English has two articles: the and a/an.

The is used to refer to specific or particular nouns. A/an is used to modify non-specific or non-particular nouns. We call the the definite article and a/an the indefinite article.

A **preposition** is a word that indicates location (in, near, beside) or some other relationship (about, after, besides) between a noun or pronoun and other parts of the sentence. A preposition isn't a preposition unless it goes with a related noun or pronoun, called the object of the preposition. For example: Let's meet before noon. Before is a preposition; noon is its object.

Commonly Misused Words & Problem Phrases

Your vs. You're

Your = possessive pronoun: Your shoes are untied.
You're = you + are: You're walking around with your shoes untied.

Accept vs. Except

Accept = verb meaning to receive or to agree.
Except = preposition meaning all but, other then.

Affect vs. Effect

Affect = verb meaning to influence.
Effect = noun meaning result or consequence.
Effect = verb meaning to bring about, to accomplish.

There vs. They're vs. Their

There = an adverb specifying place.
They're = a contraction of they are.
Their = a possessive pronoun, you are showing the reader what "they own."

Its vs. It's

Its = possessive adjective (possessive from the pronoun it): The crab had an unusual growth on its shell.
    It's = contraction for it is or it has (in a verb phrase): It's still raining; it's (it has) been raining for three days.

To vs. Two vs. Too

To = preposition.

Two = number.
Too = adverb.

Than vs. Then

Than = used in comparison statements, statements of preference, and to suggest quantities of no specific amount.
Then = a time other then now, next in time, space or order, and suggesting a logical conclusion.

Problem Phrases

- Supposed to: Do not omit the d. Suppose to is incorrect.
- Used to: Same as above. Do not write use to.
- Toward: There is no s at the end of the word.
- Anyway: Also has no ending s. Anyways is nonstandard.
- Couldn't care less: Be sure to make it negative. (Not I could care less.)
- For all intents and purposes: Not intensive purposes.
- Irregardless: Not a word. Use Regardless.
- Which: Do not use which to refer to persons. Use who.

Creative Writing Terms

Abstract: Something that exists in theory rather than reality; can also refer to a quality or condition rather than to specific detail. An abstract description relies on impressions and lacks the specific, concrete detail that a reader can imagine.

Allegory: An extended metaphor that presents a subject (a moral, an idea, etc.) disguised as something else (characters, landscape, etc.).

Analogy: A figure of speech that compares, often in the form of a simile or metaphor. Often used in explanations, analogy expresses a correspondence, equivalence, or parallelism between two things due to an element that they share.

Antagonist: Any character in the story that opposes the efforts of the hero or main character (see Protagonist).

Characterization: The author's expression of a character's personality through the use of action, dialogue, thought or commentary.

Climax: The most exciting part of the story, usually where the conflict is resolved.

Concrete: A material object or specific tangible detail, rather than an abstract state, quality, or generality. A concrete description is one that contains specific details that the reader can easily visualize or imagine.

Diction: The use of words, including range of vocabulary, the choice of wording, word order, and style of use.

Didactic: Instructional or informative literature.

Double Entrendre: A phrase that can be interpreted in two different ways.

Epic: A long narrative poem, told in formal, elevated style that focuses on a serious subject and chronicles heroic deeds and events important to a culture or nation.

Epilogue: An appendix to a text or other work intended to wrap up any last loose ends of the plot.

Euphemism: A phrase used in place of something disagreeable or upsetting.

Eposition: The beginning of the story, which introduces the characters and setting; also introduces the conflict, for which the action of the story will take place.

Falling Action: The aftermath of the climax, where the remainder of the story falls into place and the reader's questions are answered.

Figure of speech: An expressive use of language, such as a metaphor or pun, used to suggest an image or comparison. In a figure of speech, words are not used literally.

Flash Fiction: A piece of fiction written in less than 500 words.

Genre: A genre is a category of writing that has a particular kind of content or structure, such as narrative, mystery, urban, sc-fi, etc.

High Concept: A storyline that can easily be described in one sentence and seems to be especially unique and commercially viable.

Hook: A narrative trick in the lead paragraph of a work that grabs the attention of the readers and keeps them reading.

Hyberbole: The use of exaggeration for emphasis (such as referring to something as "the best ever"), not meant to be taken literally. If used too often, hyperbole loses effect.

Imagery: The sensory detail (not just visual) referring more specifically to figures of speech, which produce mental images for the reader.

Irony: When a person, situation, statement, or circumstance is not what it seems to be, but the exact opposite.

Motif: A recurring image, object, idea, situation, feature, or phrase that helps unify a piece of writing. Motif can also be used to refer a situation common across many works, such as the "heroic quest" story or the "rags-to-riches" tale.

Narrative structure: is about two things: the content of a story and the form used to tell the story; story and plot.

Oxymoron: A figure of speech combining contradictory words for descriptive purposes. For example: Jumbo shrimp.

Plot: Specifically, the plot is the sequence in which the writer arranges the events for the story.

Point-of-view (POV): The point-of-view refers to the narrator who relates the story to the reader. The narrator, often (but not necessarily) a character in the story, is the eyes, ears, and voice of the story.
- 1st person or a story told by "I."
- 2nd person or a story addressed to "you."
- 3rd person or a story in which the story characters are "he" and "she," and the narrator is not usually a character.

Premise: The question or problem that is the basic idea of a story.

Prologue: The preface or introduction to a story.

Protagonist: The main character in a literary work; the hero.

Resolution: The end; all the loose ends are tied up.

Rising Action: The majority of the plot takes place here. Dialogue, scenes, character interaction, descriptions, building tension, and more occur here. Think of the last book you read – the rising action took up most of the pages of that book.

Satire: The literary art of ridiculing a folly or vice in order to expose or correct it.

Self-publishing: A branch of publishing in which the author publishes his own works, cutting out the middlemen and raking in all the profits him or herself. With the advent of computers and desktop publishing programs, this approach has become increasingly viable.

Setting: Where the story takes place, the setting should have plenty of details. It helps a reader imagine what's happening.

Story: refers to the raw materials of a dramatic action as they might be described in chronological order.

Style: The manner of expression of a particular writer, produced by choice of words, grammatical structures, use of literary devices and all the possible parts of language use.
- Theme: A theme is a unifying motif of "message" of a story.
- External Struggle: Man vs. Man
- Internal Struggle: Man vs. Himself
- Moral Struggle: Man vs. Society
- Struggle Against Fate: Man vs. Nature

Tone: The author's implicit attitude toward the reader or the people, places, and events in a work as revealed by the elements of the author's style.

Voice: The style, tone, and method of writing which an author composes a work.

Dramatic Structure

Narrative structure: is a literary element, and is generally described as the structural framework that underlies the order and manner in which a narrative is presented to a reader, listener, or viewer. The narrative text structures are the plot and setting.

A drama is divided into five parts, or acts, which some refer to as a **dramatic arc**: exposition, rising action, climax, falling action, and denouement. Although this analysis of dramatic structure is based on five-act plays, it can be applied (sometimes in a modified manner) to short stories and novels as well, making dramatic structure a literary element similar to narrative structure, but more defined.

Dramatic Structure Elements:

Exposition: The portion of a story that introduces important information to the audience; for example, information about the setting, events occurring before the main plot, character' back stories, etc. Exposition can be conveyed through dialogs, flashbacks, character's thoughts, background details, in-universe media or the narrator telling a back-story.

Rising action: A series of related incidents builds toward the point of greatest interest. The rising action of a story is the series of events that begin immediately after the exposition (introduction) of the story and builds up to the climax, these events are generally the most important parts of the story since the entire plot depends on them to set up the climax, and ultimately the satisfactory resolution of the story itself.

Climax: The turning point, which changes the protagonist's fate. If the story is a comedy, things will have gone badly for the protagonist up to this point; now, the plot will begin to unfold in his or her favor, often requiring the protagonist to draw on hidden inner strengths. If the story is a tragedy, the opposite state of affairs will ensue, with things going from good to bad for the protagonist, often revealing the protagonist's hidden weakness.

Falling action: The conflict between the protagonist and the antagonist unravels, with the protagonist winning or losing against the antagonist. The falling action may contain a moment of final suspense, in which the final outcome of the conflict is in doubt.

Denouement ("day-new-ma"), resolution, revelation or catastrophe: Comprises events from the end of the falling action to the actual ending scene of the drama of narrative. Conflicts are resolved, creating normality for the characters and a sense of catharsis, or release of tension and anxiety, for the reader.

Generating Ideas

Before you begin writing, you need to generate an idea. If you are writing non-fiction, usually you'd have an idea before writing, but if you are looking to write fiction, here are some techniques for generating ideas:

1. Pull from your own life: jobs you've had, family and friends, relationships, hobbies, interests, etc.
2. Draw from the world: places you love, political issues, social problems, celebrities, TV shows, etc.
3. Ask the 5 Ws and 1 H questions: Who? What? When? Where? Why? and How? Use to generate topic ideas, possible angles to take on the

topic and the most pertinent information to include when addressing the topic.
4. Freewrite: Set aside a time frame (like 15 minutes) and write whatever comes to mind. Don't worry about typos, spelling or any other surface-level issues of grammar and style. When you are done, read through what you have written. You will no doubt have a lot of filler in your text, but there will also be golden nuggets of insights, discoveries and other little gems in there that you can pick out and develop for your projects.
5. Use an 'everything book': I use an 'everything book' to retain and collect any ideas I may have at any time of the day. It's a notebook which I always have close by. In it, quotes, ideas, and cooking recipes are all jumbled together.

Developing Characters

It seems the number one way you learn more about your characters is simply by writing about them. Unfortunately, when this process occurs while you're writing your story, it can show.

Awkward, uneven character development in your completed piece can be the result. One way to get around this is to write scenes with your characters that aren't even a part of your story, but help you develop and get to know them. You should always know more about your characters than your readers do, such as:
- Their temperament, how they would react to certain situations, their personality.
- Their values, beliefs, how they fell about the world and humanity, hobbies, interests, etc.

World Overview

The world overview is not from a character's point of view, it is a God's eye view of the arena or setting of your story – the world or worlds you wish to explore in your story. It's a sketch of a place, and what is going on in it.

Creating Conflict

Conflict is what drives any story. Without conflict and tension between characters or objects in a story, the "story" would be boring. We often think that to create conflict we need to show spectacular events. For example, a car chase, an argument between lovers, a fistfight, or the threat of a nuclear explosion. Or we think of conflict as some kind of internal suffering: depression, longing, or pain.

But the truth is that, if events and emotions were the only elements of conflict in our stories, we'd have some pretty flat stories. Conflict, in good stories, is not about spectacular events or painful emotions. Good conflict is about values. A value is something you admire, something you want.

Here are some examples of things you might value: Money/Wealth, Friends, Your little brother, Getting good grades, Justice, Compassion, Ferraris, Power, Respect.

There are two types of conflict: external (conflict between the protagonist and the antagonist) and internal (the fears and insecurities that a protagonist has to overcome in order to get what he or she wants).

You now have two basic ingredients for an excellent story: external conflict and internal conflict. Know that your internal and external conflicts should overlap throughout your story. Once your characters find out about each other's fears and weaknesses, you better believe they will use them against each other mercilessly as they fight to make their dreams come true.

There you have the basics. To study further, I suggest you get the book *English Grammar for Dummies*, by Geraldine Woods.

A QUICK GUIDE TO JOURNALISM

INTRODUCTION

Chances are you have already done some writing. Perhaps you've written poetry or short stories or essays. Perhaps you've written opinion articles. In journalism, we endeavor to inform readers about news such as a change in law or important events. Sometimes we tell stories about people or organizations. We do this by first reporting on the story. We interview people and we conduct research from books, documents and articles in other publications. Whenever possible, especially if we are reporting an event, we incorporate our own observations. Only after we've gathered all the ingredients do we start writing the story.

This handout is a guide to the nuts and bolts of journalism. It tells you about the basic rules and principles for how to pull together an article. The bottom line, however, is simple: a good article is one that grabs the attention of the reader and doesn't let go. That means starting with an interesting first sentence. It means making sure that your quotes are powerful, and that you have details that help the reader see your story in their mind. It also means that all your facts are correct and attributed to trustworthy sources, and you are writing as objectively and clearly as possible.

Journalism is hard and journalists hone their craft their entire career. We bear a big responsibility to report and write with integrity. But know this: your voice matters. Reporting behind the wall matters. History is shaped by those who record it.

Most news stories are written in a style called "the inverted pyramid." Imagine an upside-down triangle: the wide section at the top represents the first paragraph of the story, while the pointy section at the bottom represents the very last paragraph. The top paragraph contains the most important information in the story. The second paragraph contains the second-most important batch of information. And so on until the last paragraph.

More Info: We usually write news stories like this because our readers often only have a couple of seconds to spend on our news story, so they need to be able to see what the news is right away. If they want to learn more, they can read another paragraph and get more information.

They can stop at any time and still know how many people died in that accident last night and what time the school board meeting is tonight.

LEDES

A lede (also sometimes spelled "lead") is the opening sentence or paragraph of an article. Its purpose is to hook the reader's attention and establish the main information or questions needed to understand what comes next in the article. Effective ledes are concrete and focused, use active language, and avoid clichés.

More Info: There are two main approaches to writing ledes:

- **Straight news:** In a standard news story, the lede contains a summary of the story's essential information, and answers at least some of the "five W's" – who, what, where, when, why (and how).

- **Features:** A feature lede delays essential information in favor of appealing to the reader's emotion or curiosity. This lede style may open by setting the scene, providing an anecdote, or offering a quote. Since feature ledes don't get right to the point, journalists often choose to include a paragraph farther down in the article that clarifies that story's main idea and provides necessary context. This paragraph is called the nut graf, since it explains why the story matters, in the proverbial nutshell.

Examples:

- **Straight news lede:** "The European Parliament voted Tuesday to ratify the landmark Paris climate accord, paving the way for the international plan to curb greenhouse gas emissions to become binding as soon as the end of this week." [Rebecca Hersher, NPR]

- **Feature lede:** "When they heard the screams, no one suspected the rooster. Dechardonae Gaines, 2, was toddling down the sidewalk Monday lugging her Easy Bake Oven when she became the victim in one of the weirder animal attack cases police can recall." [Kelley Benham French, St. Petersburg Times].

ATTRIBUTION

A key part of writing a reliable news story is attribution – letting your readers know where the facts in your article come from. Aim to attribute if the information in your article: indicates a point of view (i.e. opinion or emotion), is subject to change (i.e. annual statistics), was not personally witnessed, or is not commonly known or independently verifiable. You can choose to integrate this information in the form of a direct quote, a paraphrase (a restatement in your own words), or a summary of the facts.

More Info: There are many types of sources a reporter can use, including:

- **A person:** identify initially by full name and title, such as "Lt. Sam Robinson." All subsequent references use only the last name, or the title when relevant ("Robinson," the lieutenant"). Information sourced from people can come from verbal interviews, a speech, or a written document.

- **A publication:** this includes newspapers, magazines, books, public records, and research documents. Titles of published material should be italicized. Also provide the names of book authors as well as the names of any institutions affiliated with research, i.e. Stanford University or Vera Institute.

- **The writer:** firsthand observations do not need attribution.

Examples:

- "Jimmy Daniels, a 7th grader at Sadler Junior High School, was dead at the scene with a bullet wound to the head, **said Detective Robert Medley.**" [Tulsa World]

- **"Press Secretary Beverly Hubble said** Grassley is to be treated for a tightening of muscles in his lower esophagus that interferes with the passage of food." [The Des Moines Register]

- "Salt River floodwaters, which have swept away tons of garbage from landfills alongside the riverbed, will leave behind filthy pools of stagnating water laced with rotting material and hazardous bacteria, **according to a Valley environmentalist**." [The Arizona Republic]

- "Over the last three months, six executions in the United States have been stayed or rescheduled because of constitutional issues regarding the method of execution or who can be present in the death chamber, **according to Reuters.**" [San Quentin News]

- "**The Independent notes** that before 2003 all those with felony convictions in the state of Nevada could not juries or vote unless they individually petitioned the Department of Public Safety or were granted a pardon." [San Quentin News]

WRITING DOs AND DON'Ts

- Do write in a simple, direct way. Stay away from convoluted sentences and fancy words. Just tell people what happened.

- Don't sprinkle qualifiers (adjectives and adverbs) throughout your text. They often smuggle opinions into your news story.

- Don't use more words than necessary to communicate an idea.

- Don't repeat yourself.

- Don't tell people that someone was "heroics; tell an anecdote that shows exactly how "heroic" he was.

- Don't use the first person in a news story. Only use the "I" in a feature if your story is highly relevant in that context.

- Don't fall in love with your own writing. Cut sentences and paragraphs mercilessly when necessary.

INTERVIEWING

Interviewing is about getting the key information that you need to fill out the and How of story while also building trust with your source. Think of it as a conversation with another person in which your goal is to try to get more information.

More Info: There are two main types of interview questions:

- **Close-ended questions**: This where you ask a question that a person can answer with a yes or no, without elaborating. They are good for getting a straightforward answer, but they don't really allow you to get the interesting details you need for your story. They work well when you just need to confirm or deny a fact and have a limited time to ask the questions. But they can be boring for the person being interviewed. They don't allow you to build a relationship with your source and you can't usually use the answer as a direct quote in the story.

- **Open-ended questions**: This is where you ask a question that requires a person to give an extended response by making them tell a story of what happened. This can help you create a scene. Open-ended questions allow you to pick up on the voice and vocabulary of the person speaking, provide richer details that you can use to enhance your writing, open the door for new questions that you may not have thought to ask originally, and allow for more conversation between interviewer and interviewee. The downside is that the source could take the conversation into another direction with too much irrelevant detail so an interviewer must politely retain control of the interview.

Examples:

- **Close-ended question**: "Did you see anything in the room?" **Answer**: "Yes."

- **Open-ended question**: "What did you see in the room?" **Answer**: "There were lots of people dancing, bright lights and tons of food on the table."

NOTE-TAKING TIPS

Always make sure you ask the correct spelling of a source's name, their title or position, and their age. Also jot down the date of the interview. Put a star in your notes next to all key quotes or pieces of information. This will later help pinpoint information or quotes that you really want to use in your story.

- **NEVER** put words in a person's mouth by suggesting they say something in a certain way.

- **NEVER** pay or offer any services or goods for an interview.

- **NEVER** make up an interview with a source or make up a quote someone didn't say.

USING QUOTES EFFECTIVELY

When writing a story, whether it's hard news or a feature, quotes are a must. Quotes are important because they can show emotion, bring a character alive, provide a description that brings a reader into the story, provide further explanation for a point you are making, or give an anecdote. You hear soundbites on television. A quote in print is just that:

a soundbite. You wouldn't waste space on video with a boring person's comments. Don't waste space on your print story either.

- **DON'T** put too many direct quotes back-to-back in your story. Let your writing shine through.

- **DON'T** make up a quote.

- **DON'T** take something out of context to make it fit what you want to say.

- **DON'T** "massage" quotes – don't make them "sound better" than they were originally said.

More Info: There are three main types of quotes:

- **Complete direct quotations**: The reporter uses the entire statement a person made because it was so well stated that they couldn't state it better themselves.

- **Partial quotations**: The reporter takes portions of the entire direct quote. It changes the language of the quote but not the meaning of the original statement while still retaining parts of the original sentences. Partial quotes can be useful when the person gets very convoluted about what they are saying but still has a few good lines that you want to maintain.

- **Indirect and Paraphrased Quotations**: The reporter decides not to use any of the original language of the statement but instead paraphrases what the source is saying and attributes the information to them.

Examples:

- **Direct quotation:** "I couldn't believe what was happening as I saw people start running in every direction," said Jane Smith, an eyewitness to the shootings. "It was as if we were in a bad Hollywood movie."

- **Partial quotation:** Jane Smith, who was closest to the scene of the shooting, said witnesses felt "as if we were in a bad Hollywood movie."

- **Paraphrase:** Jane Smith, who witnessed the shooting, described the chaos of the scene as something out of a Hollywood movie.

NOTES:

This primer is meant to be a general guide based on the principles of journalism in the U.S. However, jails and prisons may differ in their rules and regulations depending on the publication.

[Source: Prison Journalism Project]

WRITING WELL FROM INSIDE PRISON

By John J. Lennon

I had just finished a deep-dive interview and was daydreaming in my cell, listening to Halsey on my tablet through Audio Technica headphones. I was pacing and thinking about the material. I tend to get emotional when I think about my subjects because I often relate to their struggle – externally, internally – to overcome the complication of this prison life. That's empathy. That's what journalism has taught me. I imagine what the story will look like in the slicks (glossy magazines), how the illustration or photography will pop in the well – the splashy two-page spreads in the back of magazines. I see "the deck," the few lines that tease the story. Those are feature stories, the pinnacle of print journalism. That's what I do. From my cell.

I've been locked up nearly nineteen years now. Back in 2010, I started learning how to write in an Attica creative writing workshop taught by Doran Larson, a volunteer English professor. A handful of prisoners attended once a month. Spotting a great opportunity is like seeing a great story – you're not going to have a voice whispering in your ear telling you "this is it." I was cocky, hardly Larson's favorite, but I hung on to his every word and never missed a class. The workshop was geared toward published work, and a few of my first essays were rigorously critiqued in class before I mailed them to magazines, and they were published. I developed my signature style: journalism meshed with memoir. Today I'm a contributing editor for *Esquire* and a contributing writer for *The Marshall Project*. Recently I was asked to be an advisor for *The Prison Journalism Project*.

In this essay I describe my writing process and how I consider story. I'm writing mostly to the aspiring prison writer and journalist. We've partnered with several publications with the hope that this piece will find its way inside.

As a feature magazine writer, I substitute the who, what, where, when, and why that a traditional reporter uses in a news story with character, theme, plot, scenes, chronology, and motive. In "This Place is Crazy," a story that appeared in the 2018 summer issue of *Esquire*, I wrote about Joe Cardo, who suffered from schizoaffective disorder and used to pick up cigarette clips in the Attica yard. I observed him and nestled next to him. When he told me his story, it reminded me of my brother Eugene's struggle with mental illness, and so I wove those memories through the story. The piece wound up having three narratives – Joe's, Eugene's, and mine. It took two years of restructuring and rewriting, with help from a great editor. The story's peg, which is journalism lingo for a topic that is relevant in society, was this: Ten out of every eleven psychiatric patients housed by the government are incarcerated. Ground the specific in the general. That's the key.

According to Graydon Carter, Vanity Fair's former editor in chief, the best magazine stories have these elements: access, narrative, disclosure, and – always – conflict. When you think about it, who's got better access to story than the prisoner? I mean, we live among some of society's most colorful characters. Other journalists parachute into prisons, conduct interviews, and then leave. They can't truly know the characters they interview or the prison culture. They don't breathe the air, eat the food, feel the tension. They aren't affected by prison politics and violence and monotony. The scenes they write are almost all reconstructed instead of witnessed firsthand, which produces some of the best writing. My access has been my edge.

Narrative is simply how you set up the chronology of events. Thing is, there's nothing simple about it. Knowing where to put scenes and how to keep the tension and when to break for digressions is tricky. If you want to learn how to spin a yarn, I'd say you have to always analyze the stories you consume – a movie, an NPR segment, a magazine article. Structurally, feature pieces in magazines have a lot going on. I reverse engineer them. I underline, write in the margins, bracket the opening hooks, the nut grafs (the core premise of the article), the exposition on history of the issue to which the stories are pegged, the backstories on the protagonist, then back to the rising action scenes. Not every story has all these elements. The legendary writer John McPhee says that structure is not a template. I read the pieces front to back, back to front. "The art exists purely in the arrangement of the words," says Philip Gerard, a writer and professor at University of North Carolina Wilmington.

A bit about disclosure and conflict. "This Place is Crazy" was a personal story with characters, scenes and action. After the opening scene in the yard, where I introduce Joe Cardo and explain his situation, I digress and blend in important information on the history: "By locking up people with psychiatric diagnoses, we've boomeranged back to the way things were done in antebellum America." Then I go on for a bit about the history. That's disclosure: teaching the reader. Most people prefer to learn while being told a good story. Magazines do that well.

There's a measure of conflict every time an incarcerated person (especially one like me, convicted of murder) publishes in a national magazine. But I'm a big believer in telling the reader why you're in prison, even if it has nothing to do with the story. Guys that write stories for, say, *San Quentin News* don't necessarily need to confront this, because it's a prison newspaper and readers know the context. But the context is different with freelancing – when readers are on the outside. Your stories will be among those of traditional writers. That can make it both jarring and fascinating for readers to see your story in a national magazine, which is why you need to explain how you wound up in prison. They can handle it. (I get that this can be difficult, especially with heinous crimes and innocence claims, and I'll probably write a whole other piece on prison writers revealing their crimes, but you can be candid and contrite – even if you say something like this: "Look, I'm ashamed of what I did ten years ago. I'm not asking for your forgiveness. I've yet to forgive myself. But I do want to tell you this story about ....)

But what's the story? *Here's Writing for Story* author Jon Franklin's definition: "A story consists of a sequence of actions that occur when a sympathetic character encounters a complicated situation that he confronts and solves." Character – their wants and desires – drives story. If it's a personal narrative, you are the character. In *"The Apology Letter,"* published last November in the *Washington Post Magazine*, I explained coming to terms with remorse and how I came to feel summoned to write an apology letter to the family of my victim. With a more journalistic piece, I would say the story, and theme too, comes from the character you are writing about. To find story, then, you should always be in conversation with your peers. Tell them your story, listen to theirs. Writing is a solitary act, but reporting and hunting the story is not. Hollywood loves happy endings. But real-life resolutions are often more internal and abstract in magazine features. Characters, as Jon Franklin suggests, don't always resolve their situations. At the end of "This Place is Crazy," my brother dies, Joe Cardo is released but still struggles on the outside, and I'm still in prison. But in another sense, I've arrived as the writer. At the end of the "Apology Letter," I'm grappling with my identity, one of the major themes in the piece. "Am I the writer or the murderer? I've come to realize, regretfully, that I will always be both."

When I'm stuck and unsure with material or about to embark on a big story, I turn to my favorite craft book. The ingredients for success are in the chapters: story, structure, point of view, character, scene, action, dialogue, theme, reporting, story narratives, ethics. Jack Hart's *Storycraft*, the complete guide to narrative nonfiction, is written from the editor's perspective, which is important because editors are the gatekeepers. They say what's hot and what's not. I'm constantly in conversation with editors. They're not teachers, they're doers. I learn by watching what they do to my stories; they restructure paragraphs so the chronology of the narrative flows smoother, and they cut and cut – to increase the story's velocity. While the editors I've worked with might not tell me what they are doing, reading Hart I see how they operate – that's his genius. He also borrows from other craft experts – Robert McKee, Jon Franklin, William Blundell, Ted Conover – and assembles what's relevant in utterly readable prose.

Hart's book is the kind that jolts ideas from vague notions into real story pegs. When reading the chapter on explanatory narratives, I came up with an idea to pitch *Sports Illustrated* on a story about parlay betting and fantasy football in Sing Sing. An explanatory narrative doesn't follow the character-complication-resolution story arc; rather, it describes a process with "close-to-the-ground specificity" with scenes (action) and digressions (explanation), back and forth. The story ran earlier this year in the pre-Super Bowl issue. It wound up causing me some problems down the line, because some people around me felt I had revealed too much. Unlike other journalists who often vanish from the lives of their subjects once stories run, I remain here, in the middle of the action. That's the complication of being a journalist in the joint: you've got to face the heat. Later, a prison administrator asked me, "Why would you write a story knowing it could cause you problems?" I responded, "Because I took a shot!"

I say we all need to take a shot. Dream up big stories, imagine your name in the bylines of the slicks. At the same time, be humble enough to know what you don't know. Mail your essays to professors and writers and editors and beg them for blood on the pages. I'm not a good writer, but I am a good rewriter. The Prison Journalism Project is a good place to start. They'll give you some feedback, not a whole lot, but take what you can get. They may post it, or even help you get into a major publication. Keep in mind that I started with shorter pieces, about a thousand words, until I got a grasp of narrative.

Check this out. I once sent an essay to a woman who created a website for prison writers. She was paying $10 for pieces about salacious prison experiences. She was a true-crime TV producer, and I suspected that she was looking for material. She read my essay and told me it was good, but I was being unrealistic to think a national magazine would publish me. I felt stupid. Then I rewrote the piece and sent it to *Esquire*. It went on to become the National Magazine Award finalist in feature writing and was anthologized in *The 2019 Best American Magazine Writing*. *Esquire* paid me a good amount of money for the piece. Because the *Washington Post Magazine* essay was about my crime, I donated the money I received; the issue, written and illustrated by currently and formerly incarcerated people, won the 2020 National Magazine Award. Now there you have a happy ending.

About the Author: John J. Lennon is an incarcerated journalist serving a sentence of 28 years to life in Sullivan Correctional Facility. He was previously incarcerated at Sing Sing where he hosted a podcast. He is a contributing editor for *Esquire Magazine* and a contributing writer for *The Marshall Project*. John was a finalist for the 2019 National Magazine Awards in Feature Writing and received an Honorable Mention for the 2019 Molly National Journalism Award.

12 SECRETS TO IMPROVE YOUR WRITING STYLE!

Now that we understand some writing basics, let's discuss a few tips that will really improve your writing and take it to the next level. Prisoners are known to use the longest words they know (usually out of context), or think they know, in an effort to try and appear smarter than they really are. This usually backfires, because they use the word(s) incorrectly and end up looking like a schmuck. Another thing I've noticed is that prisoners are often not organized or clear with what they are trying to say. This is something you need to get down if you are serious about this game.

The following tips, once you have them down, will take your writing to the next level.

Communicate; don't try to impress. There is a happy medium between reading so tough you need an IQ of 180 and material that is helpful only if you have difficulty falling asleep. The comfort zone of the average reader is about the eighth-grade level, so practice the old rule of KISS ("Keep it simple, stupid"). Studies show that eighth-grade readers can understand fairly easy sentences with an average of fourteen words. Remember, we said "average." You may have a two-word sentence and then a whopper. Just be sure it is basically a simple declarative sentence. If it becomes too long and unwieldy, break it in two. You can use words such as *and, but, additionally, yet, consequently, therefore,* or *accordingly* to divide sentences easily.

Use short words instead of long ones. For many writers who typically pride themselves on a strong, versatile vocabulary, this is difficult. Stickler three-, four-, and five-syllable words should be avoided. Recondite slows down most anyone: yet family and company – also three-syllable words – totally acceptable. It comes down to using good judgement.

Use the right word for the job. Word choice is vitally important. Mark Twain observed, "The difference between the right word and the almost right word is the difference between lightning and the lightning bug." Are your words colorful? Specific? Descriptive? Don't have a man walk. Rather, let him amble stride, stagger, or shuffle along. Avoid beginning most of your sentences with "the." Try not to develop "I" trouble: overuse of I quickly bores the reader. Rephrase the sentence to do away with this repeated reference. Watch for repetition of words within close proximity. Using the same word over and over again (unless it's for emphasis) is a sloppy way of writing.

Avoid ambiguity. Rewrite anything that is unclear. A story is told that FBI Director J. Edgar Hoover decided he didn't like the margin format used for a letter he had dictated to his secretary. So, he scribbled "watch the borders" on it and gave it back to her. She dutifully retyped the letter and sent if off to the top FBI agents. For the next two weeks, dozens of agents were placed on special alert along the Canadian and Mexican Borders. Think through any confusing areas. What do they mean? Could they be misinterpreted? Take the word terminal, for instance. It means entirely different things to a computer operator, an electrician, a bus driver, and a physician.

Keep a wary eye on overall language. Foreign words and unfamiliar jargon confuse the reader. Likewise, "in vogue" terms date your manuscript and may appear ridiculous five years later.

Guard against clichés. These are overused, trite bits and pieces of speech that are part of everyone's conversations. "Money hungry," "Sly as a fox," "Grows by leaps and bounds" are all clichés. When we write, it's important to pare away worn phrases; replace them with more original phraseology. Clichés are a sign of lazy writing. Think of a fresh, new way to say it.

Delete redundancies and needless words. Why say, "He stood up to make the announcement"? (Have you ever seen anyone stand down?) Early pioneers should be simply pioneers: in the not too distant future = soon; due to the fact that = because; until such time as = until; combined together = combined. Get the idea? Watch your writing for conciseness. Have you pared away all unnecessary words? Eliminated repetition? Abolish words such as very, really, just, and other qualifiers that don't serve a definite purpose.

Brevity beautiful. Train yourself to shed the padding that comes from years of cranking out student papers. It's been said that if you run your pen through every other word you have written, you have no idea what vigor it will give your style.

Inject your writing with liveliness. Use similes or metaphors to show comparisons. A simile uses "like" or "as": His personality is as bland as oatmeal. A metaphor suggests resemblance: Her face blossomed with affection. Such additions help readers relate to what you've written.

Put more zip in your manuscript with analogies. They help make or illustrate a point. An example of an analogy: Life is a hundred-yard dash, with birth the starting gun and death the tape.

Relate anecdotes; another important fact of nonfiction writing. They are stories or examples that illustrate and clarify the points you wish to make.

Use the active voice to achieve readability. In the active voice, the subject of the sentence performs the action rather than receiving it. Here's an example:
    The active voice: The wind slammed the door shut.
    The passive voice: The door was slammed shut by the wind.
    How much more powerful is the active version? Here's a hint for spotting the passive voice: Look at the verb phrase. It will always include a form of the "to be" verb, such as *is*, *are*, *was* or *is being*.

For additional horsepower be specific! Look for ways to support general statements with details. Think of your writing as a funnel. At the top is the general statement, then it narrows down to a specific incident. This targets the reader's attention toward one given example. Rather than saying the woods are full of trees, say the woods are full of aspen, spruce, and pine.

Transition smoothly. This is another hallmark of good writing. Are there graceful bridges between sentences, paragraphs, and chapters? Some words and phrases that serve as transition bridges are *still, on the other hand, another, next, however, of course, then, finally, but, yet, unfortunately, in short, once again*.

THE WRITE SECRET

I'm going to give you one of the greatest secrets in the business of writing. You ready? Here it is: If you want to become a successful writer, you must...drum roll, please...write! Yes, writing consistently is one of the best things you can do if you want to be a successful writer.

> *"If you want to be a writer, you must do two things above all else: read a lot and write a lot. There's no way around these two things that I'm aware of, no shortcut."* – Stephen King

Writing is your craft, your trade, what you're hoping to sell to the world. If you want to be a master, you must write with the same dedication that Kobe stayed in the gym taking shots with. There is no way around this; there's no magic bullet that will allow you to skip this part of the process. (If this seems obvious, you'd be surprised at how many prisoners talk to me about wanting to be a writer, and six months later, still have not written anything.) No matter how many books you read about writing, though you will certainly pick up jewels, you must grow your skill by doing. And the same thing goes for publishing, too.

> *"Never stop writing. This Is every successful writer's secret."*
> – David Gaughran, author of *Let's Get Digital: How to Self-Publish and Why You Should*

What you need to do is write your very best book using all the information you know thus far. During this process – of writing, then publishing the book – you will learn many things. Once you're done with the book, start working on your next book, being sure to incorporate all the things you learned from your last book-writing experience. When you write this "next" book, you will learn a few more things that you didn't learn while writing and publishing the previous book. When you're done with this book, you repeat the process again with the next.

> *"It is by sitting down to write every morning that one becomes a writer."* – Gerald Brennan

This is, by far, the best way to learn to write, and publish, and be successful at it. Each book works as a learning curve. You should expect to write and publish a good 10 books before you really start to get it down (though the learning never really ends). And remember, you must give every book your best shot, using all the info you know. Trying to rush through a book so you can hurry and get to the 10th will not work. You must go through the labor pains of putting your best foot forward with each and every book.

> *"I often feel that the skills I learned writing one novel don't really kick into gear until I start the next."* – David Gaughran, author of *Let's Get Digital: How to Self-publish and Why You Should*

What you don't want to do, as tempting as it may be, is keep going over the same book over and over and over, just because you keep learning something new each time. If you do this, you will never publish the book, because each time you go over it, you will learn more that you will then have to go back and fix; then the process will repeat itself.

It becomes a never-ending cycle, and you will never finish the book. This is where 80/20 Publishing comes is. When you book is 80 percent or more to perfection, it's ready to publish. 80 percent (whether they know it or not) will satisfy the market. Then, take what you learned and apply it to the next book. Each time you complete a book, if you did it right and pushed yourself to the max, you will be exhausted, and this is how you grow – like when working out.

Building a writing and publishing career is a building process. Very few writers hit a home run on their first book. Reason being, they don't have the experience they need to hit the home run. Again, you should expect to write and publish around 10 books before you really start to get it down. I say writing and publishing, because the publishing phase, based on the information you get back from the market, will hope you hone your craft. You will learn what the market wants from you, and what they don't. This is key, and the market never lies. So, it's not the same as writing a book and just setting it on your locker; though that's certainly better than not writing the book at all when it comes to fine-tuning your writing abilities.

Using the analogy of an upcoming rapper, consider your first 10 books to be mixtapes that you're using to hone your craft and promote yourself with. What I mean is, when you learn of a new rapper from another state, though they may be new on your radar, they likely have dropped several mixtapes. People from their city, and whatever fans found them online, may have been aware of them for several years before you hear of them. The same thing works with your books. You may write a book or two and be yard famous, or even semi prison famous if they're popular enough, but it may take you 10 books before people across the country, especially folks on the outside, really become aware of you. When they of learn of you, they may think you're new to the game, only to learn you've got 10 other books (that they will hopefully now go back and buy). This is how it works. You're likely to be very disappointed if you expect anything different. Again, this is a building process; you can't get to layer 10 without first doing layers 1-9.

"It took me 10 years to become an overnight success." – Mark Cuban, Billionaire

And books aren't the only things you should write. Books are time consuming, expensive to produce, and they're a lot of work for you and your people. So, don't just think books, books, books. If you have a blog, that can help, but you should be writing and submitting to as many genre-appropriate publications, online and print, as possible.

This helps build not only your name and audience, but your contacts, too – your network. Let these other publications distribute your writing, and, essentially, build you up. They have an audience you likely don't have, but need to have. They have a platform. You want to get in front of their audience and invite these people to be your audience. This is how you build an audience – a platform. It amazes me how much prisoners neglect to do this. They simply do not understand the value.

Right now, my goal is to get published by as many publications as possible. I am trying to have my name everywhere it needs to be. I have over 25 books, so for me it's about growing my name, brand, and audience, and via the least expensive way possible. You know how a player on the streets will try and smash as many bitches as possible so his hit list is extensive, thus, elevating his player status? The more the better, right? This is the concept I'm using when trying to get articles and stories published by other publications. I'm tryna smash 'em all! The more names (relevant publications) on my hit list, the better. This is how you build a platform! Writing more books is great for several reasons, but you also need to write for other publications so you can get in front of their audience, or nobody will know about your books.

MY WRITING PROCESS

A lot of people ask me what my writing and building process is like – how I get my ideas, how I put them together, etc. – so I figured I'd include it in this book.

I'm an idea guy. Coming up with ideas is the easy part for me. I come up with a lot of ideas. I then filter out the ones I'm least passionate about, the ones that are probably the hardest to pull off, or that I don't see being profitable enough for me to invest my time. That leaves me with the best ones, which I write on a piece of paper, like a list, and hang up on my wall. This allows me to look at it throughout the day to see if anything on the list is trying to tell me anything.

At any one time, I might have 4-8 books in the works. Mind you, I might have ideas I want to do, but this doesn't mean I jump right to it. I might not get to it for a year, two, or three, but I'm aware of it, collecting info, and writing down ideas as I think of them. I keep all of this in a manilla envelope, labeled according to whatever book it's for. If the material becomes too much for a manilla envelope, I move it all into one of those cardboard Priority envelopes.

When I finally feel it's time to work on a particular book, I usually write an outline, if it's a story, or a list of contents I want to include if it's a how-to or info book, like this one. An outline is a list of things, like events, etc., that I want included in the story. Once I create this list of contents, I put them in the proper order. This is an important step in the process because it's the bones or frame of the story – what I use to but I'd my story around – and the more detailed, the better. I then use this like a roadmap. And this doesn't have to be concrete, either. As I work the story, I might come up with better ideas I didn't have before and make adjustments as I go.

Once I have the outline, I write about the first thing/event on my list. After writing everything I want to say on that part of the story, I start making a transition to the next thing on the list. I continue doing this until I've written the whole story, from beginning to end, no matter how long or short. When I'm done, at least with this part of the process, I begin to edit – take away the bad parts, detail out the good parts, add to the thin parts, insert parts I didn't think of originally, etc. While doing this, I don't care about spelling or anything, I just want to get the story out on paper. I don't trip on names, either.

If I'm not sure of what names I want to use, I will just use any names I can remember easily and differentiate in my mind while writing the story. I can go back and change them later. From here, I basically just tweak on it until it's what I want it to be. I just go over it again and again and again, polishing it until it's a shiny piece of gold.

"I tell you this because good writing is not writing it's rewriting, or editing."
– Gurmeet Mattu

But as you probably notice, I don't write a whole lot of stories. I mostly write how-to and info books, like this one. When I do write a book of stories, it's usually a book of short, nonfiction journalism-type stories that, together, as a collection, create a book. These are easier and more fun for me to do. I don't like working on one story for too long. I get burned out and lose interest. With how-to and info books,

I can just focus on one chapter at a time and they don't have to really transition into each other. So, it's like individual pieces that I can collect and put together in the form of a book. Take for example the book of California prison stories I'm working on. For this book, I'm just writing individual stories about primarily famous people and events that have happened in California prisons over the last several decades. Each story I write, which is more like a detailed magazine article, will end up being a chapter to the book. Or, for example, my upcoming book on street kings. I'm just writing nonfiction article-type pieces/stories on individual street kings, like Rich Porter, Freeway Rick Ross, Supreme, etc., and when I have enough, I'll put them together in the form of a book and publish it. When I have enough for another book, I'll publish it and call it volume 2. See what I'm saying? So, I might actually work on a book in this way for a few years, writing pieces as I'm inspired to, but I will have a few other books I'm workin on in this way, too, at the same time.

That's how I wrote this book. I've had the idea for this book for a few years already, but I was in no real hurry to knock it out, because for one, I have to really be feeling a project before I can get into it. There's a feeling I get when it's the right time. For two, I had too many other projects going one and for three, I felt like I needed to learn a few other things in order to give you the best book possible, and I wanted to learn them based on actual experience, not just by reading books, like most of these other info-authors do.

Once I finally started feeling the energy that it was time to start working on this book, I pulled out my envelope and started putting my already-typed chapters in the best order I could in an attempt to try and get some type of organization. I had so much material that I'd collected, though, that it was overwhelming, and I couldn't figure out the best way to start. I tried typing a list of all the chapter titles and subjects I already had, to see if looking at it would tell me something. However, I made little progress. Trying to catch a wave doesn't always happen quickly or easily, even for a seasoned writer like myself.

> *"Focus on one step at a time.... You're standing at the bottom of a set of steps that reach to the top of a massive stadium. Just the thought of climbing to the top can be paralyzing, because the task is so daunting. But you can take one step. It doesn't seem like much because there are so many more steps ahead. But even a seasoned athlete can't ignore those single steps. It's the only way up. There are no shortcuts to the top. You build a writing career one word at a time.*
>
> *It's important to have a clear goal, like completing a manuscript. But once it's set, you need to focus on individual steps. Keep the goal in mind, because it keeps us moving in the right direction. Taking single steps helps you overcome inertia and build momentum."* – Writer's Market

I began reading chapters that I already had, looking for anything that would grab and inspire me. I still got nowhere. I then decided I had too much material and I began throwing out anything I knew I wouldn't use. Then I picked just one chapter that needed worked on and focused solely on that chapter. I read the chapter a couple times and the material I had for it, then I thought about it for the rest of the day while I tended to other business like working out, cleaning my cell, etc. From this I started to catch my wave.

I started coming up with the direction I wanted to go with the chapter. I obsessed over it, even waking up several times during the night to write down ideas. By the time I woke up the next morning, I was ready to go. I pulled out my typewriter, loaded it with an old fabric ribbon. (what I use to type my rough drafts) and some regular lined paper, drank a shot of Folgers, and started purging all the things I had come up with over the last day or so. I do this as fast as I can, while maintaining the best order I can, but I don't worry about spelling or any of that shit. My goal is to just get the words out while I have them.

Once I catch my wave and get into my zone, I usually can't stop thinking about my project. Once I'm done purging one topic or chapter on paper, I'll look at my list of topics and see which one grabs me, then I'll purge everything I have on it. I'll do this for a few days, maybe a week, and when I start to feel burned out on the purging phase, I'll take a break by going over the pieces I purged and start editing them with an ink pen – rewording sentences better, rearranging the order of the paragraphs if needed, etc. By the time I'm done, the paper will look crazy, unable to be understood by anyone but me. Sometimes, if the paper starts to get too crazy, I will type it again with all the changes I've made so I have a cleaner copy, then I'll go over that copy several times. Then I'll usually put these up for a few weeks so I can clear my mind of them. When I go back over them with a fresh eye, I get a closer idea how readers will experience it when reading it for the first time. Once I got it down right, I'll type up a clean copy and put it in my file.

I'm explaining this to show you that nobody, not even James Patterson or Stephen King, write their books in one shot. I've seen so many prisoners try to do this; especially ones who have never written a book before. Sometimes it takes a minute to catch your wave. All of this is okay. Put all your material to the side and just focus on the one you feel the most. It may take a day or two to really catch your wave, but once you start to catch even a tiny one, start writing. Just write! At first your thoughts might be all over the place. It doesn't matter. After a few paragraphs you should start to catch your rhythm. Remember, just purge all that you want to say. Be sure to leave lots of space on your page – margins, etc. – because you will need room to write all your changes, inserts, adjustments, etc.

This is my process, just to give you an example of what I have to do to write these books. As you practice, you will come up with a process that works best for you. But to give you another example, from someone else, here's an excerpt from *Think Outside the Cell*, a book written by Joseph Robinson while he was incarcerated in a New York prison.

"I'll admit, after I got the intoxicating excitement of starting a book for the incarcerated and formerly incarcerated – a business book at that – I began to have doubts as to whether I could actually complete it. Initially, I was intimidated by the amount of time, commitment and research writing this type of book would demand of me. I'm sure that some of my uncertainty came from the fact that over the years I'd begun, and never finished, several books. But I was determined to see this book to fruition. I was determined to make it happen!

The first thing I did was take a few sheets of paper and begin brainstorming about the kinds of topics and information I thought would motivate my intended audience (you) to really think outside the cell. I wanted to make sure the book had all the pertinent business and legal information to get you started on your way to realize your dreams.

After hours of excited brainstorming, and a few days of trying to make sense of the multi-directional scribbling I'd put down on paper, my initial book outline began to take shape. I went back and forth with various chapter titles until I felt I had ones that captured the essence of what I wanted to say. I placed topics and information from my brainstorming session in bullet format underneath appropriate chapter headings.

There was no way I could predict how the final book would turn out. All I knew was that I'd give it my best. I was very fortunate to have a professional writer as my wife. I sent her a copy of my initial chapter outline, and she helped me rearrange and organize my thoughts. She helped to make sure that I had a smooth, logical flow in the way the chapters unfolded.

I knew from the beginning that if I wanted to complete this project, if I wanted to overcome bouts of self-doubt, I had to break this project down to size. I had to make it manageable, doable.

At the time, I was a facilitator for the prison's Transitional Services Program, where I conducted daily orientation classes for men who were new to the facility. My program assignment consumed six hours of my day, affording me little time to dedicate to writing a book.

As much as I enjoyed teaching, I decided to change my program to something that did not require much of my time. I changed to a pantry job in the mornings and evenings. Basically, I served breakfast and dinner chow to the men in my housing unit for all of 20 minutes. I had the rest of the day to do as I pleased. Well, not exactly, but you know what I mean.

With my edited outline as my guide, I carved out three hours every morning (my thinking is clearest in the morning). Instead of setting out to write a book, I focused on writing four to six pages a day. Often, I wrote more. Pages turned into chapters, and chapters turned into the completed book you are now reading.

It took me three months to write the first draft of this book, and another six or seven months of revising and editing. Actually, my wife (and later, her sister) did the bulk of the editing. I did cursory edits while writing the pages and chapters, but I didn't want to get lost in the editing process, as many people do. I simply wanted to write. I wanted to unleash my thoughts, not curtail them. So, I just let the words flow from me to the paper. Five edits later, I had my completed manuscript."

GREAT WAYS TO GENERATE IDEAS ON WHAT TO WRITE ABOUT!

A lot of guys ask where I get my ideas on what to write about. For me, ideas are the easy part. Figuring out what ideas to put aside so I can focus on the biggest "winners" is the difficult part. But for those of you who are unsure of what to write about, here are some tips to help you figure it out.

1. Take a lot of showers.

Ask twenty successful freelance writers where they get their best ideas, and it's safe to say nineteen of them will say, "in the shower." There's even some science to back them up – possibly about negative ions. But who cares, as long as it works, right?

2. Put your subconscious to work.

Remember that one writer in twenty that doesn't get ideas in the shower? Odds are he would tell you that the best ideas seem to bubble up out of nowhere. That, some say, is the subconscious mind at work. But you don't have to sit back and wait for your subconscious to start bubbling. You can give it an assignment. Once, Napoleon Hill, one of the founders of *Success* magazine, was trying to come up with a title for a new book. He had a talk with his subconscious before he went to bed. "I've got to have a million-dollar title, and I've got to have it tonight," he said (and he said it out loud). "Do you understand that?"

Apparently, his subconscious got the message, because at 2 A.M., Hill woke up, bounded to his typewriter, and banged out the title. Hill's book, *Think and Grow Rich*, went on to sell more than twenty million copies.

If you try Hill's technique, the results may be mixed. Some mornings you may wake up with an idea you've asked for. Other days you'll wake up with a good idea but on an entirely different subject. The rest of the time you'll just wake up.

3. Read everything you can get your hands or eyes on.

The best writers not only try to keep up with the fields they cover but read just about anything in sight. Few of the things you read will pay off in an immediate story, but they all help feed that mysterious idea machine in your head.

Books ... Poke around the library. Let yourself get lost in unfamiliar aisles. Check out the new releases at the bookstore. If you are in prison, browse the book catalogs from SureShot, Books N Things, or Bargain Books. This can help you identify trends and see what people are interested in.

Magazines ... Read the ones you want to write for, of course, but look at others, too. You'll learn some new things, discover new ways to tell a story, or maybe even stumble onto a promising market or two. Don't leave out old magazines, either.

Newspapers ... Your local paper can be a terrific source of ideas. You may see a story in your local paper that's ripe for telling practically as is in a book or national magazine. It may be a local trend that's yet to be widely written about or a local person whose tale could be made into a story.

Junk Mail ... Everyone is inundated with junk mail on a daily basis, and you've probably considered all that mail to be worthless clutter. But with a change of perspective, you'll find it can be a great source for ideas. Analyze those announcements for new products and stores, annual events, and human-interest subjects. Look at them all and save the most thought-provoking ones.

4. Listen up.

Some of the best story ideas come from listening to your friends, neighbors, cellmates, etc., tell you war stories, or talk about their ideas. *Loyalty and Betrayal*, the book I did with Armando Ibarra, came about from me hearing him tell war stories to my celly all day. I thought they were interesting and felt that others would, too. Most of them included the Mexican Mafia, and his fallout with them. Though he couldn't personally write all that well, I had him write it the best he could on paper. I edited the story and published it. It is now one of my bestselling books.

5. Tap into your own experience.

Forget for a moment that you are a writer. What's on your mind, just as a human being? If you've wondered about something, chances are other people have, too. The difference is you are a writer and can look into the subject, write about it, and maybe even get paid to do so. Remember all the events in your life – the good and the bad – are part of your material as a writer.

6. Get to know some PR people.

Public relations professionals often have great story ideas before anyone else. The trouble is, of course, is that it's their job to put a spin on the idea that benefits their clients. The other trouble is that they're out to get their clients as much positive publicity as much as possible, so if you received a story tip from them, a few dozen other writers probably did, too. That said, you'll find PR people are worth paying attention to. If nothing else, they can sometimes get you access to key experts and provide background information that you'd otherwise spend a lot of time digging up on your own. Just remember that their agendas and yours aren't identical.

7. Keep notebook handy.

As you go through your day, you cannot even begin to anticipate everything and everyone that will cross your path. Nor can you anticipate every thought that will enter your brain. That's why you should always have a notebook with you – so you are ready to jot down any idea that might present itself. Don't trust your brain to store these ideas until you have time to write them down. Put them on paper immediately so you don't risk forgetting a million-dollar-idea!

These are not the only ways to find good story ideas, but they are a good start if you're stumped. Remember, there is no right or wrong way to find an idea. Always be open to receiving them. They are all around you.

WRITE TO MARKET

What I'm about to explain to you is one of the most valuable of all secrets within this book. It's controversial to some, but we don't care about that. We only care about winning. What's this secret called? It's called Writing to Market.

Who, or what is this "Mr. Market"? Mr. Market is my writing and publishing mentor. He's the most successful writer and publisher in the world. He is who taught me the secrets of the game. He is why I am winning. You must pay very, very close attention to his lessons. If you do, you, too, will be rewarded with money and fame from your writing and publishing endeavors.

What is the process of Writing to Market? Writing to Market is picking an underserved genre that you know has a voracious appetite, and then giving that market exactly what it wants. It means that before you write word one of your book, you already know you're going to have fans waiting to buy it. It may seem impossible to do this, but believe me, it's absolutely achievable if you follow closely. Here's how...

First, do not write a book and then try to figure out who to sell it to – like most people do. Doing so is a mistake. Instead, before you write even a single word, figure out who your market is going to be – who you want to sell your books to. Keep in mind that it has to be a market you can effectively reach and compete. For example, I come from hip hop. I'm knowledgeable in the "urban" market. So, my first idea was to write books for the urban market – fiction and nonfiction urban crime stories, etc. So, I studied the genre to pinpoint the elements (something I will explain a little later), and I began writing and publishing great urban crime novels. However, I ran into a wall when trying to sell them. Why, if I had such great books, was it difficult to sell them? Because you can't sell something if people don't know about it, and notifying the urban-book buying community about my books was not within my reach at the time. 1) I have no internet access to promote to the urban-book buying community on the outside myself, and with limited resources I could not afford to hire someone to do it for me. And 2) There are lots of inmates who buy urban books, but to advertise to them via magazines such as *XXL, The Source,* and *Don Diva* was too expensive. Luckily for me, however, without intended strategy, when I published my first group of urban crime novels, I also published an informational/self-help book for prisoners. And while it was difficult to get my urban crime novels to move with my advertising resources (or lack thereof), my prisoner informational/self-help took off.

So, what lesson did my mentor (Mr. Market) teach me here?

1. I can reach inmates much easier than I can the outside market.

2. With the resources I had at the time, the inmates I could reach are more interested in informational/self-help books than urban crime novels.

When my mentor teaches, I listen. So, I readjusted my strategy. I would make prisoners (with whom there are millions) my primary market and outside folks my secondary market. I would focus first on my primary market, and I would give them exactly what they "told" (or taught) me they wanted. The market is *never* wrong.

Do not make the (common) mistake of thinking that, just because a market is bigger, it is easier to reach and pull money from. This is not the case. It has to be a market you can effectively advertise and promote to. For example; for me, it was easier and more realistic to afford advertising (one effective way of reaching people) in prisoner-based publications like *Prison Legal News* than *XXL, The Source, Don Diva*, etc. Do not overestimate your resources and abilities, like I did, and like most people do. You need to be ruthlessly honest with yourself.

Next step...

Once you figure out what market you can reach effectively, don't give them what *you* want, give them what *they* want or need so bad that they will reach into their pocket and hand you some of their hard-earned money. How do you do this? You listen! They will tell you by what they are buying. So that is the question in which you need an answer: What will make the market I can effectively reach, reach into their pocket and hand me over their money? You must identify the top subjects/answers to this. You must learn and understand the market in which you plan to take aim at.

Once you identify the top answers to the above question, pick which of those things you can do best and easiest. Sometimes it's not what you want to do, but what you *can do* effectively. For example, for my current market, prisoners, I'd love to be able to write legal/law books. That's one of the best subjects for my target market. 1) Every prisoner needs some sort of legal help. 2) Legal books are expensive, often $50 or more. However, I'm not knowledgeable enough on the law to write law books.

Law books have to be precise. There's no room for error. So, though it's an attractive topic, one my market is telling me they need, and one I'd like to do; at least at this time, it's not for me. It doesn't fall into my category of what I can do best and easiest.

So, what am I good at that I can provide prisoners with? Well, I know prison and the prisoner lifestyle. With over 20 years in prison, I'd say I'm an expert. I'm also a beast when it comes to business, as it's my passion and I've spent much of my time studying it. I can literally write *The Hustler's Bible*. A lot of prisoners are entrepreneurial – drug dealers, hustlers, have had to learn to make something from nothing for survival purposes. Like everyone else in the world, they certainly have a desire and need to make money, but have just not been taught how to do so legally. Bam! I got it! I can teach prisoners (and street hustlers) how to hustle and win legally, using the prisoner and business knowledge I have, but by putting it in terms they will ingest, understand and appreciate! I can do it in my voice, which is primarily "urban" and informal, so that it's less "stiff," more entertaining, and different than anyone else's who may try to weave into my lane! This is something I can do better than anybody. I'm not one of the best, I'm *the* best.

There's my lane – my niche.

Primarily....

You didn't think I gave up on my original plan of writing urban crime novels, did you? Giving up is what I *don't* do (another secret to success). I'm just following the steps to get to where I want to go the way my mentor is directing me. A lot of prisoners buy/read urban books; I just could not afford the demanded advertising costs when first starting. I will have to build to the bigger market. So, meanwhile, I'll focus my primary efforts on books that my easily-reached prisoner market is telling me they want, so I can make my money, and I'll advertise my already-done urban crime novels inside those books so word can start to spread without additional cost to me. This is the order my mentor – The Market – has taught me. And, he has assured me that, by following his directions, and "paying my dues," I will build the resources to promote and advertise my urban crime novels properly so that I get the desired outcome/success. (Then, he continued, by following his proven methods, he will not only make me rich and famous, he will make me a publishing boss so that I'm not only able to make myself the number one incarcerated author and publisher in America, but also publish urban crime novels by other inmates, and books that I cannot myself do that my market is telling me they want – legal books! But this is getting ahead of the current lesson. Gotta stay focused.)

The market does not lie, ever. So, though it wasn't my originally desired plan, I listened.

> *"The road to success is not a straight path."*
> – Unknown

Now, let's get onto the next step....

Once you find your market and niche and figure out what they want that you can provide with quality, buy the top-selling books in your lane, or closest to what you want to do, and study them. Whether it's romance, military science fiction, mystery or psychological thrillers that you want to write, buy 3-5 of the top selling books and study them. Closely.

For example, when I decided I wanted to write urban crime books, from my prison cell, the first books I bought was *Prison Stories* and *Street Legends Vol. 1* by Seth Ferranti. Why? Seth was a prisoner writing books similar to what I wanted to do, and he was making some noise. The market was responding positively. He was a great example for me to study. (Note: What's the biggest jewel I received from Seth? That it's about *execution*. There are a lot of prisoners who have written books. What differentiated Seth was that he actually *followed through and got his to market*. I'm sure there are many books sitting on prisoner's shelves around the country that are better than Seth's (and mine), but he followed through with his, and that makes all the difference. He wrote and published his books from a federal prison somewhere in the country, and here I was in a California prison cell with them in my hand. Valuable lesson.)

In addition to Seth's books, I bought 50 Cent's *From Pieces To Weight* from someone on the tier. Oh, my god, the writing was horrible! It's like someone didn't even give 50's book a basic edit, even though we all know he has to have the resources to do so. He's 50! That said, he's 50. He has a name and fanbase I don't have, so he can get away with things I can't get away with. We are not the same. At all. However, it was comforting to see that even 50's book was not perfect.

In addition to Seth's and 50's books I ordered a bunch of books from RJ Publications – buy 3, get 1 free. I don't know if they were written in prison by prisoners or not (RJ is not a prisoner), but RJ is much smaller than 50, so at least he was more comparable to my reality. I must've read 8 books that RJ published. (RJ's books may or may not have been best sellers in the genre I wanted to enter, I'm unsure. As a prisoner, they are what I had access to, and they were advertised in *XXL* magazine. Good enough for me. Later I read and studied *True To The Game* and *The Cartel*, which are top-selling classics in the urban genre. To follow this step exactly, I should have looked for the top sellers written by prisoners who self-published, since that was exactly my situation, but I did not know then everything I now know, and why I'm able to write this how-to book using a true story.)

When reading these books, I studied more than just the story itself, I studied all of what I call "The Elements." I dissected them, in other words. I paid attention to the page count, the word count, the font size, how they were marginalized and formatted, and how the covers looked.

Of course, I also paid attention to the elements of the storylines. The goal was to figure out the common elements of my example books. Because, as I discovered, there are common elements, both "major" and "minor." This is one of the top secrets that successful authors know: The successful books must contain the required common elements for that genre. This is a major key. When you read your example books, pay very close attention and you will see them. They are in every genre; meaning, every genre has its own set of common elements. Why? Readers expect them. If you want your book to be successful, you must provide the key elements that the readers of that genre love. Readers want the elements that are familiar to them, but they want you to use them in new and interesting ways. You must use the proper elements, and you must employ them like a master.

Here are a few examples of major and minor elements. I'll use other genres than my own, because if you want the game on urban books, check out my book *How To Write Urban Books For Money & Fame*, with TCB author King Guru. Here we go...

Genre: Romance
Major:
- Happily, ever after. This is the cornerstone of nearly every romance novel.
- Happy for now. Some romances use this, but it's more niche.

Minor:
- Hero and heroine meet.
- Hero and heroine have a conflict.
- The story will reach a point where it looks like the hero and heroine won't make it.

Get the point? All successful romance novels have some or all of these elements. Do not try and reinvent the wheel if you want to improve your chances of connecting with your readers. Even houses that look different are primarily built the same way with the same elements! Let's do a few more...

Genre: Military Science Fiction
Major:
- Humanity attacked by mysterious new enemy.
- Humanity attacked by long vanished enemy.
- Overbearing and incompetent military leadership.
- One ship and crew must save us all.

Minor:
- Aging starship (think Battlestar Galactica).
- Maverick captain (think Captain Kirk).

Genre: Mystery
Major:
- Female amateur sleuth caught in mystery by accident.
- Hot cop or FBI agent who is investigating the case.
- Mystery solved in a happy ending (no cliffhangers, ever).
- Almost no violence, and if it occurs it isn't described in detail.

Minor:
- Protagonist owns a shop of some sort.
- Vic is usually unpopular and everyone had a reason to murder them.
- Wisecracking, matchmaking granny or auntie.
- Takes place in small town.

Pay attention when you read the books in your genre and you will realize the common, must-have elements. There are countless elements for countless genres. You don't have to use every single one, but pick the most commonly used ones that you like the best and use them. If you can understand and nail this, your 60 percent of the way to writing a marketable book.

Always keep in mind this question, whatever genre you choose: What do your readers want? Why are they reading your book? What problems are they trying to solve, or what needs are they trying to fill? When you have those answers, be sure to provide it to them. That is the secret of the game. If you want an uphill battle, write what you want to write, the way you want to write it, based on your emotions, desires, feelings, and artistic ideas, ignoring the Element rule, then try to find a market for it. You will most likely fail, and remain broke. I tell my authors all the time: The market does not care about your feelings or art, especially when you are unknown. The market wants what it wants, and it will tell you if you listen. You must figure out what it is, then provide it. You take the mandatory elements, then create your art around that. That has to be there. Do not let your readers down if you want their money.

Now, let's get on to some more secrets.

80/20 PUBLISHING

This next jewel is one that will help you push through the writing process effectively so that you, unlike so many others, actually get to the publishing phase – aka, actually get to market with your book(s). What is it? It's a secret known and used in life and business by the most successful people in the world. Here we are going to apply it to publishing. It's called the 80/20 Principle. What the fuck is the 80/20 Principle? I'm glad you asked.

In short, the 80/20 Principle states that 80 percent of your success comes from 20 percent of your efforts. This means that 20 percent of your success comes from 80 percent of your efforts. In other words, 80 percent of your book's success/profits are a result of 20 percent of your efforts. The key is for you to identify what 20 percent of your efforts (low input) are giving you 80 percent of your success (high output), and what 80 percent of your efforts (high input) are only giving you 20 percent of your success (low output). Then, you begin to cut out the 80 percent of efforts that are only giving you 20 percent of your success/profits, and you multiply the 20 percent of efforts that are generating in 80 percent of your success, money, fame, etc.

This is the secret to how to achieve more with less effort, which is one of the great secrets used by all the most successful people in the entire world. It's one of the most valuable secrets/methods I've learned in life and business in general. I live by it, and I use it in all aspects of hustlin', but here we're going to apply it to writing and publishing – getting to market.

To apply the 80/20 Principle yourself, your job is to identify what 20 percent of your efforts as a writer/publisher are getting you 80 percent of your success. For example, writing every day? That's a 20 percent effort that would bring you 80 percent of your success because it's allowing you to create more product and improve your writing process, which is your bread and butter. Searching the internet or doing things that can be outsourced at a cost per hour less than what your time brings in, that's an 80 percent effort. But, even with outsourcing, you need to consider the cost per reward. For example, do you really need to hire an editor? The 80/20 Principle states that 80 percent is good enough, and at least 80 percent of the market agrees. See what I'm saying? If you are able to get your book to 80 percent perfection yourself, how much would it benefit you to spend a couple thousand dollars and wait four more months (or whatever) to publish it so that you can have an editor go over it again and again to correct a few things that may not make a difference in sales anyway? Again, this is if you can get your work to 80 percent perfection yourself. If you can't, you may need to hire someone to help to get it to at least 80 percent – market satisfaction. You following me here?

Do not interpret this as me saying it's OK to pump out a bunch of garbage. That is not the case at all. 80 percent is not garbage! What I'm saying is, the money, time, resources, etc. that it takes to capture some of the remaining 20 percent might be more trouble than it's worth, and not matter to (or even be noticed by!) a reader anyway. I liken this to an artist who draws. The artist is going to make mistakes. But, are they mistakes only *he* sees? If nobody can see what he sees as a "mistake," is it worth throwing the drawing away and spending another two months doing it over? I can assure you one thing, even if you do it over, it's still not going to be perfect. In the words of Robert Chazz Chute: "You should strive for excellence, not perfection." You need a great story. You need tight pacing. You need good prose. You need believable characters. And, of course, you should never publish a book without proofreading it. You need it to be at least 80 percent to perfection. I personally proofread all TCB books before they are published (an 80 percent activity, probably, because I can outsource it to someone as good or better for less than my time is worth, but I like to make sure all TCB books have my DNA). They are not perfect, but they are surely at or above 80 percent. They are as good, if not better than most the books in my genre (I know this because I studied my genre's elements, as I explained earlier). Nobody has complained, if they've even noticed. In fact, here's a "secret" and an example of what I'm talking about...

I type all my books on an old-school typewriter, in my prison cell. Then I send them out to get scanned so they can eventually be published. Now, when you scan a typed page, it scans as an image – like a picture – and you can't then manipulate the text for formatting, etc. In order to be able to manipulate the text, you have to run the typed pages through an OCR program. This Optical Character Recognition program recognizes each character (letter) and breaks up each word into individual characters (letters) so that it then can be manipulated. You follow me? Now, the problem is, the OCR program is not 100 percent accurate. Sometimes it misreads some characters (letters). For example, an "a" might read as an "e" or an "o" if the "a" is not dark/pronounced enough on the page. A lowercase "p" might turn to an uppercase "P". A letter L might read as an "I" or "1". See what I'm saying? It also removes most the spaces and indentions between paragraphs for some reason. But I go through and fix all this because it's necessary if I want to reach the 80 percent of perfection quality. However, if you look closely, sometimes the style of my quotation marks differ. Sometimes they are the two small straight lines, which is how my typewriter types them, and sometimes they are the two small curved lines, which is a different font that the computer has. Same with my dashes. My typewriter doesn't have dashes so I put two hyphens together. Well, when this goes through the OCR program, sometimes it reads as two hyphens together, and sometimes it reads as a proper dash. Now, after my books are scanned and formatted, they are sent to me to proofread. I mark the corrections and return the manuscript. Never are all of my markings adjusted properly, so I proofread it again and send it back (all of this is something I should probably be outsourcing, by the way). All of this going back and forth requires a lot of time and money. Now, when doing this, my main priority is getting the misread characters/letters fixed because they affect the spelling of my work, and also getting all the paragraph formatting corrected, etc. Why? All of this is easily noticed. It falls under the 20 percent of activities that result in my book's 80 percent to perfection. But what about the quotation marks and dashes? If you've seen these in my books, it's not that I didn't notice them when proofreading my shit. I'm actually very OCD when it comes to my work. It's that, going back and forth to correct them, over and over, eats up a shitload of resources – time and money – and they don't make a big difference in the story, message, lesson, etc. And this is if the reader even notices them! And of those who do, only 20 percent would even care! Get the point? I leave some of the mismatched quotation marks and dashes because to nitpick them would be more trouble than it's worth. It would be an 80 percent input that only resulted in 20 percent (or less) output.

 Remember, listen to Mr. Market. He is never wrong. He will tell you whether or not you are reaching 80 percent of perfection, whether on your own, with help, or whatever. Most people who are trying to capture a piece of the remaining 20 percent of perfection are the same ones with books still on their shelves, where they will remain forever, probably. They will never be satisfied and they will always be polishing their book until it's just right. It will never be perfect, so they will probably never get to market with their shit – their "masterpiece." Whereas Seth (remember the story?), whose books were great reads, though not perfect, got his shit done and out from his prison cell somewhere in the country, and had them in my hands, in my prison cell, in California.

> *"One trap less experienced writers can fall into is trying to write the perfect book. Let me save you several years of your life: There is no such thing as perfection in this business....it just can't be done. Accept right from the outset that perfection is unattainable."* – David Gaughran

Your books will never be perfect. Trust me. James Patterson has typos in his shit. What's important, and what your goal should be, is continuous improvement. With each new book, you want to be a better writer, and to have a more efficient process for getting them to market.

If you are not already familiar with Heinlein's rules, they most certainly relate to this Principle.

1. You must write
2. You must finish what you start
3. Refrain from rewriting, except to editorial order
4. You must put your story on the market
5. You must keep it on the market until it has sold
6. You must work on something else

Heinlein published 32 novels, 59 short stories, and 16 collections! Asimov published over 500 works! Do you think either of them wrote six drafts of every book? Fuck no. And we shouldn't either. It's fine to write a couple drafts for your first book or two because you're still learning the fundamentals – you may not yet be able to reach the 80 percent of perfection on draft one of two. But you should always be looking for ways to improve the quality of your writing, and your overall process.

> *"Writers are far better off writing five books than spending five years trying to write the perfect book."* – David Gaughran

Don't put out a bunch of garbage. But don't polish the same book for years on end trying to reach so-called perfection. You need to get books out! What good is a masterpiece that's just sitting on a shelf in a prison cell somewhere, unknown to the market/world? Get your fuckin' book(s) done and out; learn, improve, and keep pushin'. This is how you get money and fame from writing and publishing.

> *"Perfection is the enemy of profitability."*
> – Mark Cuban

> *"Everything you write doesn't have to be your magnum opus."*
> – Bob Bly

SIMPLIFY, AND CONCENTRATE YOUR FORCES!

One of the greatest jewels I can give you in any business, including jailhouse publishing, is to simplify. I cannot express this enough. Do not overcomplicate your process. Each step in your process eats profit. Again: *Each step in your process eats profit.* To simplify, use my "Hustler's Mathematics," aka The 80/20 Principle. I explain what this Principle is in previous the chapter titled 80/20 Publishing. For a deeper understanding of The Hustler's Mathematics, check out my book *The Richest Man in Prison*. There, I give a complete breakdown of the science and mathematics, which applies to all aspects of business, and life.

Too many prisoners over-complicate things, including their publishing plan (as even I did when I first started), by thinking they can do more than they actually can.

Getting things done from prison is extremely difficult, as we have limited resources and are forced to rely on others for help. We tend to have these grand ideas, which is cool, but not always so realistic. Just because we can think something up doesn't necessarily mean it's realistic to pull off, from a prison cell, where other people, those on the outside, will have to do a lot of the work.

For example, when I first started, I took on way too much. I produced and published way too many books, way too fast, and worse, I dealt with way too many prisoners. My "grand" idea was to build a whole team of Street Lit writers, like a hip-hop record label would have rappers, and also, because I'm loyal, as soon as I thought I was "on", I reached out to my friends who write and put them on. Problem was, I wasn't on like I thought.

Just because you have a book published doesn't mean you're on. Getting your book published is only a small fraction of the publishing business. The actual selling, promoting and marketing of the book takes the lion's share of work and resources, and because I was using all mine producing more and more books and dealing with other prisoners, I ended up neglecting this part of the process.

In fact, as a prisoner, I suggest you focus your publishing efforts solely on yourself, and even if you want to put your friends and other writers on, don't. It's more trouble than it's worth. Trust me. I know from experience. The prisoners you deal with are not going to know the business the way you do (as you'll learn by doing), but they will likely think they do, maybe because they've read a book or ten about self-publishing, and probably because their cellmates have told them they are going to be the next John Grisham or JaQuavis Coleman. These guys will give you a book, or most likely a bunch of pages with writing on them that they think is a book, and then they will sit back in their cells expecting to collect millions. Prisoners ignorant of the way this business works, and all that it takes to be successful, will have unrealistic expectations, end up disappointed, and likely cause you and someone you intended to help to have a falling out.

While trying to educate these prisoners and keep them abreast of what you're doing, and what they should be doing, you will spend an enormous amount of time and energy writing them letters (if they are not in your prison), explaining to them how things really work versus how they hope and expect them to. If you're not allowed to write prisoners directly, you will have to use a middleman to do all the mailing, which adds extra work for those who are out there trying to help you. Feel what I'm saying? In my case, my prison stamps the actual pages of my letters with a big red prison stamp. So, I have to type my letters, then my people have to scan them using the OCR software, which causes all kinds of misreads and formatting issues, then send them to whoever they're to go to. So just me sending a letter to someone in another prison adds a ton of work that most people won't ever think about, or even know about. Remember: Every step eats profit! For example, had my people not had to do all the extra work to fix and send my letters, they could be contacting a magazine about an interview, designing an ad, adding to my online profile, or something else that will get us more sales. Think anybody I write thinks about all the work that goes into getting my letters to them? Of course not. Removing this entirely would simplify my process; redirecting the efforts would raise my profits.

You want to concentrate your forces. Concentrating your forces and simplifying go hand in hand. Don't overcomplicate things and spread yourself too thin. Break your process down to the simplest form possible. As time goes on and you learn more, re-evaluate your process and see if you can break it down even further. Then do it again, always using The Hustler's Mathematics. Part of doing this is focusing on yourself – your career – and as bad as you may want to, don't fuck with other prisoners unless you truly, truly have it like that, which you probably don't. And if you do decide to work with other prisoners, be sure to insist that they read this book so they get an idea of how publishing from prison truly works.

Ironically, one of the reasons I'm writing this book now is to simplify my process, so I can send it to the prisoners I'm dealing with. I'm also currently going through my entire company and cutting away everything that I don't need. Though I'm more established now, I'm not *increasing*, I'm *decreasing*. Anything that does not add to the bottom line is getting cut. Strunk says "Omit needless words." I say, "Omit needles steps and people in your process."

TIPS TO SIMPLIFYING & CONCENTRATING YOUR FORCES

1. Create a 1-book business. A book like *The BEST Resource Directory For Prisoners*, or *Inmate Shopper*, can be a 1-book business. A Mixbook can be a 1-book business. A 1-book business is a book that allows you to publish all your content under one title, like a magazine; that you can publish a new issue yearly or bi-yearly, and that provides you with other sources of income, like perhaps the selling of ad space. This is a 1-book business. You won't publish any other titles, and you won't need to. Everything you write and do will be combined and sold under this one title. This is an excellent way to simplify, concentrate your forces, and brand, as you will be focusing all your resources into one title.

2. Write a series. If you don't want to create a 1-book business, write a series. For example, *Underworld Zilla*, *Underworld Zilla 2*, *Underworld Zilla 3*, etc. This way all of your efforts are put into marketing one title instead of several. It's extremely difficult to get the word out about your book from prison. So, when you do, continue to capitalize on your efforts by using the same title. Furthermore, if the first book in the series is good, those readers are likely to buy book two. It's easier to keep someone along for the ride once they've bought into a series they enjoy, invested time into it, connected with characters, etc. The same thing works for a nonfition or how-to book, too. For example, *The Millionaire Prisoner*, *The Millionaire Prisoner's Guide To Buying & Selling Stocks From Prison*, *The Millionaire Prisoner's Guide To Publishing From Prison*, etc. Remember: You don't need a lot of books, you just need a few good ones you can go hard with.

> "To become a real star, Nicholas [Nicholas Brealey, publisher of *The 80/20 Principle*] must work a great deal less. I have a theory that if he published half the number of books, and put all his effort into these, he'd make even more money." – Richard Koch, author of *The 80/20 Principle*

3. Apply The 80/20 Principle to everything. Focus on return on investment (ROI). Anything that doesn't bring in a positive ROI, cut it. Don't do anything just for the sake of doing it. Pay attention, keep score. If something doesn't bring you profit, either in the form of money or other benefits, cut it. Constantly re-evaluate and edit as you go.

4. Stick to a niche. Find your "thing," something you're passionate about and can be successful with, and stick to it. Don't jump around. When I started, I was writing urban fiction, prisoner info, true crime, how to hustle & win legally (business and entrepreneurship). Each one has a different market I had to try and reach with limited resources. This is not how you want to start out. It's more effective to spend $1,000 marketing one thing than $100 marketing 10 things. Don't even think about touching a second genre until you've gotten all you can out of the first one, and when you do work in a second genre, try to have it something still somewhat related to the first so you can try to still appeal to the audience you've built. For example, my Street Lit fans would likely be interested in moving with me to my "How to hustle & win legally" books.

5. Can you automate? Automate anything that's automatable. For example, I'm not a big fan of prisoners spending their resources on social media because the ROI isn't there. However, if you have a blog on your website – and you should – you can set it up to where your blogs automatically post to social media, and this makes social media worth having. In my chapter on Legal Books I explain how Zach Smith largely automates his selling process. Selling e-books can be largely automated. Always look for ways you can automate your process, and if it pays more that it costs, do it. This applies to outsourcing, too.

6. Publish each book fully. Don't think your work is done when you've uploaded your book to Amazon, then jump into another project. Play your book out fully, using all the information in this book, then work on your next book. If there are 100 steps to successfully publishing a book, uploading your book onto Amazon might be step 10. You still have a lot of work to do if you want your book to be successful

"Conserve your forces and energies by keeping them concentrated at their strongest point. You gain more by finding a rich mine and mining it deeper, than by flitting from one shallow mine to another – intensity defeats extensity every time. When looking for sources of power to elevate you, find the one key patron, the fat cow who will give you milk for a long time to come." – Robert Greene

PLATFORM

A lot of times you hear about an author platform. An author platform is very important, though most incarcerated authors don't have one. But what exactly is an author platform?

An author platform is basically the combined resources you have to promote a book. So, this can be your social media pages, if you have followers; your website, e-mail list, mailing list, and blog. If you have a podcast, radio show or TV show, that would be considered part of your platform. For example, Wendy Williams is on the TV right now. When she has a book or some other product to promote, she simply mentions it on her talk show. If you're the publisher of a popular magazine geared towards the same market as your book, the magazine would be considered part of your platform. I publish *The BEST Resource Directory for Prisoners*, which is extremely popular, all over the country. It's considered part of my platform because it has a large audience and I can promote anything I want inside.

I'd go on to say that your network or relationships can be considered part of your platform, so long as they will help you promote your book. For example, say you write urban books and you have a friend who's a successful street lit author with 20k Instagram followers, and he or she will promote your book for you. You could consider that part of your platform. Or, say you have a hot wife who's an IG model and has 50k followers, and your book is an erotic novel who your wife is on the cover of, and she can promote it to her followers. That can be considered part of your platform.

Solid resources you have in print publication can be considered part of your platform. Say your book is geared towards the *Prison Legal News* market, and you have an "in" with *PLN* where they will publish an article you write where you soft-sell your book, or you have a friend who does book reviews for *PLN* and he can write a favorable review for you. This is another way your network would be considered part of your platform.

Your platform is critical to your career as a writer/publisher. A lot of guys can write books, but without a platform, they will have a difficult time getting the word out and selling them. As an author and/or publisher, you need to spend time building your platform. Don't be like the idiots who write a book, then sit back and do nothing, yet expect it to sell a whole bunch of copies, and when they don't get what they didn't put into it, they are disappointed. Building a platform is a critical part of the process.

BOOK COVER

Experts say a great book cover is probably your best marketing tool. I agree. I'd also like to add book title to the list of most-important things, but the old cliché "Don't judge a book by its cover" is said because of just that; people *do* judge books by their covers. This is a fact, and there's no way around it. So, make sure yours is the best quality you can possibly get.

> *"Your book cover is your number one marketing asset. A great cover design will grab customers' attention and compel them to buy."* – Karla King, author of *Self-Publishing Boot Camp Guide*

By far, having the cover of a book done is my favorite part of the publishing process. I love a great cover. I'm OCD about them. I try to make sure the image on my covers are a pictorial representation of what the book is about. And I must say, I have the best covers in the game. #Facts

People often ask me where I get my covers, but this is one secret I won't share. My covers are a part of my branding. I use the same designer for almost every one of my books. My goal is for you to see one of my covers and immediately know it's a Mike Enemigo/TCB book, just by the artwork. Why? Because I'm the only person my designer does book covers for. He's not a book cover designer, he designs album covers for rap artists. So there lies one secret: I don't use a traditional book cover designer who does graphics for every other book publisher. I use a guy who does graphics for rappers. And you can do this, too, if you want to try and stand out and brand yourself from the rest. That said, each genre has its own look and style of artwork. You want to make sure your artwork fits the genre you write so you don't confuse potential customers. Having the wrong style of artwork for your genre can be detrimental to your book's success.

How much should you pay for a cover? Where do you get them?

Cover prices vary. You will pay anywhere between $20 and $300. You shouldn't pay more than that, because you don't have to, and if you are, you're doing it wrong.

You can find a lot of great designers on Instagram. Search "Graphics," "Gfx," "Art," and "Designs". Anybody who has those words in their name will appear. Then you go through each one until you find someone who does the style you like. Most of the artists on IG will create you a cover for under $100. If you want an urban look, try Kince Designs. He's an artist in Mexico and he's really dope.

For the cheapest covers, go to Fiverr.com and type "book covers" or "book cover design" into the search bar. You may also try adding your genre to the search, like "urban book covers," or "fantasy book covers," etc. You'll find people from all over the world who will do a cover for $20 and up. If you want to find an artist that usually does CD covers, type "mixtape covers" or "CD covers" into the search bar. Several will appear and you can look through their samples to find someone you like. Keep in mind, you typically get what you pay for, and since people certainly judge books by their covers, cover artwork probably isn't where you want to try and cut costs. That said, there are some guys there who will give you some decent work for around $40-$50. And again, I'm very picky when it comes to artwork, so if I think it's decent, you will likely agree.

Here's what I suggest. Before contacting any designer, gather 2-4 covers that you really like. Then, when you contact the designer, ask him or her if they can do something like the examples you're providing. You should pick somebody who posted examples that are already in the same area of style as your examples, and if possible, refer to the samples of theirs that you like. Then, when you send your design instructions, be sure to point out what you like from their samples, so they know what it is you're going for. For example, "I really like the font and layout of the text of the cover for *The Streets Have No King*. I'd like mine done like that, but with the words of my title. I also really like the money graphic on the *Dutch* cover I sent you. If you can give me a money graphic just like that, with the blood, it will work for me perfectly." See what I'm saying? You want to be as specific as possible. Don't leave it up for your designer, who, if you use Fiverr.com, is probably from a different country, to try to read your mind regarding what you want. Be specific so you increase your chances of getting what you want.

Here're a few examples of how I write my cover designs. Remember, I typically work with the same guy each time, so we've developed this "system", which works for us. You may need to add a few details if it's your first time working with someone.

RE: COVER DESIGN FOR HOW TO HUSTLE & WIN: SEX, MONEY, MURDER EDITION

Size: 5.5" x 8.5"

Company: THE CELL BLOCK PRESENTS (Please put this across the top in Minion Pro font)

Title: How To Hustle & Win (I'd like this big, in the middle, in the same font used for the Grand Theft Auto video game)

Subtitle: Sex, Money, Murder Edition

Authors: MIKE ENEMIGO and KING GURU (Please use our "logo" fonts)

Color scheme: Your choice

Concept and Design: This book is a "game guide" that covers all aspects of The Game, like Sex, Money, Murder, Selling Drugs, Prison, etc., and I'd like the cover to represent that.

Design: I'd like the layout of this cover to be "sectional", just like the design for Grand Theft Auto video game cover. In each section I'd like a different picture that represents an element on The Game. For example, an old-school Cutlass on big rims, a trap house, guns, money, jewelry, maybe a dead body, and something that represents sex and/or prostitution.

$$$$$

Keep in mind, my guy did this, and because he's from the streets and does rap-style graphics for a living, he understood everything I described. He knows what a trap house is. For someone else, I may need to explain. Or, better yet, show.

Let me give you another example...

RE: COVER DESIGN FOR UNDERWORLD ZILLA

Size: 5.5" x 8.5"

Company: THE CELL BLOCK PRESENTS (Please put this across the top in Minion Pro font)

Title: Underworld Zilla

Authors: MIKE ENEMIGO and KING GURU (Please use our "logo" fonts)

Color scheme: Same as attached example graphic

Design: Attached is a copy of the CD cover for Hus Mozzy: Mozzy Ova Zery Zang Youngin.

I'd like the artwork for Underworld Zilla to be just like this, but instead of what he has collaged inside the gun, collage the images I'm sending you.

$$$$$

For this cover, I sent my designer a CD cover that inspired how I wanted my graphic. The CD cover has a gun on top of a gray textured background, and inside the gun is a collage of the guy with money and other stuff. This allowed my designer to see exactly what I wanted. I then sent him the images I wanted him to collage inside the gun, which are images that represent elements of the story – a white stripper with red hair and a big ass, money, weed, a swat team. etc. Again, this was the guy I pretty much always use, and I trust his work. However, I still try to give him the best example(s) and the most info possible. And the graphic came out perfect, just how I wanted it.

Keep in mind you will likely pay one price for the front, but a little more for the front and back. And you should always request your "source file". Having this will allow you to make adjustments later. Without it, you can't. Most people on Fiverr will charge you an additional fee for your source file – usually $10-$20. But again, you want this.

To save costs, I usually have my own people do the back cover – like add text, etc. Because I work with my designer so much and have given him so much money, sometimes he throws in a graphic for the back cover for free. But I always have my people add the text. That way, not only is it cheaper, it's easy for me to have an adjustment made without having to contact my designer. It's not difficult for someone with basic Photoshop experience to add or adjust text. If you don't have someone for this, however, you may need to just go ahead and pay your designer to do it for you.

"If they like the cover, they will read the blurb. If they like that, they will read the sample. If they like the sample, they may purchase the book. If they enjoy the read, they will tell more people. This is word-of-mouth, and it is the only thing that has ever really sold books." – David Gaughran

PUBLICITY STUNT

I was online searching, trying to find everything I could on how to possibly succeed as an author in the Street Lit genre. I watched every YouTube video I could find with interviews of the major players, I read every article I could find about Street Lit authors becoming successful, I studied their Google profiles, and I looked at their social media pages over and over and over again. I finally decided I had nothing to lose by messaging a major Street Lit author directly, telling him I was a fan and incarcerated Street Lit author, and asking if he had any advice he could share on how I could take my game to the next level. Hey, why not ask? If he ignores me, I don't lose anything. If he answers, however, I might come up on a major jewel. So, I hit him up.

Guess what? He responded!

The response was quick. He thanked me for the love, then told me his career really took off when he got himself a publicist. A minute later, he sent a recommendation for one he uses. Bam! I was in the game!

I emailed the publicist; told her she was recommended by so-and-so. I told her a little about myself, and that she could learn more at my website. I wanted to know how much she charged. Then I waited, hoping for a response and an affordable price.

Then next day she responded and told me she was impressed by all the books I've done from prison, and the versatility of my writing, being that I've tackled a few different genres, rather than just one. She told me she charges $2,500 for 90-day representation, but that she would give me a deal for half off if I hired her within the next 3 days. She said she really felt she could help me take my brand to the next level. She explained that she doesn't work with just anybody (she's by recommendation only, and under contract with a major network – something to do with TV), but since I was recommended by a major client, she would be willing to work with me.

I was excited. I told my girl that I was going to hire this publicist, and that it was going to take my career to the next level. My girl seemed less excited, and told me to think about it longer – give it some real thought. During this time, my girl did some research and couldn't find anything on the publicist. I, too, did some research and couldn't find anything. But this person is major, and by recommendation only, so I felt that justified why we couldn't find any info on her online. She wasn't some low budget, anybody-can-hire publicist. And to be honest, I thought she was probably doing this on the side, unbeknownst to the major network she's under contract with, so she wasn't trying to broadcast what she was doing (and thus, by recommendation only). But my girl wasn't convinced and told me not to fuck with her because she didn't trust her. However, my girl don't trust nobody, no matter what, so I felt like she was being negative and pessimistic. I got upset because she was telling me not to fuck with the publicist, but she wasn't offering me an alternative solution to be successful. I'm in prison; my options are limited. This is the closest I'd gotten to a major player. What else was I going to do?

So, I paid the publicist – $1,250.

During the first month, she told me things were going good – she was preparing my "campaign," and everything was on schedule. I'm excited because I'm finally going to get some much-needed publicity via things I couldn't tap into myself, like urban magazines, blogs, and websites. After a month was up, she told me it was time to begin, and she sent me a logo. The logo was my name, Mike Enemigo, in some really cool font. I'd already had one I'd been using for several years, the "MIKE ENEMIGO" you see on my book covers, which I like, and created myself. I was skeptical about changing from what I'd already used for so many years, but what she sent was cool, and since she knows more than I do, and I didn't want to seem uncooperative, I went with hers. Along with the "still" logo, she sent me a few digitalized versions to pick from. A digitalized version is where the screen will show, say, a drop of ink falling. Then, when the drop hits an invisible surface, the "splash" turns into your logo – something like that.

A day or two later she sent me a Facebook banner that she said would be more effective than the one I had. Unfortunately, the banner was the wrong size, and my website's URL was wrong. It said cellblock.net instead of thecellblock.net. No worries, I had her fix this. I didn't like the graphic, but again, I didn't want to complain and come off as difficult to work with. After all, this was a major player in the game. What do I know, right?

Next, she told me to download an app that I can't remember the name of. What the app was, though, was a social media content curator. You can type in keywords and the app will send you news stories that come up, as they come up, that have those words. I think I tried to get articles on stuff like prison, laws, crime, mafia, cartel, El Chapo, etc. – stuff I felt would fit my brand. The app was free, but you can pay a fee and gain access to more stuff.

A few days later she sent me two 17-second videos to post on my social media. They are videos where 5-6 of my book covers would flash onto the screen, one at a time, move around, go out of focus then come back into focus, and so on. They looked really good and a hip-hop instrumental played in the background. Unfortunately, the way they were emailed to me made it difficult for me to move them around – to my social media, other people's emails, etc. And though she said I'd be getting three, I only got two.

After the second month she told me it was time to launch my social media campaign, and that I'd start to see my followers rise drastically, as she had a database of over 50 thousand emails. She said once I got enough followers, a steady stream, she would see about getting me a blue check on Instagram – the "verified" check. I figured this was the big play, as she was going to use the email list, she's collected of Street Lit buyers/fans from the major authors she's represented. Over the next few days, my followers on Instagram did rise, from around 90 to about 2,000. I looked at who the followers were to see if they looked like Street Lit consumers. Most were from foreign countries, like the Philippines, and those in South America. I wasn't sure if they bought Street Lit, but I'm willing to sell my books to anyone who will buy them. Hey, maybe that's the secret – the real money is out the country! Within the next few weeks, however, the followers dwindled down to about 400. After the 90 days were up, we were no longer under contract, so if I wanted to continue with her, I'd have to pay another $1,250.

As you can see, I wasted the $1,250, just like my girl told me I would. I was very disappointed; my desperation caused me to make a bad decision that cost me a lot of money.

Everything I got from the publicist; I could get on my own. The "logo" was just a cool font. Anybody could make the logo if they selected the font and typed my name – MIKE ENEMIGO – then put "MIKE" on top of "ENEMIGO." That's all it was. The logo can then be digitalized by someone on fiverr.com for around $20.00. Several people offer the service. The social media content curating app can be downloaded by anyone, for free.

The two videos, I later learned how to make. They were "template" videos where you just insert still shots – like the kind I explain in the chapter on videos. You can do this for free, too. No special resource or skill needed. The Facebook header sucked, and as soon as I was no longer working with her, I replaced it with something better. I have the dopest graphics in the game, so that part is easy for me to get done. And the IG followers weren't from some "special" list, they were from one of the companies that advertise constantly on everybody's IG that they will increase your followers. They are fake followers people use to make their pages seem more poppin' than they really are.

So, the question is, should you hire a publicist? Fuck no. Your money can be much better spent. Of course, I had to learn this the hard and expensive way, but now I'm telling you, so you don't have to. The only other way I'd ever use a publicist again is if it was one recommended by a prisoner or someone that I know well, in the same genre as me, and who personally had great results using him or her.

THE SECRETS & STRATEGIES TO PUBLISHING SHORT STORIES & REPORTS FOR PROMO & PROFIT

As an upcoming writer, one of the best things you can do is get something (of quality!) to market as soon as possible. But writing an entire book is a lot of work, will take a lot of time, and can be intimidating for the novice. However, you don't have to start your writing career by penning an entire book. Nor should you. There are ways to start small, and build, which is not only easier, but wiser.

In addition, whether you are writing your first book or tenth, getting your name out there, and word about your upcoming book(s), is everything, and this takes promotion. Promoting from your prison cell without a lot of money or resources, like social media, your options are limited. You can advertise, and advertising is good, but it's very, very expensive to do, and it will eat up a lot of your profit – the very profit you will be working so hard to make.

The solution to both of these problems, and by far the best strategy for prisoners, lies in my Secrets & Strategies to Publishing Short Stories & Reports for Promo & Profit. Like most things, this is something I had to learn the hard way, but luckily for you, you now don't have to. Let's get to it!

Reports

If your goal is to be an infopreneur, and you want to write a how-to book, rather than starting with an entire book, you can start with short reports on your subject of expertise, or another, strategically-chosen, well-selling topic. In fact, as a prisoner who likely has very few resources, for an upcoming infopreneur, I'd say this is the best way to start. It's much easier and cheaper to get started; you can go to market and start selling faster; it can act as part of your learning curve before going "big" with your entire book; you can use it to start getting your name out there to your target market; you can use it to promote your upcoming books; and you can make a few bucks from it (or a lot if you want to), then use the money to fund your larger, upcoming project(s).

Here's a little-known secret about Special Reports: If they are of quality and full of value, they can sell for a lot of money.

I've made a lot of money selling Special Reports that I've written. I branded them under the collective title of TCBU – The Cell Block University – and the topics ranged from *How to Do Your Time Wisely*, to *Prison Workout Techniques*; to *How to Turn Your Mailbox into a Money Machine*, *How to Hustle and Win Legally When You Get Out of Prison*, and more. I might've had around 100 reports available through TCBU.

And I'm not the only prisoner who's done this with some success. Josh Kruger sold a Special Report titled "*How to Get FREE Pen Pals*," and another titled "*How to Win Your Football Pool*." He later included both of these in his book *The Millionaire Prisoner: Special TCB Edition*, published by yours truly. If you're truly interested in being prosperous from prison, I suggest that you buy a copy of this book immediately. Another prisoner, James L. Valentine offered seven reports, one of which – *How to Have a Local Businessman Give You $400,000 in Addition to Receiving $35,000 and a New Car* – was priced at $100.00. Others were priced at $25.00 and $50.00.

So now you're convinced you should start by writing short info reports, but unsure of what you should write about? The best-selling topics for how-to reports are how to make money or achieve prosperity in some way; how to get girls or more sex; how to improve your health, both physically and mentally; and since you're in prison, I'd say anything that will help prisoners improve their experience, lifestyle, or legal situation.

With the above in mind, what do you know about? Are you an "expert" on anything? Maybe you found a way to get your restitution reduced from 40k to 5k, or at least an effective way to challenge it, and you can write a report teaching other prisoners how they, too, can do it? I can see a report like this being very successful. What prisoner wouldn't be willing to pay $10.00-$20.00, or more, for a report that teaches them how to basically squash a significant debt? Or maybe you found a way to get your case overturned, or your sentence reduced, in a way that many other prisoners could possibly qualify for? Maybe you found a way to make money from prison, legally, or a surefire way to get girls to write you from pen pal websites? Who doesn't want that? Maybe you know something entirely different, that has nothing to do with prison or prisoners, like James L. Valentine, and you have the ability to get in front of people who would be willing to pay you for your information? Maybe you are a former drug dealer who invested in the real estate game prior to prison, and you can market a report to fellow hustlers interested in real estate titled "How to Flip Houses in the Hood for Huge Profits"?

If you don't already have an expertise, what do you have a need for that others would also want to know, that you can research, master, then teach to others in the form of a Special Report? You don't have to be a literary genius to write one of these reports. In fact, the easiest way to create one would be to buy some how-to info, maybe a book or two, or perhaps even a Special Report, read the info, then set it aside and write a better version with more elaboration, or from a different point of view. If you're too lazy to do this, there are even reports you can buy that come with reprint rights. These you will just have to photocopy; no writing involved. Then advertise them to the proper market and fill the orders when they come. Of course, this is the worst option of all, as reports with reprint rights will be sold by many others, and you won't be offering anything unique.

The key to being successful with this is not in the length of the report, but to provide value. The more value you provide, the more you can charge, and people will be happy to pay. Again, if you charged $20.00, or even $50.00 for a Special Report that told people the secrets to getting rid of a restitution fee of several thousand dollars, nobody would have a problem paying for it, even if it was only one page long. In fact, something only a page long would likely mean you found a way to simplify the process, making it easier for the person to do it, which is actually better – so long as it worked, of course. The value here, for the prisoner, would be a simple way to get their restitution reduced, for "only," say, $50.00. For you, of course, the value is selling a single sheet of paper with info for $50.00! So, don't get hung up on length, focus on value – providing great, valuable information. If you can do this, people will be happy to give you their money. And if it's legit, they will buy from you again, which is how you really make money – with repeat business. Remember: It's much easier and cheaper to sell again to a happy, existing customer than to try to reach and win over a new one.

If your Special Reports are directed towards prisoners, to get the word out about them you can advertise in my book, *The BEST Resource Directory For Prisoners*; *Prison Legal News*, perhaps starting with a classified ad as it's the cheapest, then build from there; or *Inmate Shopper*. If your how-to report is directed towards people on the outside, you can advertise very inexpensively via the many mail order publications available for "opportunity seekers." For a list of mail order companies/dealers, and to learn more about the mail order business in general, which is heavily related to self-publishing, be sure to get yourself a copy of my book *Mailbox Money: How to Turn Your Mailbox into a Million Dollar Money Machine When You Get Out of Prison!*

Another great thing about producing Special Reports, aside from what's already listed, is that you can later put all of your reports together in the form of a book. I did this with my TCBU reports, turning them into *Get Out, Get Rich: How to Get Paid LEGALLY When You Get Out of Prison!*; *The CEO Manual: How to Start Your Own Business When You Get Out of Prison!*; *The Money Manual: Underground Cash Secrets Exposed!*; *and Mailbox Money: How to Turn Your Mailbox into a Million Dollar Money Machine When You Get Out of Prison!* Some of the Special Reports were even made into chapters for my book *The Prison Manual: The Complete Guide to Surviving the American Prison System!* Shit, I might even turn The Secrets & Strategies to Publishing Short Stories & Reports for Promo & Profit! into a Special Report and use it to not only make money, but promote my upcoming masterpiece, *Jailhouse Publishing for Money, Power & Fame!* book.

If selling reports, you will need someone on the outside to fulfill the orders when they come in, ideally to a P.O. Box you will have set up. It's best if you have a loved one, such as your wife, mother, sibling or trusted friend fulfill the orders, which will mostly consist of putting a copy of your Special Report in an envelope and mailing it off, but if you don't have anyone, all is not lost. Simply contact one of the several mail order dealers listed in my *Mailbox Money* book who's already in business selling reports, and ask them to distribute yours for a split. You won't have much trouble finding someone to work with you. These guys are in business to make money, and they're already doing it anyway.

Booklets

Once you've mastered the business of Special Reports, you may want to graduate to booklets, which are, I'd say, 20,000 words or less, though there's no set length. The actual definition is "A small thin book that gives you information about something."

For a booklet, you can add a few of your reports together, maybe for a more comprehensive explanation. Typically, Special Reports are easier to sell at a premium than booklets, and booklets are also going to cost you more to manufacture, which means less profit for you per copy. However, there's no rule that says you can't call your booklet a Special Report, yet manufacture it in the style of a booklet, like I did with my Special Report booklet, *The Ladies Who Love Prisoners: Secrets Exposed!* You may wonder why you'd want to produce your report in a way that's more expensive for you, while at the same time not allowing you to sell it at as high a price, but there are two major reasons. For one, producing a booklet will help you learn the production aspects of book publishing, as you will have to have a cover made, the interior text formatted, then everything uploaded to Amazon, etc. The other major reason lies in distribution; a booklet will allow you more options. For example, your reports will be printed on regular 8.5x11 copy paper, and Amazon won't sell and distribute those. As I explained, you will have to have a loved one or mail order dealer do that. But Amazon *will* sell a booklet, as will other companies who distribute books to prisoners if this is something you desire, like *SureShot, Inmate Shopper*, and so forth. Like most things, you have to weigh the pros and cons when deciding your strategy.

When I officially launched my publishing company, The Cell Block, in 2014, I published two booklets. One, *The Art & Power of Letter Writing for Prisoners*, was around 9,500 words, and I priced it at $9.99. "Letter writing" was actually two chapters out of the first book I wrote, *Surviving Prison*. I wasn't ready to publish *Surviving Prison*, and wanting to launch TCB with as many books as possible, I decided to take out chapters "*Letter-Writing Like a Pro*" and "*Pen-Pal Websites: The Secrets*" and publish them as a booklet. And thank God I did, because it ended up being a hit! I had no idea! I sold a ton of them! (I attribute part of this to the fact it was picked up by book distributors like *SureShot* and *Inmate Shopper*, where it's still sold to this day.) This was the market's way of saying, "We will give you our money for this type of book," and that's when I knew I had to elaborate on it, so I published *The Art &*

Power of Letter Writing Deluxe Edition in 2018, which has also been very successful.

As mentioned above, *Letter Writing* isn't the only booklet I've dropped. I once got into a beef with an incarcerated rapper, who I, along with a friend, was forced to stab back in 2010. After the incident, the schmuck, who told, went online – social media and various top-tier hip hop sites – trying to assassinate my character, and lying to the fans about the incident. So, I responded to the blog, online, but then I turned the response, which was lengthy, about 6,500 words, into a booklet so I could easily distribute it to prisoners who don't have access to the online blogs, and sold it for $9.99. This booklet was also a hit.

Don't underestimate the value or power of a booklet, which also can later be added to a book, or made into a bigger book if the market responds favorably.

Short Stories & Articles

Writing short stories or articles, depending on your genre (short stories for fiction, or a nonfiction story; articles for nonfiction, like how-to books), is a great way to start in this business. If you can get your Short or article published in a magazine or some other established publication, it's a great way to get your name out there, and your target market familiar with you. By definition, Shorts are under 10,000 words, but I'd say 7,500 is a good amount, unless you are writing for a magazine with limited space; they will likely have a word limit you have to abide by. And when I say established publication, I mean any publication in your genre that has a bigger platform and fanbase then you do.

Do not underestimate the value of this, as so many prisoners do, as even I did at one point in time. This is something I had to learn the hard way. Listen to me: Promoting yourself from prison is very hard to do, and also very expensive. But it is critical to your success as a writer, because no matter how great you are, if nobody knows about you, they cannot buy your books. You may think social media is the answer to getting your name out there. If you were free, I'd say you're right. But as a prisoner, you have to depend on someone on the outside, who is busy, to keep it maintained for you, and depending on someone else is never a good thing. And you can run ads in whatever publication, if you have the money, but I promise you, ads are very expensive, and they are going to eat your profit more viciously than a school of starving piranhas will eat a dead body floating in the Amazon – if you're lucky enough to profit in the first place.

But if you can get a dope short story or article published, preferably as many as possible? You now get your product – not an ad about your product – in front of your potential customers. This gives them a sample to see whether or not they want to fuck with you, and if they do, you are likely to make a sell, and hopefully even gain a fan. Look at it this way: I pay $1,500 for a full-page ad in *Straight Stuntin* magazine. This means I have to sell $1,500 worth of books just to break even. But if I can get them to publish a short story or article relevant to the topic of my book(s), and establish myself to the reader as an expert or dope author, this can persuade him to buy my book – or at least get him closer to doing so, perhaps more effectively than an ad, if done right – without me having to pay the $1,500, which means everything I sell as a result of the short story or article is profit. This is so important, I now require all TCB authors to give me at least three short stories or articles for each book I publish, relevant to the specific book, so that I can do my best to get them published in the appropriate, established publication.

The reason I say "publication" instead of magazine, is because magazines are not the only place to target with short stories or articles. If your shorts stories or articles are geared towards the prison audience, you can submit them to me for possible placement in *The BEST Resource Directory for Prisoners*; or Freebird Publishers for possible placement in *Inmate Shopper*. If what you write is related to laws impacting prisoners, or prisoner conditions of confinement, etc., you can submit to *Prison Legal News* for possible publication. These are all established publications that will get you in front of prisoners all around the country, if this is what you desire. I also have a couple short story collections in the works – *Trap Tales* (short urban stories) and *American Prison Stories* (short prison stories). I'm creating these specifically to be a promotional platform for TCB and other incarcerated authors. I plan to run a heavy promotional campaign for these books that includes magazine ads, giving away hundreds of books free to prisoners around the country, and more. The point is to get our work in front of as many readers as possible, so that if they like what they read from a particular author, they can then purchase their book(s). Yes, I've learned that even giving away books for free, which is quite costly, can be less expensive than ads. (Note: If you wish to submit to *Trap Tales* or *American Prison Stories*, send your very best work to The Cell Block; P.O. Box 1025; Rancho Cordova, CA 93581, or email them to info@thecellblock.net. Do not write your prison address on the pages of your story. Only write your first and last name, and what state you're in. My people will keep record of your full address. Include with your submission, on a separate page, a brief bio, being sure to list any books you may have available. We have the right to edit, and we do not pay for submissions. We will, however, send you a copy of whatever book your work appears in, if you make it into one of our books.)

If you can get paid for any short stories or articles you submit to an established publication, great! I urge you to get the bag. But do not bypass an opportunity to get your name and work out there via an established publication who doesn't pay, because you think you should be paid. Too many prisoners, ones with no name and who've never sold a book, think like this. Perhaps this is the reason why we don't know their names, or have never bought their book(s). Do not be arrogant and foolish like such prisoners. Established publications don't need your story or article, you need the established publication's platform. Even I, who has a rather large platform, will give a free story or article to another publication, perhaps one with a platform less established than my own, so long as they have a solid platform, one I'm trying to reach, and one I may not be reaching with my own.

Getting your name out there is extremely valuable, as you will otherwise not sell books. So, remain humble and focused on your objectives. Your goal needs to be to get yourself out there, at little or no cost to you. Do not underestimate the value of this.

And get this; if you have a book already written, it's not hard to find and interesting part, edit it accordingly and make a short story, then submitting it to the appropriate place(s), to promote the book. King Guru and I have made several Shorts out of scenes in the *Underworld Zilla* series that we offer free to any publisher with a platform. I also mail these out to fans who've been loyal supporters of The Cell Block to keep them in the loop of what we're working on.

E-Shorts

If you're working on a fiction novel that you want to promote to people on the outside, you want to publish an e-short first, relative to the upcoming book, possibly a prequel, and give it away for free, or .99 cents. An e-short is a short story that you publish electronically – a short e-book. From the e-shorts I viewed online, I'd say an e-short should be between 20 and 40 e-pages.

As we've established, writing a book takes a long time. And then you don't even know if the market is going to be interested in it. This means you may spend an enormous amount of time and money, all for nothing. In addition, in case you don't know by now, getting your name out there and promoting from a prison cell is very difficult and expensive. So what you want to do, while working on your book, is drop an e-short as quickly as you can, on Amazon and other e-book sites, so you can get the word out about your upcoming book while you work on it. This will not only allow you to start spreading the word, but also get feedback. To help spread the e-short around further, you can get in touch with websites and blogs in your genre, ones who have lots of traffic, and work something with them, where they can give it to their web visitors for free. This will help you get your story in front of potential buyers of your full-length novel. For example, I have a book titled *The Mob* coming out with inmate-author PaperBoy. *The Mob* is about Bay Area rappers in the drug game, and one of the rappers is Mac Dre, who's like a God in The Bay. There are several Bay Area hip-hop websites with large followings, like Thizzler.com, RapBay.com, AllBayMusic.com, and DopeEra.com, and *The Mob* is geared towards their exact market. Before I lost my last cell phone, I was in the process of negotiating a deal with these websites, where they would give *The Mob* e-short away free. This would get *The Mob* in front of over 200,000 viewers. We would also then be able to read the comments and see what people like and dislike about the story, allowing us to use the information while finishing the novel, all the while, getting people to know and hopefully talk about *The Mob* for the next year (or whatever, we're in no hurry) while we finish it.

I also use *The Mob* and other e-shorts to capture e-mail addresses from urban readers who visit my website, thecellblock.net. I give them away free, but the person (and hopefully future buyer) must insert their e-mail address to receive the download. Now I have their e-mail and can e-mail them directly when the book is done, or a similar book. If we did our job with the story and made it interesting and entertaining, this person is likely to buy the novel when it's done. We may even gain them as a TCB fan, where they then buy our other books.

I also publish my e-shorts on Amazon and sell them for .99 cents. (I can't give them away free on Amazon without signing up for KDP Select, which is an exclusive deal, and that would prevent me from offering the Short on my website where I'm able to capture e-mails, something I can't do on Amazon, so I'm not willing to sign up for KDP Select.) Not only does selling the book for .99 cents help promote it by offering it at such a low price, if you push it enough, you may even make a few bucks you can then invest into the publishing of the full-length novel.

E-Shorts are a must if you want to promote to people on the outside. Offer them for free or .99 cents, allowing potential readers of your upcoming novel a risk-free entry point into you world. Get this done as soon as possible, then promote it via as many low-cost ways as you can.

Novellas

If you're working on a fiction novel, you definitely want to get short stories relevant to your novel published in as many magazines and short story collections by more established publishers as possible. But again, these will usually have some sort of word limit you have to meet. But if you want to write a longer piece, it would be a great idea for you to publish a novella. A novella is between a short story and a novel; over 10,000 words, under 50,000. A novella is similar to an e-short, but a little longer, and not necessarily distributed in electronic form. Novellas can be done in any genre, but romance and erotica novellas have been especially popular, making a few self-published authors rich.

The Mob, which I discussed in the previous section was made into an e-short with the specific intention of using it to promote *The Mob* online. But how do you use this same strategy to promote to prisoners, who may need a printed product? In the case of *The Mob*, since it has some length to it, around 17,000 words, I made it into a print copy, which would classify it as a novella (though on the shorter side), that I sell for $6.00. With the cost of printing and mailing, etc., I don't profit from the $6.00, the $6.00 I charge is just to cover my costs. I give this story away free online for the purpose of promoting the upcoming novel. So, my goal here is not to profit from the novella (although you can sell novellas for a profit), it's to give the reader the lowest possible price without me losing money, so I can get it to as many people as possible, and promote *The Mob* to as many potential customers as possible. It basically works as a way for me to promote *The Mob* for free, which is critical, as so many other ways we have to promote from prison is so expensive.

In addition to what I've explained thus far, on some ads I offer the $6.00 *Mob* novella free with the purchase of $40.00 or more, of any of our other books. This not only allows me to get the word out about *The Mob* at little or no cost to me, it also encourages customers to spend a little more than they would have, in order to get a free copy of *The Mob*. As I write this, I have *The Mob* in my ads for *Straight Stuntin* magazine, *Kite* magazine, and *State V. Us* magazine. PaperBoy, who's writing *The Mob,* is in another prison working on it along with a few other projects. We're in no rush to publish the full novel because the longer the novella and e-short is out, the more it promotes our upcoming book, and this increases the likeliness of it being a success.

Do not sleep on the importance of getting word of your story out as soon as possible. But instead of just talking about it, which you should also be doing to any- and everyone who will listen, put out a sample of what's to come, and make sure it's something that, whoever reads it, will be standing in line eagerly waiting for the novel to drop so they can buy it. And don't do this with the expectation of profit; instead, do it with the objective of getting free promotion, promotion that would otherwise cost you thousands of dollars, for the book you later plan to sell.

As they say, "A penny saved is a penny earned," and this is especially true when publishing from prison, where most of us don't have a lot of pennies to work with.

To see a great example of a novella that you can use to promote an upcoming novel, order *The Mob* by sending $6.00 or one NEW book of 20 Forever stamps to The Cell Block; P.O. Box 1025; Rancho Cordova, CA 95741.

WRITING FOR ONLINE PUBLICATIONS

Getting word out to the people about you, your writing and your books is one of the most important things you can do, but also one of the most difficult. One of the best ways to do so is to write for online publications, like blogs or magazines, who already have an audience. Depending on what you write, there are several publications that will publish your work, some even specifically requesting writing from prisoners.

It is also easier to get something published by an online publication than it is a print publication. Reason being, the space online is unlimited, whereas the space for print isn't; and therefore, the print publications are much pickier about what they will accept.

While most prisoners focus on trying to submit to print publications because they can get a copy of the publication and view their work, gaining a sense of accomplishment and pride, do not ignore the online, digital publication opportunities that are available, just because you may not be able to see your work personally. These days, other than prisoners, everyone is online, and if you want to get in front of people, online is certainly the place to do it. And remember, you want to build a digital profile. This is done with one piece at a time. From my experience, it's never one thing that really gets you there, it's an accumulation of all the things I've mentioned regarding this subject. Each thing you have online is like one more crumb adding to the trial of crumbs that lead back to your books.

Check the resources at the back of this book for several online publications that will publish work from prisoners. And don't forget, at the end of everything you write, be sure to give a 3-4 sentence bio, and point readers back to your website, blog, and/or article-related book.

YOUR AMAZON AUTHOR PROFILE PAGE

If you have a book on Amazon, you can have your outside assistant create you an Author Profile. This is an amazing resource. It's very easy for your people to create, and it's free to do.

An Amazon Author page is basically your author profile, right there in the Amazon book store. And you can do quite a bit. For example, you can upload your author pic and bio, a few additional pics, a few videos, book reviews, blurbs, links to your website and social media, and if you have a website with a blog, you can set it up to where your blog automatically feeds to your Amazon page. You can even list your prison address if you want (in your bio). In addition to all of this, all of your books will show right there on your page, where they can also be purchased. Almost everything you would have on your author website or social media pages, you can have right here on your Amazon page, and once it's created, it doesn't require any maintenance (unless you want to change something).

Do not skimp on this, as so many people do, including some of the top-dog authors. This is a resource you definitely want to take advantage of.

Make sure your author bio is fully optimized and keyword rich. Keep in mind you can adjust your bio depending on where you're using it. For example, on the back of the book, I might not put as much as I do online, where I need to be sure to include keywords to help search engines find me.

Below is an example of how I write my bio in print versus online.

Print

Mike Enemigo is America's #1 incarcerated author who has written and published over 25 books. He's inspired by emotion: hope, pain; dreams and nightmares. He physically lives somewhere in a California prison cell where he works relentlessly creating his next piece. His mind and soul are elsewhere; seeing, studying, learning, and drawing inspiration to tear down suppressive walls and inspire the culture by pushing artistic boundaries.

Online

Mike Enemigo is America's #1 incarcerated author who has written and published over 25 books. He specializes in both fiction and nonfiction, true crime, gangs, prison stories, prison culture, street lit, urban books, urban life, how-to books, self-help books, and books for prisoners. He's inspired by emotion: hope, pain; dreams and nightmares. He physically lives somewhere in a California prison cell where he works relentlessly creating his next piece. His mind and soul are elsewhere; seeing, studying, learning, and drawing inspirations to tear down suppressive walls and inspire the culture by pushing artistic boundaries.

See the difference? In my online bio I include several keywords I want to be associated with. Some may even be redundant, such as street lit, urban books, and urban life, but it's because each of those are terms someone would use to find urban books, so I wanted to be sure to include them all.

You want to be sure to take advantage of every opportunity you have to be found and to sell yourself. Also, you will have to have a separate page made for Amazon UK if you want the folks there to have access to this info (which you do). Lastly, don't forget to link everything you have together!

METADATA: THE STRATEGIES

As a jailhouse publisher, or aspiring one, I bet metadata is probably something you've never even heard of. Or if you have, maybe from reading a book on self-publishing, it's likely you didn't fully understand it, and most certainly don't realize the importance of it. But let me tell you something: optimizing your metadata is extremely important.

What is metadata? Well, it's data about data. Metadata is critical for your book's discoverability, and to optimize it is free, so as an incarcerated author with little resources, this makes it even more vital for you.

Metadata consists of things like your book's title and subtitle, author(s), book cover, price, categories, description, keywords, etc. Some of these elements are pretty self-explanatory, but others aren't, and are certainly worth explaining in detail as there is a strategy to utilizing them effectively.

Book Title and Subtitle

Book titles are critical. And gone are the days where you only need to come up with something sensational so that a potential buyer would pick your book up off a bookshelf. With Amazon and other online bookstores now being where most people will discover your book, the best titles are now those that are attention grabbing, sensational, *and* will come up in a search engine when people are searching for books like yours. This means the including of keywords, and it's true for both fiction and nonfiction, though sometimes more difficult to accomplish with the former.

For fiction, many authors will often decide on a title that they find artistically appealing. The problem with this, however, is that it often won't mean anything to a potential reader, as they would have to read the story for it to make sense. For example, my book *Money iz the Motive*, with Cascious Green, which is Street Lit, was originally titled *Kano's Struggle*. *Kano's Struggle* fits the story perfectly. Problem is, it doesn't reveal its relevance until you start reading the book, and since nobody knows who Kano is to care about his struggle, nor is it sensational or genre specific, or SEO friendly, it wasn't going to help us sell any books. This is why I changed the name to *Money iz the Motive*. Anyone who is a fan of Street Lit should know a book titled *Money iz the Motive* is likely on some street shit. Though this doesn't help with our search-friendly goals, as I didn't know about that at the time, it's a step in the right direction from *Kano's Struggle*.

Creating a search-friendly title for a fiction book can be a challenge, but one trick is to add a subtitle. This is another thing I didn't know at the time of titling the *Money iz the Motive* book, but I could have added a subtitle like "The Greatest Urban Book of All Time," or "One of The Greatest Urban Books of All Time." This would have gotten the search-friendly term "urban book" or "urban books" into the title, would have confirmed to a potential customer that the book was indeed an urban book, and the hyperbole may have tempted the potential buyer to become an actual buyer. Mark Edwards, a successful self-publisher uses another trick. As one who writes mysteries, he often lists his subtitle as "For Fans of Dan Brown and Stieg Larsson." This is akin to me having put *Money iz the Motive: For Fans of JaQuavis Coleman and K'wan*. Clever! Good news is, since I'm the publisher, I can adjust the title whenever I want.

For nonfiction books, coming up with genre-clear and keyword-rich titles and subtitles is much easier. For example, if I was to write a book on the Mexican Mafia, I could title it, *The Mexican Mafia: The Rise and Fall of One of America's Bloodiest Prison Gangs*. "Mexican Mafia" is a term someone would search if they were looking to buy a book on the Mexican Mafia, or even online looking for information on the Mexican Mafia. The title also has the terms "Prison," "Gangs," and "Prison Gangs," also words one would search if interested in the subject.

As another example, say you were going to write a book on self-publishing. You would want the title to have "Self-Publishing" or "How To Self-Publish" in the title. Those are words someone looking for a book to teach them how to self-publish would search. If your title has them, you greatly increase the chances of your book being among the ones that come up.

In any case, if you cannot find a way to include keywords in your main title, be sure to include them in your subtitle, as both are search friendly. For example, my book with Armando Ibarra, *Loyalty & Betrayal*, was originally titled just that – *Loyalty & Betrayal*. But it's a story of one guy's battle with the Mexican Mafia, and wanting to capitalize on the search-friendly term Mexican Mafia, I added the subtitle "My War with the Mexican Mafia." Now people searching for the Mexican Mafia, a major element in the book, can find it easier. To give you one more example using the self-publishing topic, say you insisted on titling your book *Write to Eat*. You can then add the subtitle "The Secrets to Self-Publishing Successfully," or "How to Self-Publish Successfully," and this would allow you to benefit from the search-friendly terms "self-publishing" and "how to self-publish."

A great title is one of the best marketing moves you can make. And best of all, aside from a little creativity, it's free. Do not waste this opportunity.

Description

A great description is another very important element of your book's success. Remember, the goal of your book's cover and title is to get the potential customer to read your description. Not many people will buy a book without reading the description, so make sure yours is top notch.

The description is part of your sales process, where you're pulling your potential buyer in, one step at a time. Don't waste this space and opportunity. Every line you write should compel the reader to buy your book.

There are subtle differences between how you write a description for a book that is fictional, versus a book that's nonfictional, versus a how-to book. Here are some examples.

Fiction

For fiction, you generally don't need to go on and on about the plot, twists and turns, characters, etc. You want your description, which is often called a synopsis, to seduce and tease the reader. You want to say what will make the reader want to buy the book to learn more.

Description for *Underworld Zilla*:

When Talton leaves the West Coast to set up shop in Florida, he meets the female version of himself: A drug-dealing murderess with psychological issues. A whirlwind of sex, money, and murder inevitably ensues and Talton finds himself on the run from the law with nowhere to turn to. When his team from home finds out he's in trouble, they get on a plane heading south...

That's a really good book description. If gives you just enough to know what kind of book it is, the general idea of what it's about, and enough of a tease to make you want to buy it to find out what happens.

Nonfiction

For a nonfiction story, it's similar to how you'd write a description for a fictional story. However, it might have more opportunities for you to add keywords.

Description for *Conspiracy Theory*:

Kokain is an upcoming rapper trying to make a name for himself in the underground scene of Sacramento, California – home of rap stars Mozzy, Lavish D, C-BO, and Brotha Lynch Hung – and Nicki is his girlfriend.
  One night, in October, Nicki's brother, along with his best friend, go to rob a house of it's $100,000 marijuana crop. It goes wrong; shots are fired and a man is killed.
  Later, as investigators begin closing in on Nicki's brother and his friend, they, along with the help of a few others, create a way to make Kokain take the fall.
  The conspiracy begins...

The *Conspiracy Theory* description is also really good. And here I name real rappers from the city it takes place in hopes of attracting their fans. Let me give you another example.

Description for *Loyalty & Betrayal: My War with the Mexican Mafia*:

Chunky was an associate of and soldier for the notorious Mexican Mafia – La Eme. That is, of course, until he was betrayed by those, he was most loyal to. Then he vowed to become their worst enemy. Though they've attempted to kill him numerous times, he still to this day is running around making a mockery of their organization.

Loyalty & Betrayal: Special Deluxe Edition contains the original *Loyalty & Betrayal* book that started it all; "The Lost Chapters," which is the prequel to the original book; the brand-new release of *Loyalty & Betrayal part 2*; and an exclusive, never-before published interview of Armando "Chunky" Ibarra detailing what life has been like since the release of the highly controversial *Loyalty & Betrayal* story. You will never guess how this book ends. You do NOT want to miss this...

How-To

For a how-to book, it's all about listing the benefits the reader will get. You don't have to list every benefit, but you should list enough to sell the book. Remember, all it takes is one of the benefits to sell the book, but you never know which one of the benefits will appeal to a particular reader. Here's an example of what we did for *The Millionaire Prisoner*.

Description for *The Millionaire Prisoner*:

Why wait until you get out of prison to achieve your dreams? Here's a blueprint that you can use to become successful!
The Millionaire Prisoner is your complete reference to overcoming any obstacle in prison. You won't be able ot put it down! With this book you will discover the secrets to:
- *Making money from your cell!*
- *Obtain FREE money for correspondence courses!*
- *Become an expert on any topic!*
- *Develop the habits of the rich!*
- *Network with celebrities!*
- *Set up your own website!*
- *Market your products, ideas and services!*
- *Successfully use prison pen-pal websites!*
- *How to get FREE pen pals!*
- *And much, much more!*

This book has enabled thousands of prisoners to succeed, and it will show you the way also!

A Few Additional Description Tips

Though the space to write your description and other text might be limited on the back of your book's cover, the space isn't limited on Amazon or any of the other online places you may list it. Take advantage of this. Aside from a detailed, keyword – rich description, you may also want to include blurbs and book reviews. These can be very powerful, especially when they are by someone known and respected in your book's genre. Another thing I do is list a paragraph that says "You will love this book if you like:", then I list the titles and authors of several comparable books. I can't say for sure how beneficial this has been, but I believe it's better to do than to not do it, for sure. Some also say that keywords in the descriptions are not usually picked up by a search. But here I would argue, again, it's better to do than not do. Things are always changing and advancing, so if they aren't now, they very likely will be eventually. And in any case, like I always say, when jailhouse publishing, where we're working against all odds and with the fewest of resources, we need all the help we can get, so you want to fully optimize all of these opportunities.

Categories

When you upload your book onto Amazon, you will be able to list it under two categories – a main category and a subcategory. There are over 500 categories, such as Self-Help, True Crime, African American Literature, Urban Life, Suspense, Murder, etc.

There are different strategies that people use with this. However, what I suggest you do is look up books similar to yours, and whatever they list as their primary category, you do the same. This will help people browsing that category find your book, though it may be crowded, depending on the popularity or the category.

But for your subcategory, it could be wise to use an obscure category, one with little traffic, even if it has nothing to do with your book. An obscure category won't help you be found by your target market, but it can help you easily become an Amazon best seller, which comes with several perks and advantages. Check out the following excerpt from the April 2017 edition of *Entrepreneur* magazine:

"And authors have made a pastime out of hacking Amazon rankings. Brent Underwood, a partner at the marketing firm Brass Check, recently proved the point in a piece for the New York Observer. He created a book titled *Putting My Foot Down*, featuring not much more than a photo of his foot, then listed it under an obscure subcategory where few books are published. (There are 500-plus to choose from.) He asked 3 friends to download it for $0.99, and voila – Amazon listed him as a #1 best-selling author."

Keywords

Keywords are another important element to improve your book's discoverability. I've mentioned keywords in regards to creating a great title, but aside from the title, Amazon will allow you to enter seven additional keywords.

There's a whole science behind this keyword thing, and you can get books that will give you a deeper understanding, but here I will give you the basic jewels to get you started.

To recap, and possibly clarify, a keyword is a word or phrase that is associated with your book. These keywords are used by Amazon's search engine, so if someone enters one of your keywords into Amazon's search bar, your book will be among those that show up in the results. Amazon's "search" will very likely be the biggest source of traffic to your book's page, so it's very important that your keywords are correct. When figuring out what keywords you will enter for your book's page, you want to think about the words or phrases that people who are looking for your kind of book would search. For example, continuing with the self-publishing example, you would want to use the phrases "how to self-publish," "self-publishing," "how to publish a book," and things of that sort. These are the phrases someone looking for a book to teach them how to self-publish would search.

One way to test what others are using is to search the keywords and phrases you think are good, and see what comes up. If a book that is successful comes up, you are on the right track. There is a way to do a deeper search to find out exactly what words and phrases people interested in your book's subject are using to search, and that's to use Google's Adword Keyword Tool. This tool is designed to suggest and evaluate keywords for advertisers who spend billions of dollars on their Google Adwords campaign, not books, but it will still give you a great result, and it's free to use. You can use this by going to https://adwords.google.com/KeywordPlanner. Keep in mind that your title and subtitle are already search friendly (not only for Amazon, but also Google), so if your title has keywords in it, you don't need to use your allotted keyword space by including the same keywords. For example, if "self-publishing" is in your title, you don't also need to include it in your keywords.

Now, your seven keywords are set apart by commas, and in between each comma can be 50 characters (letters, numbers, etc.). You need to use these wisely. Some experts suggest you cram as many words or phrases in between each comma as possible. For example, a book on self-publishing could have "how to self-publish how to publish a book." That's two phrases that both fit inside the allotted 50-charcater space. For my book with Vernon Nelson, *OJ's Life Behind Bars*, I think I put something like "prison stories Kim Kardashian sports murder" as one of the keywords. The hope is that, whenever someone searches one of these words – prison, prison stories, Kim Kardashian, etc. – the OJ book will be among the ones that come up.

Another clever trick used by some authors is to use the names of successful authors within their book's genre, as those names are probably often searched. For example, if you're publishing an urban book, you might want to use keywords such as JaQuavis Coleman, Ashley Antoinette, Wahida Clark, K'wan, Leo Sullivan, etc. Hey, you have to use whatever advantage you can. Just be careful, though, as I'm not sure if this is permitted by Amazon or not. They do have some rules, and breaking them could get you banned from their site.

Good news is, you can adjust your keywords whenever you want, for free, so you may want to test words until you find what works best for your book(s).

ADDITIONAL ONLINE PROFILE OPPORTUNITIES

I suggest that you have as many online profiles as possible created for you, especially if they are free, as each little piece can only improve discoverability. And since we are inmate-authors, this includes inmate pen-pal sites. Most these sites invest in SEO, so for a small price, and sometimes free, you can tap in to it. Furthermore, since people who go to these sites are interested in prison/prisoners in some type of way (by finding a pen friend to write to), they may be interested in books written by a prisoner. And since we are working with minimal resources and funds, it can't hurt to try. Who knows, maybe you'll find a pen-pal, too.

The best site, in my opinion, is prisoninmates.com. For $40 a year, your outside assistant can create you a profile with your address, 5 pictures (which can be book covers), a 300-word bio, and a link back to your website. For additional fees you can add more pictures or book covers, videos, and even blogs. PIO doesn't care what name you post under – your real name, or your pen name. So instead of a pen-pal profile, you can make it an author profile if you want. If you do, however, and you want people to still be able to write you via snail mail, you will have to include your real name and address somewhere in your bio. Another cool thing is that people can email you, and PIO will forward them to you every two weeks. Of course, for this, your profile would have to be under your real name, as PIO will only forward the messages to the main name and address your profile is listed under. (This is one of the benefits of writing under your real name versus a pen name.)

For $180 a year you can have your profile "Featured." This will get your profile picture on the Home page, and most other pages, which gets you in front of pretty much everybody who visits the site. You can even advertise on the site if you have the funds, all the while pointing visitors who come for a pen friend back to your profile, website, or wherever your books are available. I've been rather successful getting pen pals from PIO, but I've not advertised on it personally, and I can't say for sure how many books I've sold because of my profile there. What I do know, though, is that, when I'm googled, the site comes up, and in any case, it provides another low-cost opportunity to be seen by people who are, at the least, interested in a pen pal.

There are other sites, however, where your outside assistant can create you a profile for free, such as intouchforinmates.com and lostvault.com. I'm not exactly sure of all the capabilities with these sites, as I've not yet added myself to them. I do, however, plan to do so shortly, and you may want to consider doing it as well. Since we as jailhouse publishers are working with limited funds and resources, it can't hurt to try. Who knows, like I said, maybe you will find a pen pal, too.

WEBSITE

Your website is your online headquarters. It's where people will come to learn about you, what you're doing, read your blog, buy your products, etc. Ideally, the other components of your online platform will come from your main website, and any time you do something, online or otherwise, you will direct people to your website – for more details, etc.

Every website needs a domain name. This is your web address – what people type into the search bar to get to your website. You will have to purchase this and pay a yearly fee. Your domain name should be whatever name you write under (i.e. mikeenemigo.com), or the name of your publishing company (i.e. thecellblock.net). However, since I recommend that you solely focus on you and your writing, it may be best for your web address to be the name you write under. This will help you concentrate your forces and brand your name.

You can have a website built affordably using free, do-it-yourself platforms like WordPress, Wix, Squarespace, etc. However, unless you have a friend or relative who specializes in one of the other platforms, I recommend that you use WordPress. WordPress is actually a blogging platform, but it offers so many great building options, it can be built just like a website. At this time, WordPress is the most popular platform to use; and again, it's free if you know someone who can build it for you, which isn't difficult to do. You don't have to know any coding. WordPress offers lots of simple-to-use drag and drop options for building and designing, and you can get free widgets to add things like e-commerce ability. For example, Gumroad offers a widget that will allow you to sell your books directly from your website. In addition to this, your outside assistant can find lots of support services for building a WordPress website. All they have to do is Google what they are trying to do and they will be offered lots of tutorials in the form of blogs and YouTube videos.

If you don't have anyone out there to build a website for you, or if it's just easier for you to outsource the work, you can find an affordable web designer on Fiverr.com. My website, thecellblock.net was built using WordPress, and I found my webmaster on Fiverr.com. Have your people go to Fiverr.com and type "web designer" in the search bar. Freelancers from around the world (mine is from Pakistan) will appear with examples of what they can do. Find one you like, tell them what you're looking for, and they will send you a quote. When I want to add something to my website, I send my guy a message regarding what I want, he sends me an affordable quote, I pay him, and it's done within a couple of days.

Depending on your resources, your website should be built one of two ways.

Simple Profile Website

A simple profile website is the easiest and cheapest to build, and requires little or no maintenance. It's basically a one-page website with all the relevant information on the Home page. For example, your picture; author bio; book or books with links to Amazon, where they can be purchased; maybe your snail mail address if you want to possibly get letters; links to your social media pages if you have any; and an e-mail sign-up form. You can probably find someone on Fiverr to put this together for you for no more than $200.

Advanced Website

An advanced website will have all the things I described above, plus more components and capabilities. It will have more pages, such as Home, About, Blog, Bookstore, Merch, Contact, etc. This will be a bit more expensive to have created if you hire an outside source, but the good news is, you don't have to have it done all at once. You can start with the basics, then add over time. This kind of website, with a blog, will require constant upkeep – to upload your blog posts. However, it's not very difficult work, and it can be very beneficial. It gives you a platform to publish anything you want, immediately, which can be powerful. It may take a minute to grow an audience, but there are ways to do it, and once you do, they are likely to be your biggest supporters – as are the folks who sign up for your e-mail list. And one thing I like about a website with a blog (other than you being able to build a loyal audience, if you do it right), is that you can set it up to feed your blog posts automatically to other elements of your platform, like Facebook, Twitter, your Amazon Author Page, etc. I love anything with automation capabilities because it helps to simplify, which, as I often explain, is key.

Additional Website Tips

Regardless of the kind of website you choose to build, make sure you keep your design simple and clean. Each time someone has to click on something, you risk them leaving. Make sure your links work, and navigation is simple. I can't tell you how many websites I've been to, even so-called "professional" ones, that had bad links, or made it nearly impossible for me to find what I was looking for. This caused me to become frustrated and leave. Be careful with adding sliders and things, too, because each flashy, spinning thing you add can slow down your website. If there's too much going on, the website will run slow, causing people to lose patience and leave. People are in a hurry and don't want to be waiting forever to get what they are there for.

Also, one of the most important things on any site is the ability to capture visitor's e-mails. You can get a free mailing list account with MailChimp for the first 2,000 e-mail addresses. MailChimp makes it very easy to add a sign-up form on your website (or blog). Many experts recommend that you put the sign-up form at the top-right of your website because that's "where people expect it to be."

> *"Let me put it this way: If, you focus solely on writing good books and can produce them reasonably quickly, have a mailing list reader can sign up to, and run the occasional promo, you can build a career out of this. A mailing list is the single most important component in developing an audience."*
> – David Gaughran

Do You Need a Website?

Now, while I think you should have a website if you have the resources to get one, at least a simple profile website, do you absolutely need one? Is it a must-have? Like most things when it comes to jailhouse publishing, I think it depends on your resources; or, maybe I should say, lack thereof. You have to figure out how to use your resources the best way possible. I have a website and thoroughly enjoy it. For several reasons. For one, I own and control it. It's not subject to surprise changes I can't control, and often don't like, such as the case with social media, or anything I use that I don't own and control. It allows me to collect e-mails, and I find it gives me credibility when dealing with people, like family members of prisoners who order books, or other businesspeople I contact to work with in some way. They are able to go to one spot and learn about me, my books and other writing, and see that I'm legit. I think as a prisoner, who people are often leery of dealing with, this is important. I think websites still have a little more respect than, say, a social media page. And one of the things I love most is that I'm able to feed my blog to all my other platforms automatically. It also makes my web presence bigger, because I'm able to concentrate everything in one spot. But remember, I've been doing this for a while. This isn't something I built day one. It's something I've added to over time, as I learn, and as I'm able. Major jewel: It's a building process.

But whether you need one or not is a decent question.

On the flip side, however, what I noticed in my research on major Street Lit authors, is that most of them do not have a regular website. I found this very interesting. Ashley and JaQuavis have AshleyandJaQuavis.com, but when you go there, all it has is a brief bio, a picture of them together, and an e-mail sign-up form. Other than that, they don't even have links to their books or anything else. It's simply an e-mail-gathering platform. And I believe it's old, too. Instead, they use social media – Instagram, Facebook and Twitter – then link their pages to where their books can be bought; in the case of Ashley, her MyShopify store. So is this evidence that the need for a traditional website is actually shrinking? Though I don't know their exact reasoning for not having traditional websites, I know they have a reason. These guys are the big dogs – *New York Times* Best Sellers. I also know that hip hop, what Street Lit falls under, has the savvyest of hustlers, often on the forefront of what's next. Could it be they feel their social media followers is their e-mail list? Their social media posts is their blog? That social media is simple to use, free, and it's where everyone is anyway? Again, I'm not sure. But if you can't get a website, it may be easier to go with the route of these major Street Lit authors. It may be cheaper, more modern, and a way to simplify your setup, which is one of the major keys. Then again, these guys are out, and already established. You're not. So, it's something you gotta weigh.

BLOG

The word "blog" is short for web log. A blog is a platform where you can publish or "post" news, opinions, stories, and, really, anything else you want. You can blog on your website, a blogging platform/service like Blogger, Moveable Type, WordPress, one of the many others, or even on social media.

Should You Blog?

As an incarcerated writer, if you have someone who will help you maintain it, I absolutely think you should blog. If you're able to get some traction, it can be a very powerful component of your platform. For example, if you write books, you will have an audience at your immediate reach; one who is already familiar with you, that you can promote to without having to depend on outside entities and expensive advertising. Those who follow your blog are likely to be your primary fans. And you can blog without writing and publishing books. Your jailhouse publishing career can solely be your blog, which, if done correctly, can be both powerful and profitable.

What Should You Blog About?

It depends. If you write books, your blog should be relevant to the genre of the books you write. For example, if your write urban books, you can post sneak peaks, interviews with other urban authors, maybe articles on other incarcerated authors who have been successful in the urban genre, like Wahida Clark and Vickie Stringer, etc. You can write short stories using characters in your upcoming book, or past books, like side stories that aren't available anywhere else (exclusives!), or maybe erotic stories (erotica is very popular!) featuring the characters in your past, present or future books. You could – and should – also post any favorable reviews that others write about you, interviews, and so on. If you write, say, about prison, and you're more like a prison journalist or "expert," you may want to write about the latest laws affecting prisoners; mass incarceration issues; all the popular prison reform activities going on with Kim Kardashian West and other celebrities; prison news; prison stories; reviews on books for prisoners, by prisoners, or about prison. If you wanted to you can write about what's going on in your prison, like a "prison reality blog," and even expose injustices going on. You could put unscrupulous guards on blast, and even give your readers/supporters a phone number to call to complain.

That said, it's not easy to create a successful blog. Today there are a couple hundred million blogs on the Internet. If you want to stand out, and increase your chances of success, there are a few tips you should follow.

Blog Tips

1. Use the proper platform. Though various blogging platforms are available, it is by far your best option to blog using WordPress. If you have a website, ideally also built using WordPress, host your blog from your website. Having someone out there build you a basic blog using WordPress is extremely easy. It is akin to building a basic author profile website. WordPress offers many free templates with basic drag and drop options for building and designing. A blog using WordPress will allow you to automatically feed your posts to your social media pages, like Facebook, Twitter, and G+, and if you have a book published, your Amazon, LibraryThing, and Goodreads author profile pages. This automation allows you to simplify your process and reach more readers with less efforts.

If you don't have anyone to build a blog for you, and you can't afford to hire someone on Fiverr, you can start blogging via social media, like Facebook, Twitter, and/or possibly Tumblr. All social media pages are pretty much blogging platforms, each specializing in different things; for example, Instagram is best for pictures, YouTube is best for videos, Facebook is best for text, photos and videos, etc.

Start with what you have and build up!

2. Ideally you are going to blog from your own WordPress setup. In this case, purchase your own domain name. Your domain name, which is your web address, should be the name of your blog. For example, I blog from my website, TheCellBlock.net. But The Cell Block is also the name of my blog, so if I didn't have a website, I'd still want the domain name to be TheCellBlock.net. Same thing if you use social media. For

example, Facebook.com/TheCellBlock, Instagram.com/TheCellBlock, etc. Also, try to have all your urls and domain names the same if possible.

3. Offer contact information. A lot of bloggers like to create an air of mystery, so they use an alias, don't post any pictures of themselves, and don't offer contact info. I use the mysterious approach with all of my writing in the sense that I never post any pictures of myself anywhere, and I write under an alias, but I do offer contact info. A lot of readers want to know who you are and be able to reach you, because it feels more personal. So use a picture in your bio profile if you can, and offer a way for readers to contact you via e-mail and/or snail mail. Who knows, you might get a pen pal out of it.

4. Have an About page. An About page is a vital blog component. It's probably the most visited page after the Home page. This is where you tell readers about yourself and your blog – who you are, what your blog is about, and why you're the best person to be writing on the subject. Tell them why you and your blog are unique. You have something going for yourself here being that you're in prison, especially if you blog about prison. This is something unique that the majority of bloggers don't have. There are a lot of blogs and websites about prison, but most are not written solely by those who are experts in the area – prisoners, like you. Use this to your advantage. Be sure to make your About page interesting, and if you have any credentials, list them.

5. Clean up the design. Personally, I love the old 2008-era MySpace design. When Facebook came out with its clean design, I thought it was boring and creatively restrictive. But I remember hearing that one of the things people liked better about Facebook, which killed MySpace, was its clean design. For whatever reason, people prefer it, and the same goes with your blog. You want it clean: a basic design that's easy to read and simple to navigate. You don't want dark backgrounds, tiny type, a bunch of sidebars and other distractions. You want a simple graphic header, a great title (i.e. The Cell Block), and a great tagline that quickly communicates what your blog is about (i.e. News, Entertainment, & Resources, From The Cell To The Block). You only have a few seconds to get your reader's attention, and hopefully keep it.

6. Stick to a niche topic. A lot of bloggers like to write about whatever's on their mind. Don't do this. Stick to a topic, or a few related topics, ideally the same as your books if you write them. I had a hard time figuring out how I was going to do this when I first started. I had the prison/prisoner news and info I wanted to blog about (and books to promote), but I also had the urban/street info I wanted to blog about (and books to promote). "The Cell Block" is primarily a prison term, and I always used a prison graphic to represent it. But with a little creativity I was able to play on the words and make it mean, "from the cell (prison), to the block (streets)," and tie it all together. My header graphic is now an image of a cellblock fading into a street block.

If you write books, make sure your blog is relevant to the genre you write because your blog is a major part of your platform to promote your books. It's where you'll be building your audience. Don't have a blog about prison if you write western novels. That's two different audiences that don't cross anywhere. Pick a niche, concentrate your forces.

7. Provide useful content. In addition to interesting and entertaining content, provide your readers with something they can use, like information. People love this shit. Tips and how-to info should be incorporated into your blog regularly. And if you aren't sure what your readers want, ask. Take a poll if you have to.

8. Write strong headlines. I'm sure you've noticed by now that everything online is found by the keywords, key phrases, headlines, etc., that you use. And this includes your blog and blog posts. Make sure you use headlines that are search-engine friendly.

9. Use blog-style writing. Blog readers don't want long, dense, book- and mag-style paragraphs. They want short ones with only two or three sentences each. Blog readers like to read fast – they skim. Using bold subheads, numbered lists and bullet points is a good idea.

10. Make sharing easy. In order to grow your audience, you need your readers to help spread the word, so make sharing easy with one-click buttons for all social media.

11. Feed your blog posts to social media. If you're using WordPress, you can set it up so that your blog posts automatically feed to Facebook, Twitter, and G+. This gives you additional distribution with no extra work, and it allows your audience you follow you in other ways that they may prefer.

12. Affiliate sales. Amazon has an Associates Program for site owners and bloggers. They offer a search tool that will allow you to find the right products and services from their site, and offer a variety of ad styles to display on your site, including text-based and banner images, which are basically digital billboards. Whenever someone purchases an item through your Amazon links, you get a commission. Even with fairly low traffic to your site, you can make a decent amount of money for doing absolutely nothing. Be sure to pick things that will be of interest to your readers.

13. Ad revenue. One method of making money with your blog is the same model that radio, TV and print media have been using forever: create something people enjoy, then charge businesses to advertise on it. If you can create a devoted following, you can convert their loyalty into cash. Ad networks such as Google AdSense will provide you with ads to post, and each time your readers click on them, you will receive a commission. Again, be sure to advertise things that will be of interest to your readers.

14. Blogvertorials. A "blogvertorial" is an advertisement that you publish on your blog. They are usually done in the style of interviews or book reviews. *Don Diva* magazine sells blogvertorials in the style of an interview for $550. You will remain on their website permanently, and they include a social media "push" with this. I sell the same thing on my blog for $100. If you want to promote something, such as your book, send the money, and let me know exactly what it is you want to promote. It must be of interest to my readers, so anything relevant to prison or the streets will work. If you are an incarcerated author, that works. Once you give me specifics, I will send you interview questions. Once you answer them, I'll post the interview on my blog, along with up to 5 pictures (they can be book covers), and a link to your website, or where your book(s) can be purchased. This will remain on TheCellBlock.net forever.

If you decide to blog, this is a way you can make additional money from it as well.

15. Sell books. Whether paperbacks or e-books, you can sell your books directly from your blog. This is a great way to make money. Say you blog about prison, and you've written a book titled *Surviving Prison* or *Prison Secrets*. At the end of your blog posts about prison (which can even be an excerpt from your book), you add a link to where your book can be purchased, or if you're selling an e-book, you can have it to where it can be downloaded right then and there. If you provide a great article, there is no better time to promote the book or books that relate to it. And if you haven't written a book because you're just blogging, one way to create a book later is to group together your related posts, give them a collective title, then sell that bitch on Amazon and everywhere else books are sold. This is how you make your blog posts and writing work twice as hard for you.

SOCIAL MEDIA

Social media is everywhere. It's huge. Watch TV and you hear about it constantly. Talk to your people on the outside and they mention it regularly. Because of this, many prisoners think, if they just get on social media, where millions upon millions of people are every day, they will then be in front of millions upon millions of people, and everyone will know their story, about their book(s), etc. But this is a huge misconception. It doesn't work like this. Not even a little bit.

Just because you're on social media, available to millions of people, doesn't mean millions of people are looking for you, or going to somehow stumble upon you. Social media is something that has to be actively worked in order to have any kind of success. You cannot just put up a profile and it catch fire. And since it's something that has to be actively worked, unless you have a cell phone and can do it yourself (which may put your phone at risk if you put yourself out there like that), you will have to rely on someone on the outside to help you; likely the same person helping you with the 1,000 other aspects of publishing. And it's a lot of work.

Personally, though I'm sure there are more, I've only seen two prisoners really have some type of real presence on social media, specifically Instagram, and that's a guy named Snubbz, and another named Shod.

Snubbz (who I think is out now) is a rapper who posted pictures and videos daily without trying even a little bit to hide the fact he was in prison, doing it all with a cell phone. I didn't ask him, but I suspect cell phones were easy to some by where he was, because to be that careless, he had to be confident that, if he lost his phone, he could easily get another. Last I checked, Snubbz had about 12,000 followers, a following he told me he built solely while in prison, and over the course of about two years.

But Snubbz is not just any schmuck starting from nothing. He's well known in our city –Sacramento, California – and he's the "big homie" of a hot rapper, Mozzy, who's from his hood – Oak Park. (I have a book titled *Underworld Zilla* with King Guru, who's also from their hood, and it even features Snubbz as one of the characters.) Mozzy has several songs with Snubbz, and also occasionally shouts him out. Snubbz is a well-respected member of their team. So Snubbz has several advantages that the average prisoner doesn't, and that must be taken into consideration when you think about the possibility of you being as successful on social media. And lastly on this, I'm not sure how much having the 12,000 followers transfered to music sales for Snubbz, so I can't tell you how beneficial any of it actually was. It might seem cool to have 12k followers, but if it doesn't result in sales for what you're doing, the ROI (return on investment) isn't there, and when doing something from prison, where resources and opportunities are few and far between, you must always pay attention to ROI on everything you do.

The other guy, Shod, is out of Georgia. I saw him grow an enormous following on Instagram. Shod is the founder and designer of The Trenchez, a clothing company. He started the company before he went to prison, but he really blew up when he posted a few pictures from inside his cell with "fresh drip" – clothing he made with a home-made needle, out of whatever fabric he could find around his cell, like various state and personal clothing, plastic from the mattress cover, etc. However, Shod, too, had an advantage. While incarcerated, he got in touch with a childhood friend, Chelse, who has her own podcast (or radio show, I can't quite remember), called Chatting with Chelse, and she agreed to help him promote his "drip." With her help, I began to see Shod's story everywhere. Last I was on Instagram, I think he had over 40,000 followers. But again, Shod not only had a dedicated friend, he had a dedicated friend who already had a successful platform, and, if I might say, is a social media marketing guru.

Now back to our writing/publishing plans. If you read any books on self-publishing, they will tell you social media is a mandatory component. "Being on Facebook is non-negotiable," says David Gaughran, successful self-publisher and author of *Let's Get Digital: How To Self-Publish, And Why You Should*. And I most certainly agree with him...if you are on the outside and can maintain it yourself. Is it, however, "non-negotiable" if you're publishing from prison, where you have to rely on someone else to do the work, and you must prioritize differently? In my opinion, to have someone actively run a social media presence for you is not a wise investment of your resources. I don't think the ROI is there. I think you will burn a lot of your resources – the time and energy of your outside assistant, and your money if you're paying them – and it won't result in sales that are worth the effort. Even if you get a couple of followers (you're not at all likely to get as many as Snubbz or Shod), the likelihood of those followers turning into customers, is small. Unless you are able to do it yourself, I personally think social media will be a huge time, energy, and possibly financial drain.

Now, if you have someone who is a social media guru, loves social media for their own reasons, wants to spend the time actively running a page (or pages) for you – engaging, etc. – and especially if you can't get this person to do anything else for you, maybe you should let them do it. Let their contribution to your jailhouse publishing endeavors be just that. And if you have a resource like Snubbz or Shod, I say definitely do it. But if you don't, it's likely to be more trouble than it's worth, and you'd be better off spending your resources elsewhere.

That said, there is one way to use social media to your benefit, where the rewards will likely outweigh the work, and that's to blog from your WordPress website, and connect the blog to all your social media pages, so when you post a blog, it automatically distributes to your entire social media platform. This virtually takes no extra effort or time than it does to post to your blog, so there is only a possible upside. You will not be providing the personal engagement your followers may appreciate, but you can post new content regularly, and easily. This you should absolutely do.

What platforms should you use?

I say, if you're going to incorporate social media to your strategy in any capacity, you should use as many of the platforms as possible. Let me explain.

If you're going to go with the automated strategy I suggest, other than creating the individual pages for each platform, which will only take maybe ten minutes each, it will take your outside assistant no more time to post to all of them than it will to post to one of them, as they will only need to post directly to your WordPress blog, and it will automatically go out to the various pages you are connected to. And if you don't have a WordPress blog, your outside assistant can use social media managers like Buffer and HootSuite, which will allow them to run all your platforms from a single interface. They won't have to go into each and every social media page individually. They will be able to insert your header, body of text, picture, and hashtags, then post to all your pages, the same as if they were doing it from your blog.

Here's the thing: You never know where you will find your audience. You might think your audience will be on Instagram, but it might be the folks on Twitter, Facebook, or even Tumblr who embrace you the most. So, if you have your posts going to all of them, you will be able to see where you are gaining traction, then you will know which one to engage with most if you're having someone out there do that for you.

I've only personally used Instagram, Facebook, and MocoSpace. My favorite to use, both with posting and following others, is Instagram. I don't like Facebook – for many reasons. That said, IG is mostly used for posting pictures. This is why it's such a great platform for "Instagram models." And they're growing in the area of videos now, too, especially since they launched IG TV. But as a writer, Facebook is probably better. And though I've never used Twitter personally, every writer seems to use it, so you obviously want to be there. I've read that blogging is big on Tumblr, so you should add that to your platform. And though G+ never caught on like the others, I think you should be there simply for the fact that it's owned by Google, the most used search engine, and I believe it will increase your SEO – Search Engine Optimization. I'm not 100 percent certain of this, but I've read several things that've led me to believe this is the case. Because of this, I not only plan to build a G+ profile for Mike Enemigo and another for The Cell Block, I'm going to build one for each individual book. For the individual book profiles, I will put the book's cover as the profile picture. For the url I will put the title of the book. For the About I will put the book's summary. Then I will link each one back to my website where the book(s) can be purchased. The more opportunities for exposure, the better. It certainly can't hurt. And it's free to do. And when you're publishing from prison, and something is free, we need to take advantage of it.

PROMOTIONAL VIDEOS

As prisoners, we don't have access to the Internet (usually), but videos are everything these days when it comes to promoting something to folks on the outside, including books. It's videos that everyone is doing. I watched a million of them on Instagram, Facebook, and YouTube. There are four types of videos that are best for promoting books. I'll explain each of them below.

Trailers

I'd say the most popular kind of video to promote a book would be a book trailer. A trailer is usually 60 seconds or less, and it acts as a commercial for the book. Think of a movie trailer, which is a short commercial that shows exciting clips from the movie, enticing you to want to go and see it in theaters. It may even have some sensational text in between clips, or in front of it. Book trailers are like that.

Now, you probably won't have the money or resources to hire actors to act out scenes in your book for your trailer, but that's OK; most people are not having trailers acted out and produced this way, not even the big dogs. Instead, they are grabbing clips off the Internet that relate to the topic of their book, and editing them together in a way that tell the story they want told. For example, say I had a novel about a street kingpin that takes place in Sacramento, California, where I'm from. For the trailer, I might start it out with some text that pops up on the screen saying, "Mike was a kingpin from the grimy streets of Sacramento, California," and in the background, behind the text, you would see video footage of some grimy Sacramento streets, feel me? I can have someone shoot footage, or I can find some on the Internet somewhere. The words would disappear, and the next words to appear on the screen might be, "He ruled with an iron fist." Here, the scene in the background might be some real-life police footage of a murder scene, maybe with a body in the street, covered in a sheet, some police cars and crime scene tape. I could find this on the Internet, and as long as it doesn't have a notifiable landmark or something in it, it doesn't even have to be a scene from Sac. Nobody would know. That text would disappear, and maybe the new text would say, "Then came Nadia." The scene behind this text might be that of a beautiful woman, maybe from a rap video, looking sexy and whatever else represented the story. You getting the point? It would continue for however long it was necessary to tell the story of the trailer – whatever you wanted the trailer to portray to seduce and hook the viewer. During the trailer you'd hear music that fits the proper vibe. For an urban book trailer about a drug lord, maybe you'd have a Migos song, or something like that.

These are the best videos for fiction. To get them done, or any video you're having someone else do, you write what's called a treatment. Basically, a treatment is a bullet list of what you want – what text, images, songs, vibe, etc. Once you have this, you find a video editor, of which there are plenty these days, as so many people are doing these right on their phones or laptops. You may pay anywhere between $50 and $300 for this kind of video, and you could probably find someone on Instagram, or even Fiverr.com. Just remember, most of the freelancers on Fiverr are from other countries, and may not be really familiar with the right look or style you're going for, so you need to be specific. In fact, no matter who you use, I suggest finding a trailer you like, and use it as an example, especially if it's one created by the editor you decide to work with. If you want to go further, you may even find the footage and scenes you want to use in the video. This will likely save you some money, and allow you to better control what you get. Of course, since you're in prison, you may need to have someone on the outside collect this for you.

Sales-Pitch Videos

Another type of video that can be done, which is much easier and less expensive, is what I call a sales-pitch video. Wahida Clark does this sometimes, where she just talks into the cameras, usually from her office, about a new book or project, or just simply dropping some jewels, perhaps about self-publishing – which then, of course, leads to some service she may offer, as this is a business, one of which Wahida is a master, and nothing is done just for the sake of doing it.

As a prisoner, again, unless you have a phone and can record your own video, you may need to have someone on the outside create this for you. If you have a hot wife, sister, etc., you can have her talk about your new book, about how good it is, maybe read the synopsis, and whatever else. This style of video is probably best for a how-to book, though it can be done for any book you have. Your "actor," which should not come off as an actor, can excitedly list the things the book covers, all that they learned, and how they benefitted, then at the end, mention to click the link in order to purchase the book. I can have a video like this done for, say, *The Hood Millionaire*. I can have one of my young students out there who's really gettin' it create this video while sitting inside his Benz. He can have stacks of money, a Rolex, chunky necklace on, and a bad bitch next to him while speaking into the camera about the book, and occasionally holding the book up to the camera. Again, it can be done for any kind of book, you just create the video for whatever vibe you're going for.

Q and A Videos

Similar to the sales-pitch videos, some authors do Q and A videos when they want to promote an upcoming book and/or increase activity on their social media page(s). That's what my favorite street lit author, Al-Saadiq Banks, did. While working on his upcoming book, *Block Party 666* (it's available now, but not when he was doing the videos I'm referring to), each day he'd drop a couple videos where he'd answer questions sent in by fans about various aspects of his career. It was storytelling at its finest, laced with jewels, as I was able to learn all he went through to get to where he's at, which taught me an awful lot I needed to know, because it showed me we've had similar struggles with this, which boosted my confidence. I intensely watched these videos of him talking, usually from inside his foreign whip or the patio of his fancy house while smokin' a 'gar. These videos, simply done, recorded on his phone and posted on IG, allowed me to get to "know" Al-Saadiq, and feel a connection with him, which is the whole point of him doing them; and what you, too, want to do. Al-Saadiq became my favorite street lit author, even though I'd not read even one of his books, just on the strength of the authenticity I felt from him, and the jewels he laced me with. I then connected with him personally, via IG, and he gave be additional jewels via direct messaging. Today I can tap in with him directly and get a response, just like that, with whatever jewels I'm asking for.

Can you make this kind of video?

Note: Since then, I have bought and read Al-Saadiq book *Caught Slippin*, which I bought because of his videos, and it didn't disappoint one bit. Is he truly the best street lit author? I don't know. He's certainly one of them, and for sure, my favorite along with my guy Dutch. True game is the ability to gain fans for your book – for you! – before they even read one.

Template Videos

Template videos, as I call them, are videos where you insert pictures into a template, then the template moves them around – brings them back and forth, makes them flash, spin, etc. They look really good, and even though the images are actually still shots, there is a lot of movement, so at first glance, it almost looks like a real, moving video.

These videos are very easy to make. And get this; remember I hired the top-tier publicist who gave me two videos as part of my package? These are the type of videos they were. After she and I worked together, I contacted her because I needed a couple videos made – ones Wahida wanted me to make – I was desperate, and I didn't know where else to get them done. Guess how much she wanted per video? $250.00! Yep. But she said she'd give me two videos for $400.00 since I was a "past client." Fuck that. I wasn't that desperate.

I went on the hunt to find another route, but couldn't find one. Then, one day on IG I saw a rapper who had one of these videos to promote his new CD. I contacted him about creating one for me, but he wasn't interested. Luckily, however, I saw a logo in the bottom corner, so I Googled it and found the app he used to make it. I downloaded the app and set out to learn it, which I did, easily, even though I'm far from a tech/Internet guy, as this shit wasn't even around when I was out. I can't remember the name of the app, but it was free to download, though you can pay a small fee for an upgraded version. Try having your people Google "free video-making app." When you find it, your people can download it to their phone. It's very easy to use.

For the particular app that I used, when you go to it, it will offer you maybe 75-100 different templates to choose from – ones that move and flash differently from each other. You click on the one you want to use, then it will have slots for you to insert photos from your phone – around seven. (I believe one of the features for the upgraded versions will allow you to add more.) You insert the photos in the order you want them to go.

The next step is where you add the music you want to play during the "video." The app has a bunch of different instrumentals you can pick from, but they suck. No problem, you can easily use your own. Whatever song to want to use, you have to convert it to an MP3. There are websites that allow you to do this for free. To find one, Google "how to convert a song into an MP3." When you go to the site, you type in the song you want, by what artist, and when it comes up, click "convert." It'll be done in about a minute. You then upload it to the video app, and save it in your file. (You can save a whole bunch of songs and have them ready to go.) Once you upload the song to the video app, you go back to the point in the video-making process where you select your song and select the song you just saved. You can even select a specific part of the song, if you want. It's all very easy. Trust me, if I can figure it out, anyone can.

As an example, one of the videos I made was for my book *Underworld Zilla*, with TCB author King Guru. For those of you who don't know, *Underworld Zilla* is about a West Coast thug who sets up shop in Florida; meets a white stripper with red hair and a big ass, who sells drugs and has a murderous secret; then he runs into a problem where he needs to call upon his folks from back home – members of the Underworld Zilla clique. So, for this video, I inserted the following seven pictures, in this order:

1. A black and white picture of a Cellblock that said "The Cell Block Presents" across the middle.
2. The *Underworld Zilla* book cover.
3. A picture of Russia Lit, a real stripper in Florida with red hair and a fat ass. It's the same girl used in the gun on the cover of *Underworld Zilla*.
4. A picture of a whole bunch of money.
5. A picture of Snubbz and Staxx, real members of the Underworld Zilla clique.
6. A picture of guns and blood.
7. A picture of the *Underworld Zilla* cover again, to end it.

All of these images fit perfectly to the story. The template I used made these pictures, which it showed one by one, in the order I listed, flash, go blurry then come into focus, spin, etc. The song playing in the background of this video is "California Nigga," by Mozzy, who's also from Underworld Zilla. I made this video in probably ten minutes. You can watch it now on my IG @mikenemigo.

I made other videos like this, too, for *How To Hustle & Win: Sex, Money, Murder Edition*; *Money iz the Motive*, and a few others. Then I started making them for friends, like Stone Ramsey, Jasmine Johnston, and others. They all thought I was the shit, with hella skills.

I'll take that.

E-BOOKS

If I could do one thing regarding this publishing thing, it would be to build my empire selling e-books. In my opinion, e-books are the best thing going if you can crack the code. The biggest reason is because, with e-books, everything is digital, which means you have no hard product to deal with, and therefore, you don't have to worry about fulfilling orders, shipping, handlining, etc. Everything is done online.

Furthermore, when you are in the e-book game, when you are ready to publish a book, you can do so at a moment's notice, and within a few hours be available all around the world. And with e-books, whether your book is 10k words or 250k words, the commerce is the same.

Having a successful e-book operation is the epitome of earning passive income, because other than ads you may have to set up, you can basically "set it and forget it." Once it's set up, everything is done online, automatically, and in my opinion, there's nothing better than an automated money machine.

Unfortunately for me, I've yet to master the e-book selling secrets. That said, I'm getting closer. I have e-books available for most of my books and producing them isn't a problem at all, but I've yet to crack the code to sell enough of them that, if I wanted to, I could rely solely on them and no longer have to deal with hard copies.

But I'm getting closer...

Now, would I still deal with hard copies if I'm able to crack the e-book secrets to success? Yes, because I sell a lot of books to prisoners – a lot of my books are specifically for prisoners. But I'm telling you now, once my e-books bring me a comfortable income, I will be brave enough to sell my hard copies the way Zach Smith sells his, and that's by promoting my books to prisoners, then directing them to my website or Amazon to purchase them. They will have to have their loved one go online and order the books, which completely removes me and my team from the ordering process. This is what I suggest you do, too.

I have a couple articles from *USA Today* that I've saved over the years that really inspired me in regards to e-books. I want to share them with you so you can see there are people making real money from self-publishing e-books. It's not easy, but it's possible. As a prisoner, this is what you should ultimately be aiming for, even if you have to start somewhere else, like I've had to do.

SELF-PUBLISHED AUTHORS ARE HITTING IT BIG WITH E-BOOKS!

In 2009, Michael Prescott's dream died, or so he thought.
After graduating college in 1980, Prescott had labored for almost three decades to become a best-selling novelist, writing more than 20 books under various names. He enjoyed critical praise and some successes.

But when 25 publishers passed on buying his thriller *Riptide*, Prescott thought the gig was up. Then, on a whim, he decided to self-publish it as an e-book.

Today, the soft-spoken Prescott, 51, is living his dream. He is one of 15 self-published authors whose e-books, often selling for just 99 cents, have cracked the top 150 on USA TODAY'S best-seller list this year [2011], threatening to change the face of publishing.

For Prescott and a handful of others, the numbers add up. Prescott says he has earned more than $300,000 before taxes this year by selling more than 800,000 copies of his self-published e-books.

Five of Prescott's thrillers have logged a total of 42 weeks on USA TODAY'S best-seller list.

"If someone in this year had told me I was going to make a lot of money with e-books, I wouldn't have believed him," Prescott says. "I thought maybe a couple of hundred dollars."

E-books are changing the way authors and readers connect

Today, authors such as Prescott can bypass traditional publishers. They can digitally format their own manuscript, set a price and sell it to readers through a variety of online retailers and devices. Amazon sells e-books via its Kindle app for smartphones and computers. Barnes & Noble sells e-books through its Nook electronic reader device and app. There is also the Sony eReader, Apple's iPad and Kobo, while Overdrive provides e-books to libraries.

Almost every day brings more digital modes for readers to obtain books in non-print forms, creating more choices for readers, opportunities for self-published writers, and challenges for traditional publishers.

E-book business is booming

According to the Association of American Publishers, e-books grew from 0.6% of the total trade market share in 2008 to 6.4% in 2010. Total net revenue for 2010: $878 million with 114 million e-books sold. In adult fiction, e-books are now 13.6% of the market.

"It's a gold rush out there," Prescott says. "Forty acres and a mule. It's the best time for an independent writer to get out there."

Forget the sensitive auteur waiting for the muse. Self-publishing an e-book requires an entrepreneurial spirit. For each 99-cent e-book sold, Prescott receives 35 cents. The online retailers – Amazon, BN.com, Apple, Sony – take the rest.

In traditional publishing, an unknown first-time author might get an advance of as little as $5,000, and then receive royalties from sales.

Prescott symbolizes how the Web can empower an author to circumvent the traditional model, in which an author signs with an agent, who then sells the manuscript to a publisher, who edits, prints and distributes the book to stores and promotes it to the media in exchange for a share of the profits.

In the past, if the manuscript was rejected, it usually sat unread in a writer's desk drawer because the alternative – self-publishing one's book – carried a stigma. A writer could pay a vanity publisher to print the book, but stores rarely stocked them and critics rarely reviewed them. (There were exceptions: E. Lynn Harris, for example, became a star selling his self-published *Invisible Life* out of his car before signing with a traditional publisher.)

Prescott was never willing to self-publish his print books. "From the start of my career, I was published by major publishing houses," he says. In 2000, Prescott's *The Shadow Hunter* – a thriller about a woman on the trail of a stalker – hit USA TODAY'S list at No. 140. His 1992 book *Shiver* was made into a 2011 movie.

But in the new world of "indie publishing," with its opportunity for self-published authors to sell hundreds of thousands of e-books, the stigma is disappearing. Plus, there are fewer fixed costs; no paper, no printing press, no warehouse, no trucks.

"It's a whole new world," Prescott says. "You're eliminating the middleman."

One reason Prescott is able to capitalize on the e-book revolution is that he already has a back list of novels previously edited and released by traditional publishers. (When his publisher lets the book go out of print, the rights reverted to Prescott.)

'It's a paradigm shift'

Barbara Freethy, a top romance writer for 20 years who has written 30 novels, says that this year, she has sold 1.3 million self-published e-book versions of 17 of her out-of-print novels. Nine hit USA TODAY'S top 150.

"There have been more changes in the last two years than the previous 18 years I have been in publishing," says the San Francisco writer, who is considering self-publishing her new book, *A Secret Wish*. She finds it satisfying to see the balance of power shift within publishing, with authors gaining more control over their work.

"It's a paradigm shift and a revolution," says J.A. Konrath, who is considered the guru of the self-publishing movement. "It's a huge win for readers," who now have access to more writers from around the world, he says.

Konrath, 41, who had modest success writing mysteries published by several traditional publishers (who still publish him), is now a best-selling writer of self-published e-books. He also runs the influential website The Newbie's Guide to Publishing.

"I am the guy who had his butt kicked by the industry for 20 years, and now I'm showing other authors what they can do so they don't have to go through the same thing," he says. "Traditional book publishers are just serving drinks on the Titanic."

Konrath has seen his income from his self-published e-book sales go from $1,400 in April 2009 to $68,000 in April 2011.

But before you quit your day job to become a best-selling e-book writer, Konrath points out that the vast number of books released in any form, print or e-book, don't sell. To become a successful writer, talent, hard work and self-promotion are important.

Meet attorney and debut novelist Darcie Chan, 37. This year she self-published her debut novel, *The Nill River Recluse*, after being rejected by more than 100 literary agents. Set in a small Vermont town, the moody mystery centers on what happened to a beautiful young bride. It spent 16 weeks on USA TODA'S best-seller list, peaking at No.6. Chan says she has sold 416,000 copies of the 99-cent e-book.

Despite the success of some self-published e-book authors, it's premature to write the final chapter for traditional publishers. In an ironic twist, several self-published e-book superstars – most famously Amanda Hocking – have landed headline-making contracts with major publishing houses, which will be releasing their titles in print and digital formats.

Hocking, 27, a life-long Minnesotan from a working-class background, has been telling stories almost since she could climb out of the crib and was writing full-fledged novels at 17.

Unable to find an agent, she began self-publishing her young-adult paranormal romances in 2010. They became huge hits; seven of them have spent 50 weeks on USA TODAY'S list in 2011.

Steppingstone to success

Her addictive *Trylle* trilogy – *Switched, Torn* and *Ascend*, starring a raven-haired royal beauty named Wendy – has surged to the top with an intensity that suggests Twilight's Bella has a rival for the hearts of female readers.

This is when things get weird. Already wealthy from her self-published e-books, Hocking in June signed a $2 million contract with St. Martin's Press. In January, the *Trylle* trilogy will hit stores – brick and mortar and online – in trade paperback. The movie rights already have been sold.

With technology enabling everyone to be his or her own Johannes Gutenberg, why would an author sign with a traditional book publisher?

"I wanted to reach more people," Hocking says. She points out that most people – particularly young teens she writes for – do not own iPads or e-readers. Hocking says it's about the story, not the device. "I wanted to write a fun book, not start a revolution."

C.J. Lyons also appreciates what traditional publishers bring to the table. A former emergency-room pediatrician, Lyons, 47, has published more than a dozen medical suspense novels with traditional publishers, as well as nine self-published titles, two of which hut USA TODAY's list this summer.

Now she has signed with a traditional publisher, Minotaur Press, a division of St. Martin's. "I enjoy working with an editor, and I think my writing is ready to go to the next level," she says.

Her new publisher, Andrew Martin, says, "I'm not buying a book, I'm building a career with an author." He says an established publishing house lets the author do what he does best – write – while the publisher offers expert marketing, editing, production and aggressive protection against e-books being illegally pirated.

In the midst of this revolution, Martin sees a silver lining for traditional publishers. In the past, editors, agents and publishers depended on their gut about whether a book would connect with readers. Now the stories are being pre-tested in the online marketplace. "It's like the old-fashioned slush pile being road tested – with the cream rising to top."

In the end, Martin selected Lyons for the oldest reason of all. "She is a storyteller. I think that speaks most to me."

WRITER FINDS RUNWAY SUCCESS WITH SELF-PUBLISHED E-BOOKS!

Without a college degree or even a hint of celebrity, Amanda Hocking has overturned the world of publishing with the young-adult paranormal romance e-books she published on her own.

In April 2010, Hocking released *My Blood Approves* – the story of a vampire love triangle through Kindle. Suddenly her novels, priced from 99 cents to $2.99, were taking off.

By February 2011, Hocking had seven self-published e-books, including her "*Trylle* Trilogy," starring trolls, on USA TODAY's Best-Selling Books list, where they would stay for 50 weeks. She has earned an estimated $2 million selling 1.5 million copies of her e-books.

The traditional publishing world that once rejected her took notice, and consequently, Hocking's empire (and bank account) has grown even bigger.

After a headline-making auction in March, Hocking signed a multimillion-dollar deal with the traditional print publisher St. Martin's Press. The deal gives St. Martin's the right to release Hocking's "*Trylle* Trilogy" in trade paperback and as e-book editions.

The first novel, *Switched* (St. Martin's Griffen, $8.99), hits stores today with a first printing of 250,000 print copies. The St. Martin's e-book edition also is $8.99. (The sequels, Torn and Ascend, are due Feb. 28 and April 24.) Meanwhile, the Trylle (pronounced "Trill") film rights have been optioned by Media Capital Rights. Screenwriter Terri Tatchell, Academy Award nominee for District 9, has completed the first draft, Hocking says.

And on Aug. 21, St. Martin's Press will publish *Wake*, the first novel in Hocking's brand-new hardcover quartet, *Watersong*. The publisher paid Hocking $2 million for the print and e-book rights. It's the tale of female siren sisters who are "strong and funny, good and bad," Hocking says.

The author will head to Manhattan soon for intensive media training to prepare for a tour through the USA, U.K., Spain, Italy and Ireland. Her website (worldofamandahocking.com) has been polished to a high gloss and her photos glamourized.

Had the e-book not been invented, Hocking today might still be unpublished. And not for lack of trying. She completed her first novel at 17, wrote constantly, took writing classes at local colleges and regularly queried agents and publishers, only to be rejected until she was already a self-made millionaire.

One expert in young-adult paranormal romance who is impressed by Hocking's imaginative powers and ferocious work ethic is Rebecca Housel. (Hocking says she wrote Switched in one week fueled by Red Bull, Sweet Tarts and ravioli. "The story was already in my head," she says.)

But Housel, who co-edited 2009's *Twilight* and *Philosophy*, and examination of the Meyer series, also believes Hocking could improve if she enrolled somewhere like the Iowa Writer's Workshop.

Reviewers haven't always been on board. *Publishers Weekly* said of *Switched*: "While Hocking grabs readers early on, thinly drawn, enigmatic characters with deliberately poor communication and a flair for high school-style drama stall the story's momentum. The plotting recovers, but the last chapter simply sets up the sequel, *Torn*."

Hocking herself appreciates professional editing. It's one reason she signed with St. Martin's Press. Other motivations included the $2 million paycheck and the chance to reach readers who do not have e-readers, perhaps a contrarian notion in the world that's becoming increasingly digital.

Plus, running one's own publishing enterprise is exhausting. "I wanted more time to write," Hocking says. She says she enjoyed working with St. Martin's editor Rose Hillard and took her advice about some characters for the paperback edition.

Hillard, for her part, says she is excited to help: get Hocking's books into the hands or more readers.

"I first discovered Amanda's work when I ordered the self-published edition of *Switched*, which had just started getting some buzz online," she says. "From the moment I started reading, I knew I had something very special in my hands. There was something uncommonly good about her work – it was unputdownable, haunting, intensely romantic and incredibly entertaining."

DISTRIBUTION

Book distribution is the way in which your books are delivered to customers. Amazon distributes your books by sending it to the buyer by way of download, if it's an e-book, or POD (Print on Demand) if it's a softcover. Draft2Digital is a distribution platform that you can upload your books to that will send your books to various other online distributors for digital download. D2D) charges 10 percent to do this for you, but it's worth it, because it would be a lot of work for you to contact each place individually yourself.

You may distribute your books yourself via a P.O. Box. I do. You can order any of my books by sending the money and order to my P.O. Box, and we will send the book(s) to you. There are two ways to distribute through this method. The first way is, you can order a bunch of books via your KDP account at the discounted publisher's price, and when orders come in, your outside assistant will need to package It and mail it off. This method may give you the biggest profit, but fulfil ling orders can be a lot of work for your outside assistant(s) – all the packaging, trips back and forth to the post office, paperwork, etc. This method is what Freebird Publishers does when you order one of their Freebird-published books. The second method is to receive orders via P.O. Box or website, then fill the orders by mailing the books directly from Amazon, but using your publisher's account to purchase the books, where you get a discount. You may not get as much profit per book this way than if you mail it yourself, as Amazon will want their piece, but it's a lot less work on your people, so when you factor that in, you're not losing much, if anything.

In any case, distributing using the POD method is my favorite, as you don't have to pay upfront expenses buying a bunch of books – where your people will also have to store them, etc. With POD, the books aren't even printed until the order/money is sent. This is the best method, in my opinion, for prisoners.

> *"Using a POD print and distribution service is a low cost and risk-free way to do business because you don't hold inventory. The downside is that it cost a bit more for POD than it does to print thousands of books with an offset press. POD printing and distribution services also take care of the sales side of*

your business. They print the book and fulfill the order as soon as the customer pays for the book. Then they credit your bank account. It's all one efficient process."
– Karla King, author of *Self-Publishing Boot Camp Guide*

There are several books-to-prisoner's distributors that may sell and distribute your book for you. At a price, obviously. Places like SureShot and Freebird may put you in their catalog and accept order for your books. Contrary to popular belief, these guys do not have a warehouse full of books. What they do Is buy an Amazon Prime membership for $100 a year, which gives them free shipping. So, when you buy a book from one of these places for, say, $15.00 plus $6.00 shipping and handling, they send you the book from Amazon, at Amazon's cost, and their profit – the bookstore's – is the $6.00 shipping and handling. This is good for you because you don't have to send them books upfront. Also, when their book catalogs go out and your book is in it, that's free promotion for your book. I've sold a lot of books like this Your money will come from Amazon, as these are basically Amazon sales. Have your people contact these books-to-prisoner's companies and ask them to add your book to their catalog.

There are a few urban books-to-prisoner's distributors, such as Wall Periodicals, Urban Reads, which Is operated by State Vs Us, Special Needs X-Press (SNX), and others. Some of my books are distributed by State V Us/Urban Reads, but I had to purchase and send them books upfront, which I don't like doing, especially with my Directory since it expires quickly and I'm always updating it. I've dealt with the guy at SNX a few times, but he played games. He had me send him books, then he never got back at me. I bought his most recent catalog and it seems as if he's only selling urban books by CASH and Lockdown Publications. The SNX guy claims he has a big warehouse full of books and distributes them personally, but I'm not sure if this is true or not. He probably uses the Amazon method SureShot and others use.

The good thing about these distributors is that they are established in their market and have a customer base. If you can get any of them to carry your books, I think it will be beneficial, especially if they use the Amazon method and You don't have to send them books upfront.

Bookstores on the outside are few and far between these days. However, if you know someone who owns a store whose audience may be interested in your book, you may consider trying to sell them out of their store for a split. For example, if your brother owns an urban barber shop, you may be able to sell a few urban books out of his shop. If nothing else, you should at least try and have fliers on the counter and posters on the wall. Same thing if you know someone who owns one of the little hole-in-the-wall stores that sells stuff, like clothing or whatever, to people who may be interested in your book. Then again, it may be more trouble than it's worth.

King Guru wants to sell his book *Underworld Zilla* from the corner store in his neighborhood, as his neighborhood is full of Oak Park Bloods and Underworld Zilla members. This may work if we were out, or had an "in" with the owner of the store. Other than that, we would have to move a whole lot of books out the store in order to make any real profit. If we pay $2.50 plus shipping per book, and we sell the books for $12.00 each, the store would likely want half the $12.00, so that only leaves us with around $3.00 profit for each book. That's pennies when considering all the work we have to do to arrange this and get them the books from prison. Then we have to hope the books don't get damaged, and we will likely have to use lots of time and energy trying to get paid, as most store owners aren't eagerly trying to pay money. It's usually up to the owner of the book/product to contact the store owner for payment, so it hardly seems worth the effort, even though it may seem like a good idea on the surface. Now, if you have someone who frequents the store regularly anyway, and knows the manager or owner well, it might be worth doing, but that is unlikely.

> *"In my experience, no matter how well your book does, bookstore owners tend to order in very small amounts, even though it's generally on consignment basis – meaning they only pay if it actually sells. And that's when it goes well. Often books can go missing, or get returned in poor condition, or you can have difficulty getting paid, and so on. Plus, physically printing and shipping and storing books is costly, in time and money."* – David Gaughran, author of *Let's Get Digital: How to Self-Publish and Why You Should*

> *"Do not dismiss the fact that, whichever route you take, you are responsible for the marketing and promotion that will*

create buzz and sell your book. That is, you can't just send the books to your distributor and expect them to sell magically. It can take years for even a very good book to rise to the top. Persistence pays off." – Karla King, author of *Self-Publishing Boot Camp Guide*

AUDIO BOOKS

Audio books, which are sold just about everywhere books are sold online, is big business right now. And it makes sense, too, with how busy people are. Traditional books, and even ebooks, demand your eyes and attention; you have to pretty much stop what you're doing and focus on reading them. (Maybe the exception being us prisoners who have learned to read a book, listen to music, and keep an ear on the TV for something we don't want to miss, all at the same time.) With audio books, however, you can listen while driving, cleaning the house, cooking dinner, taking care of the kids, or whatever else one in the busy freeworld needs to do, but who also want to get a good story in.

Most authors hire a professional reader to read, record, and produce their audio books. A pro can cost you several hundred dollars an hour. I think hiring a pro to do this is a mistake. I think you should do it yourself, so long as you don't have an annoying voice, and your voice fits the main character whose point of view the story is told from. I listened to books on Amazon by major authors, who I respect and have named in this book, that had their stories read by what sounded like a white female, when the main character whose POV the story was told from was a black thug. I couldn't believe it. And the women-reader's voice was so boring and robot-like, as bad as I wanted to hear the story in hopes of learning, I began to get tired after only a few minutes.

No bueno.

Let me give you another example. A business associate of mine, Young Doe, is a relatively famous rapper from Denver. He often raps with California artists from the Bay, like J. Stalin. (Shout out to Stalin. I got you on that.) What you may not know, even if you've heard of Young Doe, is he also wrote a book titled *The Carlos Crimson Story* under the name Charles Truth. (Personally, since he already has a fan base under the name Young Doe, I think he should have written the book under that name, but this is a different point than what I'm trying to make here.) For his audio book, he hired a well-known (and expensive) reader. I thought this was a mistake. As a rapper, one with a decent fan base, his voice is his moneymaker. His fans buy his music to, essentially, listen to his voice. Why would he not have read his own audio book? His voice is something his fans would have already been familiar with. It would have brought them memories and vibes from all their favorite songs of his, and added to the experience. This was a missed opportunity, in my opinion.

It is unlikely that you will be able to read and record your own audio book(s) while in prison (the exception being if you have a cell phone or some other recording device), but if you have someone out there to do it for you, I don't think you need to have it done by a pro. Especially if you're tight on funds. Maybe you have a brother, wife, friend, etc. who can do it for you. This can easily be done with a phone or a laptop and one of the many free apps available online. Shit, start with what you have, then upgrade later if you want. My friend, Street Lit author Jasmine Johnston, who wrote the *Hustlerz* series, asked me if she should read her own audio book, as her friend told her to do so would be "ghetto." But who knows her characters better than her? Who knows the way they're supposed to talk, better than she does? Who would put more passion into it than her? I told her I absolutely think she needed to do it.

There's another option – acx.com. Acx is a website where freelancers post samples of their reads so you can hear their voices and they have almost any style you may be looking for. You can contact someone you like and request that they take on your project. You can work two different deals with them. One is to pay them outright, and the other, if they agree, is to split the royalties of the audio book(s) 50-50. This is good if you're on a tight budget, if you can get them to agree to do it. It would help if you had some type of sales record for your book, or past books. Another thing this site allows you to do is make a profile page for your project, and the readers can contact you if they are interested in taking it on.

URBAN BOOKS

A lot of prisoners have the desire to write urban books. And given that most prisoners have experience with the street life, it's understandable. After all, several prisoners turned-street-lit-authors have gone on to have great careers: Wahida Clark, Vickie Stringer, and Leo Sullivan to name a few (more on this later).

But, and I emphasize the *but*, just because you may have the desire, and possibly an idea for a story, doesn't mean you can do it without putting in the necessary work. You must learn how to write! I say this because too many prisoners want immediate results and think they can skip this very important part of the process. You'd be amazed at some of the stuff people send me that they think will work. You cannot skip the very important element of the writing game, called, well, writing! Though you may not need to be Shakespeare, you must learn to write properly. You cannot skip this part. Trying to do so would be like trying to play basketball without learning how to dribble. It doesn't matter that it's Street Lit, learning how to write – properly! – is a mando ingredient for any kind of storytelling.

In addition to knowing how to write, you need to learn what works within the Street Lit genre. You learn by studying The Game. You study The Game first by reading the books that have been successful, and figuring out why they were successful. When I decided I was going to be a factor in the Street Lit game, I read every urban book I could get my hands on, trying to figure out the science and mathematics of them – how many pages they were, how many words per page, what size the books were dimensions-wise, what the quality of the writing was, what the common elements of each are, etc. Then, when I had the means, I asked my people to google the "top 10 urban books" to see what came up. They sent me a list. I then began to order each and every book on that list. This is the type of dedication it takes to win, in any genre.

Top 10 Street Lit Books of All Time

1. *The Coldest Winter Ever*, Sister Souljah
2. *B-More Careful*, Shannon Holmes (started writing in prison)
3. *True to the Game*, Teri Woods

4. *A Hustler's Wife*, Nikki Turner
5. *Dutch*, Kwame Teague (written in prison)
6. *Let That Be The Reason*, Vickie Stringer (written in prison)
7. *Gangsta*, K'wan (started writing in prison)
8. *Dopefiend*, Donald Goins (started writing in prison)
9. *Thugs and the Women Who Love Them*, Wahida Clark (written in prison)
10. *Block Party*, Al-Saadiq Banks

Now, if you've read my book with Joshua Kruger, *The Millionaire Prisoner*, Josh says to not spend your time reading urban books. I want to elaborate on this a bit. What he means is, don't spend your time reading urban books just to kill time, or so that you can fantasize about getting out of prison and living a thug's life. Use your time to your advantage – to learn and to build. However, if you want to write urban books, you better read at least the urban books that have been successful. This is how you learn and build as an aspiring urban book writer. Still to this day, I read a lot of urban books (reading *Ethic 2* by Ashley Antoinette right now). But, do I sit and read them for entertainment, to kill time? Fuck no. I'm in the business of writing and publishing books, including urban books, but I don't sit and read any book for entertainment. Every book I read, though I might be entertained while doing so, I read for some kind of learning purpose. For example, even though I write nonfiction, how-to, and Street Lit, when *The Girl With the Dragon Tattoo* came out, it made so much noise, I read that, too. (Good book, by the way.) I wanted to find out what it was that made it so great. I tried to do the same with *Fifty Shades of Gray*, because it made so much noise. However, I couldn't get past the first 8 pages. As much as I wanted to learn what all the hype was about, to me, the book was boring, and I couldn't do it.

Now, fortunately for you, if you are an upcoming, or even experienced Street Lit writer, there's a book to teach you The Game – *How To Write Urban Books For Money & Fame*, a book I did with King Guru, a partner of mine who writes phenomenal urban books, and who I've made a great deal of money with.

Here's an excerpt:

INTRODUCTION

What is an Urban Novel?

An urban novel is a fictional story based on the lives of individuals living throughout the inner cities of America. Some stories are based on real life events, yet the genre is centered on fiction.

And what is fiction?

Fiction is a made-up story. Therefore, an urban novel is a made-up story about people living in the ghetto.

You're up against a unique challenge whenever writing urban novels because you only have words to work with. There're no pictures, sound boards, or movie producers with computer generated special effects. Everything is done with letters we put together to create words which we then put together to create sentences. When done correctly these words will enter the imagination of the reader transforming them into an alternative reality.

Most people enjoy reading urban novels because they crave entertainment. For others it's a way for them to get away from their everyday lives. A well written story will satisfy both of those needs extremely well. Every urban novel ultimately requires its words to intermingle with the reader's mind in order to take them into a different place and time; giving them a chance to experience life through a sort of looking glass.

If you have the skills to make this happen you will have a bright future in the literary world.

The first step in writing an urban novel is having the desire to do so. Since you've opened this book it's obvious that you have the hunger to learn. That's a good sign; it's a beginning.

I started writing books while I was in prison. Needless to say, I had a lot of time on my hands. However, what I failed to realize in the beginning was that time isn't the only precursor to writing a good story. It takes a certain set of skills to write a good, entertaining urban novel. In my mind, since I knew how to read and write – the rest would fall into place. But what I soon found out was that writing a book was nowhere near as easy as it sounds.

During the first stage of my development, I was so hyped about writing a book I would tell everyone and anyone who would listen about my plans and ideas. That's when I started to see that I wasn't the only person in my cipher who had ideas for a book. Almost everyone you talk to has an idea for a manuscript; and most of them think they can do it whenever they feel like it.

Well, I'm here to tell you that not anyone can sit down and hash out a good urban novel without the proper training in craft. Writing is a craft that takes practice and skill. That's why I decided to write this book in the first place, so I can pass on the skills that it takes to write a bestselling urban novel. I can guarantee that once you finish reading this book you will have a newfound respect for story writing. You will even start looking at other people's work in a different light because you will finally have the knowledge of how the story you are reading was really created. In this book I am giving you tricks of the trade – Jewels of the Game, if you will – that in the past you may have never recognized and had taken for granted. Therefore, it is inevitable that this book is going to make you into a better writer than you are right now.

Basing your story on real life doesn't always work

It's not a secret that the best urban novel authors have some sort of tie to the streets. We've really carried pistols, sold dope and were active in the streets at one point or another. Nevertheless, just because you've actually lived an exciting, glamorous life doesn't mean it will come out as a thrilling story when you go to put it down on paper. Right off the top of my head I can give you five specific reasons as to why writing about real life can quickly become a problem:

1. Most people allow the real situation to drive the plot of the story. This stops them from exploring other alternatives that might make the story more interesting.

2. Whenever someone personally knows the characters, they are writing about they tend to neglect developing them on paper. This happens because they naturally assume the reader knows what they know.

3. Over-explanation also becomes a problem. You tend to try and explain things too much, not allowing your reader to come to their own conclusion.

4. You limit your horizon because you already know how the story begins and ends.

5. Another one of the main problems that arise when writing a story based on real life events is that the writer fails to add detail that creates emotion. This happens because they are writing from their own experience instead of from the character's experience.

Don't get me wrong, the best urban novel writers often borrow from real life events. I do it in almost all of my books. The trick is to mix real life characters and stories with just the right amount of fiction. I've found that the best way to do this is by starting a scene with the real-life situation then letting it find its own way into fiction.

You must never allow your mind to be closed off to different possibilities. Maybe you really do have a good true story, most of us do. If this is the case then try writing it from a different character's point of view. Explore the use of third person narrative and watch yourself turn into another person. Never allow yourself to be tied down by real life; leave your options open. Remember: in fiction, reality is only a small piece.

Turning facts into feelings

I can't emphasize enough that one of the most important rules about writing urban novels is to show instead of tell. If your goal is to write a realistic, believable story you need to show your character's feelings and thoughts. Give your reader a sense of how your character sees the world. In order for you to accomplish this goal you must first realize that, with creative writing, most of your formal teaching is wrong.

In school we learn to tell the teacher the facts we have learned from our lesson; to give answers from a purely logical point of view, keeping our feelings out of it. This is also how real life works in or day to day business dealings. But that's not the case when writing an urban novel.

When you embark on the journey of writing an urban novel the rules are completely different. You're not expected to state the facts like you do in a court of law. You gotta be aware of all your character's emotions and viewpoints regarding each individual situation he's presented with. Then you have to find the right words to paint the picture with so that your reader can become part of the whole experience. Think of it like this: instead of telling your readers how to feel, lead them in a way that will allow them to come to their own conclusions.

In life we sometimes have family or friends that try to protect us by giving us advice regarding real life experiences that we might be going through. Most of the time the advice is really good, but how many times do we actually listen? Sometimes you just have to learn life's lessons on your own. Well, urban novels are like that. You can definitely get your point across but you have to let the reader get to it on their own. The best way to accomplish this goal is by involving them in your story and letting them experience the world you have created for them. If you do it right, nine times outta ten, they'll most likely come to the conclusion you intended them to from the beginning.

Your story has to be realistic

In order to make your urban novel as realistic as possible you must create scenes that people can relate to. This can easily be done by appealing to all of their senses through words. You can do this by showing them instead of telling them. Here are four tips on how to show your reader what you want them to see, hear and feel:

1. Select a single character's point of view.
2. Know the thought process of that character at all times.
3. Present those thoughts and feelings as vividly as possible.
4. Give the reader these emotions at the right moment in time.

As long as you stay in the viewpoint of your main character, you will easily be able to show instead of tell. If you don't stay in viewpoint you won't be able to "tell" the story because when real people experience life they don't "tell" about it, it just happens. This also helps to keep a certain level of thrill in your story because it gives the reader the sense that anything can happen at any time. And that's want you want; your ultimate goal is to have your reader experience the story as the characters do.

CHAPTER ONE

Blueprint

A blueprint is a detailed plan. The first mistake most novice writers make is they start their book without first creating a blueprint. Even I made this mistake during the outset of a few of my projects and it always creates undue problems that could've been thwarted if I would've just taken the time to write out a plan. With experience I've created a full-proof plan and I've split it into three sections, and they go in depth so pay attention to what you read in the next several pages because I'm really giving you some deep insight into the writing game.

PART 1: BACK TO BASICS

Title

You're gonna need a working title. A "working title" is the name you'll use to refer to your manuscript while you are writing it. This doesn't have to be the actual name that you go to the printing press with but it'll give you something to call it while you're working on it.

P.O.V.

The next step is figuring out what point of view you're gonna tell your story from. The best p.o.v. is a character who is closest to the action. The most important thing about p.o.v. is that you have to stay in it the whole time you write your story.

Blurb

Your blurb is a short sentence that summarizes the entire story. It should include the conflicts, goals and motivations of the star of your story. I'll cover this more in depth in the next chapter. After you write your blurb, post it up on the wall in front of your working area.

Just fill in the blanks: (name of protagonist) wants (goal to be achieved) because (motivation for acting), but he faces (conflict standing in the way).

Story Sparks

Now we need to come up with the beginning spark of your urban novel.

"A spark" is a major conflict. Most urban novels start with a major conflict and go from there.

This first spark has to be a work of genius. This is what's gonna start the drama that will keep your urban novel going into the end. There will be other sparks but this first one has to be federal!

The average length of an urban novel is around 85,000 words. In a story of this length there should be at least three sparks. The first spark sets up the conflict. The middle spark complicates the situation and the last spark resolves the conflict and situation.

PART 2: WORKING DETAILS

The only way to have a cohesive story is to figure out all the working details, so let's cover 'em.

Main Characters

If you haven't come up with your main characters yet, this is the moment you get that done. Since you've gotten this far in preparing your urban novel, then you probably already know who the main players are going to be. This is when you should make a file for the characters that will include a checklist of information about them. Your characters will grow throughout the process of your writing, but these files will include a checklist of information on them including the basic information you'll need to start your book.

First, you need to introduce your character and that is basically listing your character's name and role in the story. Each of your main characters should bring something to the plot and this first introduction should explain that.

Physical Description

This description not only describes how your character looks but it also includes the impression he or she gives people when they first meet him. Does he look shady, trustworthy, scary or timid? There will be times in your urban novel when someone else is going to meet your protagonist and this description is what they'll see.

Occupation Description

A lot of times, someone's job or hobby shapes their personality. Sometimes the plot of the story will revolve around their occupation; especially if it's drug dealing, gangbangin, prostitution or law enforcement.

Enhancements and Contrast

If you want to create a character who your readers will always remember, he's gonna need enhancements and contrasts. An enhancement is a character trait that makes your guy above average. You really don't want a protagonist who is average or your story will be boring. This doesn't have to be something obvious like the ability to fly, but is should set him apart from other people, and it doesn't have to come out early, either. He can utilize this skill when his back is against a wall.

The contrast is a personality flaw. It's never good to have characters who are 100% good or 100% bad. If you create a bad guy with some compassion it will add depth to his personality. It's the same science with the good guy; he definitely shouldn't be all the way good because in real life no one is perfect.

People who read urban novels prefer a flawed star. It makes him realistic and they can relate to that. A strong contrast can be a secondary contrast which comes in the form of another character. If your protagonist is a level-headed individual who enters the drug world to make a certain amount of money, then gets out the game; a good contrast would be if he had a best friend who is a cold-blooded killer who lives for the fast life.

Symbolic Element

A symbolic element is something that can be added to your story repeatedly that defines your main character or his arch-enemy in a subtle way. Every time it's mentioned it gains more meaning. This can be an object, event or emotion. It can also be a scar, a piece of jewelry or another character.

This symbol can be anything, but I'll give an example: Your character can be a vigilante who is adamant about ridding his neighborhood of drug dealers. His symbolic element can be a picture in his living room of his late mother who died of an overdose. Whenever he gets frustrated, all he has to do is look at the picture of his mother and he gets reinvigorated to do what he has set out to do.

The important thing that you need to keep in mind when working with and/or creating a symbolic element is that it has to be subtle. You don't want to force it on your readers. And it's never too late to come up with this aspect of your story. You can always add it during the revision process.

Setting

The setting of your story is important because it enhances the characters, the conflict and the suspense. It also provides a landscape for your story to unfold. If the setting for your story doesn't match the plot you'll have a harder time trying to create the right mood for your urban novel.

In order to paint a vivid picture to your readers you need to describe a setting to your story. It has to match though. Can you imagine an urban novel taking place on a space ship? It wouldn't match because it's not the right genre for that setting.

You want to set your story in a place that you can persuade your readers to believe really exists. Even if it's a fictional location it should be realistic and match your storyline. Another thing you should keep in mind is that you only need to describe the parts that involve the plot of your urban novel. There's no point in describing things that don't move the story along.

PART 3: DRAMA

If you want a realistic, interesting plot, you're gonna need some conflict. Without conflict there's no story. I'm gonna go ahead and lace you on the aspect of conflicts so pay attention. You'll need the following items for all of your sparks, and you should also include these situations for all of your major characters.

Internal Conflict

In urban novels, character conflicts are what keep the characters from accomplishing their goals. He can't solve his problem until he faces his conflicts. Your audience must also be able to identify with these conflicts in order for them to be involved with the story.

Internal conflicts are emotional problems that conflict with the character's conscious. This is what keeps your character stubborn and from seeing the obvious.

If you don't recognize this conflict early your story won't be as organized as it should be. The drama will bounce around and confuse your reader because your urban novel will be flooded with unfocused ideas. Conflicts that aren't identified clearly will bore your reader and that's what you don't want.

$$$$$

If you're serious about writing urban books, *How To Write Urban Books For Money & Fame* is a must read. (In fact, no matter your genre, you would be wise to read the book, because it teaches in-depth storytelling fundamentals any storyteller needs to know.) *How To Write Urban Books For Money & Fame* will teach you the proven methods we, and the other successful Street Lit authors, such as the ones listed below, have used.

8 Urban fiction authors who overcame prison and forged lucrative careers

[By Evette Brown]

These former incarcerated authors turned their sentences into real-life experiences for millions of readers...

Dominating the *Essence* and *New York Times* bestsellers lists, respectively, street literature, officially recognized as urban fiction, has evolved into a permanent part of American literature. Telling the often-tragic stories of African-American men trapped in the gritty realities of urban culture and the women who love them and become victims of vicious cycles, these novels have captivated many in the black community and beyond.

With the success of street literature, many African-American authors have been transformed from street-savvy hustlers to literary inspirations and millionaires. Most of these prominent urban authors are using their life experiences to fuel their passion and words. Here, we feature eight urban authors who were once or are still incarcerated. They all have criminal histories, but now their experiences are used to prevent others from following down such a despairing path.

Wahida Clark

With the release of her 2005 acclaimed debut novel, *Thugs and the Women who Love Them*, the world was introduced to an emerging talent in urban fiction, Wahida Clark. The "Queen on Thug Love Fiction" immediately built a dedicated foundation of readers that were mesmerized with her depictions of a lifestyle that involved hustling, murder, and millions. Writing about the realities of the "ghetto," where loyalty is more valuable than life, Clark used her words to create a literary empire.

Though the New Jersey native is one of the most popular authors writing street literature, for most of her Essence Bestselling career, she was once incarcerated in a women's federal camp in Lexington, Kentucky. After reading a small portion of Shannon Holmes' *B-More Careful* in *XXL* magazine, Clark made the conscious decision to dedicate the remainder of her nine-year-sentence to creating the "Thug" series, thus sharing her experiences in life with the world. Since her release, Wahida Clark had used her position in literature to expose other urban authors to her audience. She is now the head of W. Clark Publishing and is now regarded as a savvy business woman and wise entrepreneur.

Kwame Teague

When *True to the Game* author, Teri Woods, discovered Kwame Teague in a North Carolina prison, a dynasty was created. Serving two life sentences for the shooting deaths of two men (he plead not guilty), Teague refused to spend his time idly, waiting for a possible release date in the future. Instead, he has penned the series, *Dutch*, a wildly successful urban fiction masterpiece that has captured the attention of many readers. Though Kwame's name is not included on the covers of any of the *Dutch* novels for legal reasons, he is the mastermind behind the words. The *Dutch* series has been banned in all state prisons for inciting violence among inmates, but that has not stopped Teague from continuing to write about these fictional characters living real-life situations.

K 'wan

K'wan is one of the most accomplished authors in urban fiction, but in 2002, he was merely a novice in the writing world, as he was the first author in line to be published by the relatively small and widely unknown company, Triple Crown Publications. Catching the writing bug while serving a short stint in jail, K'wan was literally dared to write the beginnings of the classic, *Gangsta*. It became the foundation from which Triple Crown Publications was built and evolved into an Essence bestseller and a favorite of many devoted urban fiction readers. Now, with over 10 bestsellers under his belt, a multi-book deal with St. Martin's Press, and thousands of his adoring fans that read whatever he chooses to write, K'wan is regarded as one of the leaders in the genre.

Kiki Swinson

Author of the extremely popular and successful *Wifey* series, Kiki Swinson is a living testament to the resilience of the human spirit. The Portsmouth, Virginia, writer discovered her passion for penning real-life experiences in novel form when she completed her first book, *Mad Shambles*, while serving five-years in federal prison for allegedly being the "*wifey*" of a very successful drug dealer. After being released, Swinson self-published *Mad Shambles* before pitching *Wifey* to publishing houses. Eventually, the book was picked up by Melodrama Publishing and after a sequel, Swinson delivered with *I'm Still Wifey*, *Life After Wifey*, and *Still Wifey Material* along with other popular novels. Fifteen years after being released from prison, Kiki Swinson's life as a narcotics kingpen's wifey had generated a hefty profit.

Shannon Holmes

Bronx, New York native, Shannon Holmes, was armed with nothing more than a GED and a prison record when he decided that writing about his street experiences rather than living them was his life's mission. While serving five years in prison for various drug convictions, Holmes wrote his first novel and negotiated a deal with Triple Crown Publications. His timely classic, *B-More Careful*, was the launching pad for his successful career as an author. Going on to sell half-a-million copies, *B-More Careful* transformed Holmes into a platinum commodity in publishing. After negotiating a two-book, six-figure deal with Simon and Schuster, Holmes continues to be a giant in urban fiction. His softmore novel, *Bad Girlz* sold 50,000 copies in the first week alone and he accomplished a feat that no other urban fiction author had been able to do in the past. His critically acclaimed book, *Never Go Home Again* was the first in the genre to be printed in hardcover. Now crowned as the "King of Hip-Hop Literature," Holmes has negotiated a larger deal with St. Martin's Press and released several other popular street novels.

Jihad

Seven years in federal prison served Jihad well. It awakened his conscious to the issues plaguing the African-American community and inspired him to begin writing and using his experiences to motive others to achieve the impossible. After signing a deal with Envisions Publishing, Jihad created the Jihad Uhuru Wake-Up Everybody Foundation and began creating thought-provoking characters for his popular novels, including *Preacherman Blues, Preacherman Blues 2*, and *Baby Girl*. As an award-winning novelist and *Essence* bestseller, Jihad is nine novels into his blossoming career and is in the process of adapting *Baby Girl* into a screenplay.

Vickie M. Stringer

All hail the Queen of Hip-Hop Literature! Vickie M. Stringer is a literary powerhouse. After founding the renowned publishing company Triple Crown Publications, Stringer was integral in changing the publishing world by creating a stable of urban authors with powerful stories to share with the world. Once considered the "Cocaine Queen" of Columbus, Ohio, Stringer served seven years in federal prison before realizing that she had a knack and passion for writing. After her release, stringer found Triple Crown Publications. After receiving 26 rejection letters from different publishing houses, Stringer self-published *Let That Be the Reason*, selling it out the trunk of her car at salons and barbershops. Now, she has inked a deal with Simon & Schuster to publish her successful novels including *Dirty Red* while she still seeks talent for her Triple Crown Publications, which is rumored to be worth millions. Vickie M. Stringer turned her life into a living testament to the power of determination, strong will, and the resilience of the human spirit.

Treasure Hernandez

There isn't much known about one of Kensington Publishing Corporation's premiere authors, Treasure Hernandez, but her novels are a grim slice of urban reality. As the creator of the *Flint* and *Baltimore Chronicles* series, Hernandez is a force to be reckoned with in the urban fiction genre. After her words were discord by fellow author, Carl Weber, Hernandez has been in a tunnel headed towards success. The most powerful aspect of Treasure Hernandez' journey is that she is currently incarcerated, but has released a full seven-book series, three books of a new series, and two other independent novels. Once she is released, Treasure will be able to capitalize on the career that she has established behind prison walls.

$$$$$

Think you have what it takes to be the next Street Lit star? If so, be sure to order *How to Write Urban Books for Money & Fame: Prisoner Edition*, by Mike Enemigo and King Guru by sending $16.95 plus $5.00 shipping and handling (or 4 NEW books of Forever stamps) to: The Cell Block; POB 1025; Rancho Cordova, CA 95741 TODAY! Inside you will learn the true story of how Mike Enemigo and King Guru have received money and fame from inside their prison cells by writing urban books; the SECRETS to writing hood classics so you, too, can be caked up and famous; proper punctuation using hood examples; and resources you can use to achieve your money motivated ambitions! If you're a prisoner who wants to write urban novels for money and fame, this must-have manual will give you all the game!

LEGAL BOOKS

Are you a legal beagle? Perhaps you had to learn something about the law for yourself that you can now teach to others? If your legal game is on point, writing and publishing legal books can be a great business for you. Legal books in *Prison Legal News* often go for $50.00 or more. As a publisher, I love the high cost of legal books. The reason I don't personally write them is because I know nothing about the law, other than maybe how to break it. The legal topic is one thing I know I know nothing about. When I try to read anything that has to do with the law, my mind wanders after two sentences. Hey, I know my strengths, and I know my weaknesses.

The reason I don't like to publish legal books by other prisoners, who may know the law, is because I can't personally go over them and know whether or not they are accurate or any good. In addition, the laws change too much, and I'm too busy writing and publishing other books to want to be revising the legal books over and over. I already have to do this with my Directory, *The BEST Resource Directory For Prisoners*, which is a lot of work, but at least the content is something I know well.

However, if you know the law, and you gotta know the law, because it's not cool to sell someone inaccurate information that can affect their freedom/case, this can be something worth getting into.

One thing you may not know, is that every government publication is public domain, meaning it's not copyrighted, and can be used by anyone, in which ever way they want. A lot of information in the law library is public domain, and you can use this freely to make a book – cites, case law, etc. There are prisoners who have made large books that consist of cites, case law, etc., and they sell for lots of money. Right now, in my current *PLN*, that I got yesterday, is an ad for a book titled *Qwik Legal Cites* – A legal reference book starting with Access to the Courts, ending with Witnesses. Organized like an encyclopedia but with actual written opinions of the judge. Covers major legal subjects; e.g. Access to the Courts, Attorneys, Consumer Protection, Due Process, Evidence Ex Post Facto, Fines and Fees, Government Misconduct, Habeas, Health Care, Immigration, Parole, Prisons, Religion, Search & Seizure, Weapons, Statue Interpretation, and many more." This book sells for $44.50. Not sure if it's by a prisoner, but a prisoner knowledgeable on the law could certainly put something like together.

In the same *PLN* is an ad for The *Colossal Book of Criminal Citations*. It consists of "5000+ Supreme, Circuit, District, and State Citations; 125+ Topics Covering Pretrial – Post Conviction; Prosecution & Defense Strategies Revealed; District Court & Innocence Project Addresses; Sample Motions; 500+ Legal Definitions." The book is 8.5 x 11, 800+ pages, and is priced at $99.95. All you gotta do is sell a thousand of these....

On the same ad is another book by the same author – *The Colossal Book of Civil Citations*. It consists of "1000+ Supreme, Circuit, District, and State Citations; 40+ Important Topics; Sample Motions; 500+ Legal Definitions." It's 8.5 x 11, 300+ pages, and priced at $49.99. The ad says the book is a "Must Have for Prisoners Filing 42 U.S.C. § 1983 Actions."

Most of the info in the 3 books above can be gotten right out of your prison's law library. Your job, if you want to do a book like this, is to collect all the proper information, organize it, and put it all in one book so it's easy for a prisoner to navigate and use, in their cell, without having to rely on access to the law library.

One of the best examples of a prisoner who writes and publishes legal books is Zachary Smith. I've watched him for a few years now, and I like his entire setup. We've never communicated, but he uses many of the strategies I teach in this book, which tells me he's sharp.

First, all I've seen from Zachary Smith, besides a few short stories and articles in *Corcoran Sun*, a now defunct newsletter Freebird Publishers used to publish, are legal books. So, he's stuck to one genre (a way to concentrate his forces), presumably one he knows, and has branded himself as a legal expert. He didn't mix up his brand of being the go-to legal guy by writing and publishing books in other, unrelated genres.

He has 5 books available (so far), all branded under his last name, "Smith's Guide"– *Smith's Guide to State Habeas Corpus Relief for State Prisoners*; *Smith's Guide to Executive Clemency for State and Federal Prisoners*; *Smith's Guide to Chapter 7 Bankruptcy for Prisoners*, etc. The covers all have a simple "manual style" design, and are all very similar, other than the title. They all even have the same price, $34.95, which helps keep things simple when advertising. And he has a clever tagline that says: "You'll always miss 100% of the shots you don't take. Get a Smith's Guide and take your best shot!" Nice.

JAILHOUSE PUBLISHING

I've also seen Zachary's books in just about every books-to-prisoners catalog, like *SureShot, Inmate Shopper*, etc., so he's got a decent distribution setup. I've seen him advertise his books in *PLN* with a quarter-page ad, with all 5 books on it, then point the reader to Amazon to purchase them. I like this because it automates his sales process. He didn't use his wife, family, or outside assistant to fulfill orders, which simplifies his process. It may seem as if he would lose sales only directing people to Amazon and not offering a direct mailing address, and maybe he did lose some, but this doesn't necessarily mean he lost in profit. If he used a middleman, say, a family member, even if he didn't have to pay them cash money, it would cost them in time and energy. It's a lot of work fulfilling orders, especially when dealing with prisoners who can be unrealistic, impatient, or trying to scam their way to a free product. If he used an outside assistant, he'd surely have to pay them for their work, which would cut into his profit. So it may have all evened out, all with less work, headache, and people, by putting all that onto Amazon's staff. Furthermore, a lot of prisoners who see book ads have their family members go to Amazon to order the books anyway, as they don't have the money on their accounts, or don't want to spend the money they do have on their accounts. I'm not personally brave enough to only direct people to Amazon instead of TCB just yet, but it's tempting, just to cut the cost in time, energy, money, and stress my people have to go through fulfilling orders, dealing with problematic inmates, etc.

Another person who dropped a series of legal books in a way I really liked was Kelly Patrick Riggs. Kelly dropped a 7-book series with Freebird Publishers, one book at a time, each only a few months apart, and each priced at $22.99. If you drop a 7-book series, all topics prisoners must have, each only a few months apart, it would take around two years to drop the series. This is similar to what Ashley Antoinette did with *Ethic*. If done right, this could make a real nice chunk of change.

Again, the books must be fire. If the first book is fire, odds are the person will buy the second, then the third, etc. Though not legal books, this is like what Ashley Antoinette did with her 5-part *Ethic* series. This is how you make money.

I see this being a good business for you if it's your thing. And if it is, I suggest you just stick with this, and brand yourself as the legal beagle to go to – the prisoner version of Johnny Cochran or Jose Baez. You do this by providing great information. Also ask your customers to write you with their success stories so you can include them in your sales material. As prisoners, most of us need some kind of legal help. That means most of us have a strong reason to buy at least one legal book during our lifetime. If you can brand yourself as the one to go to, you can make a lot of money. And if you brand yourself properly, are good, and are fortunate enough to be getting out someday, you can also set yourself up for a great career, as several other prisoners have done, such as the ones I showcase in my book *The Blueprint*.

MIXBOOKS

"Mixbook" is a term I created, after the term mixtape. A mixtape is an underground album, usually hip hop, where the artist doesn't adhere to the norm, and often rides in the grey area as far as legalities are concerned. For example, a rapper will rap over another rapper's beat, without permission of the owner. Mixtapes have become very popular, maybe even mainstream, though they were originally, and often still are only sold on the streets, in corner stores, or given away free, online. So, a mixbook is the book version of that. A mixbook isn't necessarily restrained by one topic; rather, it's more like a magazine, where it has various topics of interest to a particular market; maybe news, entertainment and resources, as well as pictures, perhaps that you collected from various sources.

I like the mixbook concept personally for several reasons. For one, I get bored writing one long story. I also have a lot of ideas, and as long as the ideas are related or geared towards one market, the mixbook allows me to create each of them and put them all into one book. I also originally wanted to publish a magazine, not books, but I didn't have the resources to publish a magazine at the time; a mixbook is like a hybrid of the two. I've had an idea for a long time for a mixbook titled "The Cell Block," which I'll eventually do. It's going to be geared towards the prisoner market, and it will consist of things the prisoners I aim for enjoy: short stories; legal info; tips on how to get girls from prison; resources; news; prisoner art; pics of hot, non-nude girls, etc. Basically, a little bit of all my books all rolled into one. This will likely transition into a magazine.

A book like this can be dropped quarterly, bi-annually, yearly, or however you want to do it, really. Once you get a decent fan base, this type of publication can act as a platform, too – a promotional platform where you can highlight any new books you may drop, or other projects. You can also sell advertising space to others who need your platform, which is another source of income that most other books don't have.

Because of the various opportunities it provides, a mixbook can actually be an entire business. With it, though you can, you don't need to publish other books; you can put all your resources into this one book, which may be your best bet anyway, as it will allow you to concentrate your forces. Because it's a mix of things, any idea you have will likely fit inside this book. This type of book is easier to brand, too. Whereas now I have over 25 titles I'm trying to get the market to learn about and remember, if you do a mixbook, you will consistently be using the same title/name, over and over. You will just change the volume number; i.e., *The Cell Block Vol. 1*, *The Cell Block Vol. 2*, *The Cell Block Vol. 3*, etc. Again, just like a magazine does it.

It's easy to get material for this kind of book. Other than your own writing, inmates who need a platform will submit requested content, so long as you build it up enough to where they feel they will get exposure from it – inmates who have books, who want to be prison journalists, legal beagles, artists, poets, etc. You can also cheat by getting information off the Internet that prisoners don't otherwise have access to. Prisoners don't tend to mind this. For example, all the non-nude pictures companies sell? They are just images collected off the Internet, but we don't care, because we have no other way to get them. Just like a mixtape often pushes grey area limits, a mixbook could, too, so long as it's geared towards prisoners, or some other "underground" culture who won't care. What it's about here is value. For example, if I give you $15-$20 for a fat, 8 x 10 book that has a ton of value, I don't care where or how you got the content. I'm just happy I got all that game/info/content for the dub.

Keep in mind, this type of book is not likely to be a *New York Times* Best Seller, especially if you "barrow" from the Internet or other sources, but if your goal is to make money from prison, and perhaps build yourself some type of platform, this could certainly be the way to do it. And this is something you can eventually turn into a magazine, maybe with all original content, once you build it up and gain the resources. (If you put one of these together, make sure I get free ad space for giving you the game.)

Another way to create a mixbook would be if, say, you write fiction, nonfiction, short stories, essays, journalistic articles, poems, etc., and you want to put them all in one book. Maybe you have some recipes and you also draw. You could include all of this in one book and try branding yourself as an "artist" of some sort. I'd consider this a mixbook, too.

MAGAZINE MONEY

Some of you may want to try your hand at writing magazine articles. If you can write well, it's certainly a good way to start, as it will not only help you build you name, but build relationships with magazine editors that can be beneficial when you do end up writing and publishing that book, especially with the promotional phase.

While you may not be able to get rich when just starting out, as you have to build a demand for yourself, here's some game from folks who are getting a nice chunk of money from writing magazine articles.

9 SECRETS OF SIX-FIGURE FREELANCERS

What are some things that six-figure freelancers do that regular folks don't? Turns out, making a six-figure living as a writer or journalist is not only about strategy, it's about mindset, lifestyle, and habit. After two dozen six-figure freelancers were interviewed, here are the commonalities found.

Secret # 1: They stretch themselves constantly.

Ask a six-figure freelancer if they know about content marketing and most of them will list off at least half dozen clients they have that do exactly that. Crowdsourcing? They've tried it. E-books? Most of them have self-published at least one. Not that the e-books made them any money, mind you, and not even one six-figure freelancer interviewed said that the e-book added any substantial weight to their income, but they'd tried it. They'd had the willingness to put in the time and effort into something new, even if it didn't eventually add multiple zeroes to their income.

In fact, trying new things and creating additional income streams was a common goal amongst six-figure freelancers. While most of them identified as writers and journalists, they also brought in money (both large and small paychecks) from websites, traditional book deals, books they'd self-published, speaking engagements, teaching, and coaching.

None of them were dependent on one income stream to generate all their income, which also ensured that when one part of their business was generating less cash, they were easily able to make up that deficit through other areas.

Most have pitched and been rejected (or met with silence) by *The New Yorker*.

Secret #2: They take risks.

Many six-figure freelancers advise that writers create a safety net – three to six months of living expenses in the bank – before they quit their jobs to go full-time. Yet, did they do the same when they were starting out? Mostly, no, and ironically, many of them attribute their success to that very fact. Quitting their jobs and taking up freelancing full-time when they had no other source of income forced them to hustle like no one's business. They had no safety net, no plan B, and therefore, many of them felt that they had no choice but to earn money, and earn good money at this chosen career path. By taking away the choice, they forced themselves to come up with creative solutions to problems, write when they didn't particularly feel like it, and contact clients for work even when it felt uncomfortable. They worked every single day and performed because not doing so was never an option.

Many of them attribute their current work ethic to these early days and years of training themselves to write even when they weren't in the mood.

Secret 3: They work long hours.

Most six-figure freelancers work very long and hard hours. While some manage to hit the magic number despite part-time hours (less than 20 hours a week), most six-figure freelancers work somewhere between 40 and 60 hours, and some even log in as many as 80.

The good news, however, is that many of these six-figure freelancers felt that they were working these long hours not because of economic necessity, but because they really enjoyed their work and liked putting time into helping their business grow. Most felt they could easily scale back if they wanted to without a massive drop in revenue.

Secret #4: They're in stable relationships.

Speaking of happiness, six-figure freelancers are typically in stable, happy relationships – many of them happily married for many years – or are at peace with whatever relationship situation they find themselves in. For most, a lack of drama on the home front was an important factor in ensuring that they could work through the challenges in their freelancing careers. Further, a supportive spouse or partner was, for many, essential in getting them through the lean times and the encouragement they received at home enabled them to go out confidently and perform at work.

Secret #5: They set goals.

While many six-figure freelancers sailed over the threshold without even realizing it, most actually had that number in their minds for a few years before they hit it. They worked towards the goal, keeping track of their earnings, their most profitable clients, and their hourly rate. They almost always tracked their time, had Excel worksheets filled with data about hours worked, rates per assignment, and most importantly, weekly and monthly income goals that allowed them to stay on track with the big yearly number.

For most freelancers who eventually hit the six-figure mark, it didn't happen the first year they decided to hit this number, not even for the next three. But within five years, most of the freelancers interviewed had achieved their goal. They stayed committed to it, even when it felt difficult and unachievable, and eventually found that the numbers kept growing, until they were able to hit the $100,000 mark.

Secret #6: They say no. A lot.

A side effect of setting goals and knowing what they need to bring in each month, week, and day means that six-figure freelancers often have very specific limits of what they won't accept in terms of compensation. Many have a minimum hourly rate that they mentally calculate for every assignment they're offered (typically $100 an hour) and several had a $500 baseline; that is, they wouldn't accept any project that fell below that number. Three $200 projects ended up being a lot more work, they found, than one $600 project because of the starting and stopping and mental energy that went into the three projects.

Further, not one six-figure freelancer felt any hesitation in turning down projects or assignments that they felt didn't move them towards their financial (or other) goals. They considered it a sign of their professionalism to be able to turn down work that didn't meet their needs than to take on everything that came their way. Almost all had turned down work in the last six months. When first starting, however, you should take what you can get until you can do better.

Secret #7: They join and remain a part of professional networks.

Six-figure freelancers believe in mentorship, in professional networking, in creating supportive communities surrounding their work, and partnering with like-minded people in order to work towards common goals. Most six-figure freelancers are a part of two or more networking organizations, groups or online forums, and frequently join Facebook and Linkedin groups they feel will help them connect with other writers in their industries.

They're committed to learning, and a huge chunk of that comes from these professional organizations and associations. A large number of six-figure freelancers had attended at least one conference in the last two years and several made it a point each year to set aside money for professional training, coaching, conference travel, and online courses. Most had at least two or three freelancers in their networks that they would consider close personal friends that they could rely on for support and advice. Of course, some of this you won't be able to do from prison.

Secret #8: They're optimistic about the future.

It could be argued that any writing professional at that level of income would, of course, be optimistic about the future of writing, their careers, and their earning potential, but in most cases, the optimism came first and the money arrived later, most likely a consequence of that optimism and faith. Writers who believed – and continued to believe, in the face of adversity and periods of low income – that there was enough work out there for them, were more likely to actually hit that number.

It's pretty simple, really. The six-figure freelancers who believed that there was work out there that could pay well and keep them happy, were so much more likely to turn down work that didn't pay well, to negotiate harder, and to come up with creative ways to find it. They also were much more likely to market themselves regularly because they believed that this marketing would indeed, lead to rewards. Writers who didn't believe that their six-figure share is there for the taking are often operating from a deficit mentality; that is, they think if they don't accept the low-paying work, they may not get any work at all. They're all much more likely to give up on marketing when it doesn't yield results quickly.

Secret #9: They build relationships.

Almost all six-figure freelancers had a core group of regular clients that were responsible for a large chunk of their income. Most of them said they had anchor clients, people who came to them repeatedly for work, giving them a guaranteed number each week or month that ensured a steady income and freed up hours for marketing that could be utilized elsewhere. Six-figure freelancers make it a point to keep in touch with former contacts and clients and to continue nurturing those professional relationships in big and little ways, such as calling every now and again, or sending holiday cards at the end of the year to each client. These small efforts often led to them being top of mind for clients and got them repeat work.

HOW TO MAXIMIZE YOUR PROFITS WRITING MAGAZINE ARTICLES

When writing articles for magazines, the old cliché, "Time is money," is oh-so-true.

Magazines usually base pay on word count. The editor couldn't care less if it takes you four hours or four days to get it done, as long as you give him the quality and content desired. That means it's up to you to make the most efficient use of time possible. The faster you get the work done, the more you make per hour and the more time you have to do other freelancing and make even more money.

If you are a professional writer, you want to make lots of money in a profession not usually known for that. You have to be organized to accomplish your goal. You need to get organized to maximize your output and minimize your effort. Start by developing a timeline.

Put together your action plan. How much are you getting paid for this article? How much do you want to make per hour? Divide the second figure into the first to decide how long you'll devote to this project. Say you're getting $750 for a one thousand-word story. You want to earn $125 an hour, so that means you should devote six hours to this project. (Note: As an inmate author, you should not expect to make this much, at least for a very long time. It takes time to build up to this level.)

Next, think about how much time you'll need to write the story. If you've always been a fast writer, assume you can turn out one thousand words in about an hour, then maybe spend another hour or two rereading and editing, double-checking facts, and putting the first draft into final form. So, in this example, that would leave you about four hours for research. etc.

By taking this information approach, you'll find that you can increase the money you earn writing. For example, Robert Bly started freelancing full time in 1982, and except for the first year and the next, he has earned more $100,000 a year as a freelance writer for over twenty consecutive years. In 2001 he grossed $500,000, as he did the year before that. He continues to prosper because he has figured out how to think like a businessman as well as a writer.

This illustrates that making a six-figure income is a realistic goal for even an average freelance writer. Bly's never written a best-seller, nor has he sold a script to the movies or television, but he knows how to make the most possible money out of his work. Follow these suggestions to help you achieve your moneymaking goals.

1. Get serious about money

If money is not your concern, you can write whatever you want, whenever you want, as much or as little as you want, without regards the fee you will be paid, how long it will take you to write the piece or the likelihood you will sell the piece. But if you want to make $100,000 (preferably a year!) as a freelance writer, you need to avoid the poverty mentality that holds so many writers back from earning a high income.

A doorman in New York City earns around $30,000 annually. If an unskilled laborer can make $30,000 for opening a door, surely you can earn $50,000 to $100,000 for your skills.

2. Set daily revenue goals

To make $ 100,000 a year, you need to earn $2000 a week for fifty weeks. For a five-day workweek. that comes to $400 a day. Will people pay you $400 a day for writing-related work? Do you have to make $400 each and every day? No. Some days you'll be writing queries or doing self-promotion and earn nothing. Other days you'll get in to a writing groove, finish a $1,000 article in six hours, and still have time to write more queries. You're safe as long as your average revenue is $400 a day, or $2,000 a week, or about $9000 a month. Again, this is not how you will start.

3. Value your time

If you earn $100,000 a year and work forty hours a week, your time is worth at least $50 an hour. You should base decisions about how you spend your time on that figure. If you spend an extra half-hour to go out of your way to save $10 in office supplies, it costs you $25 in lost productivity, and you are $15 in the red. The only thing you get paid to do is write, research, and think for your clients and publishers. All other activities are nonpaying and therefore should be farmed out to other people who can do them better and more cheaply than you can. If your time is worth at least $100 an hour, then virtually any service you can buy for under $100 an hour – including lawn services, handymen, and tax preparation – you should outsource (the 80/20 principle!). You don't need a full-time secretary to outsource routine office work and administrative tasks. Plenty of bright high school and college students (or inmates) are eager to work with writers for the glory, glamour – and a relatively modest fee.

Of the two resources, time and money, time is the more valuable. You can always make more money. But time is a nonrenewable resource. Once it's gone, you can't get it back.

4. Be more productive

Develop habits that help you get more done in less time. The easiest is simply to get up and start work an hour earlier than you do now. That first hour will be your most productive, because you can work without interruptions before the business day starts.

5. Nix writer's block

Profitable writers write consistently, every day, whether the mood strikes them or not. The best way to maintain a steady output and avoid writer's block is to have many projects on different subjects and in different formats.

Try this fail-proof method. If you're writing a magazine ad and get stuck on the headline, put it aside and switch to a different writing assignment you are working on for another publication. If you need more info to proceed with the second assignment, put that aside and work on yet another.

6. Get paid more

You may read articles and letters in writer's magazines that go something like this: "I was writing for a long time for a magazine that paid ten cents a word. Finally, I told the editor that could not work for less than fifteen cents a word. At first, he said no, but I stuck to my guns and, by gosh, he paid it. See, you could get paid more for your writing!"

The practice of going to low-paying markets and trying to convert them into high-paying markets is unproductive. Even if you get an extra five cents a word – which in this example represents a 50 percent pay hike – you're talking about only $50 more for a one-thousand-word article.

If you really want to start making big money from your writing, don't haggle over nickels and dimes. Don't try to get a penny-a-word market to pay two cents a word, then feel pleased that you doubled your fee. Instead, target high-paying markets and assignments, such as large-circulation consumer magazines.

Moving to higher-paying assignments accelerates your climb to the $100,000 a year mark. It's much easier to meet your goal of $400 a day when you get $2,000 per project instead of $200.

When considering the profitability of assignments, calculate your earnings per hour rather than per project or per word. If it takes you ten eight-hour days to do a $2,000 feature article for a magazine, you make $25 an hour. If another magazine hires you to write simple articles for their publication for $500 each, and you can do two per day, you make $125 an hour. Again, 80/20 principle!

7. Create a demand

To earn six figures as a freelance writer, you have to be pretty busy most, if not all of the time. Writers who suffer prolonged periods without work will have a difficult time meeting their revenue goals. To ensure a full writing schedule, you have to create a demand for what you are selling. And one way to make sure you are always in demand is to specialize.

You can specialize in a subject: money, sex, crime, power and fame. Or you can specialize in a format or medium: how-to articles, women's articles, or writing for online venues.

Must you specialize? No. But as a rule, specialists earn more than generalists, are more in demand, and have an easier time finding work than generalizing.

A few more words about specializing:
- Being a specialist and a generalist are not mutually exclusive. You can develop a specialty – even several specialties – and still take on general assignments.
- The narrower your specialty, the greater your value to clients and editors who need someone to write on those subjects. An example of a narrow focus is mutual funds, a subtopic within the broader area of investing and personal finance.
- The less popular your specialty is with other writers, the greater your competitive edge. If you are only one of a handful of known experts on your topic, the demand for your writing services will exceed your supply, and you can pick and choose your assignments.

8. Get repeat business

The most profitable assignments in freelance writing are repeat assignments from current clients. Why? Because you are familiar with the client and his organization, what you need to learn about him diminishes with each new assignment. You can charge the same price per job, or maybe even more if he likes you. And you can do the jobs much faster because of the knowledge you have accumulated.

How do you get lucrative repeat assignments?
- Give every writing job your best effort. The more satisfied the client, the more likely he is to give you another job.
- Provide excellent customer service. Don't be a prima donna. Clients avoid working with writers perceived as difficult or demanding.
- Ask the editor for another project. Often you won't get the work unless you ask.

Making significant amounts of money as a writer is very possible, but it won't just happen. You must work hard to create opportunities and improve your efficiency as a writer. Believing you can do it is essential. Don't let the stereotypical notion of the struggling writer limit you. You can break that conception and make a healthy living as a dedicated freelance writer.

HOW TO SELL YOUR OWN SUBSCRIPTION NEWSLETTER FOR HUGE PROFITS!

If you have special knowledge in a particular field about which others would enjoy reading, you could easily begin your own subscription newsletter. With a little time and effort, you could develop it into a widely distributed publication – and make lots of money in the process!

Newsletter publishing appeals to many different people because of its relative simplicity and minimal initial investment. Yet, it can be highly profitable. According to one report, newsletters produce an estimated two billion dollars in revenue annually! Although usually composed of just a few pages, newsletter subscriptions can run upwards of $100 annually. You can see how easy it is to make a handsome profit!

If you publish an eight-page newsletter with an $80 subscription price and you sell only 1,000 subscriptions, you will take in $80,000. Even if your cost is 50%, you will still realize a profit of $40,000. And even if you have to write all the articles yourself, it would still be a part-time job at best. Yes, newsletter publishing can be very profitable!

To choose a topic about which to develop a newsletter, take a look at yourself and your interests. What areas appeal to you? Do you have a particular hobby? What types of books do you like to read? What do you do in your spare time? Do you have a particular skill? Most likely you will discover that you can turn your interest or hobby into a profitable newsletter. Turn your interests into income!

What type of information will you include in your publication? Your newsletter may summarize information taken from other sources, such as magazines or books. You cannot copy other people's articles word for word, but you can rewrite the information and use it in your own articles. If this is your aim, stress to the subscribers that you will save them time by sifting out the important news from all the other "fluff" they generally have to plow through in order to find out what they need to know. You can gather stories for your newsletter from many sources. You can summarize articles from professional journals or from the national wire services. But, be careful not to violate the copyright laws when doing so.

One of the best sources for news – in almost any field – is the so-called information Superhighway, known as the Internet. With outside help, you can have someone "subscribe" to E-mail groups whose members daily write back and forth to one another discussing developments in their fields of interest. They can print and send this to you. This data can be summarized and expanded into long and short articles for your newsletter. Many of these letters can be printed directly into your newsletter with no editing needed. Although the data is technically public domain, you could ask the author's permission to publish it by sending him or her an E-mail message. Best of all, the information often comes from the world's leading experts in the field, making your newsletter a top-quality publication!

If your newsletter is widely read, you may be sent query letters by potential writers suggesting future stories they would like to write. While it may at first glance appear expensive to pay for stories, it is really not. Most publications pay only five to ten cents a word for stories. Some pay a flat fee. If the story looks good and you can negotiate an agreeable price, go for it!

Here is a partial listing of some of the types of newsletters that are being published today.

Internet Tips
Inside Professional Sports News
Investment Advice
California Lifer Newsletter
Book Reviews
P.L.U. Max
Inside Hollywood Gossip
Bookseller News
Prison Legal News
Criminal Legal News
Aspiring Writer's Tips
Hip Hop News
Free Items
Voices.con
Insider Newsletter
Parole Metters

If you have access to a personal computer, your task will be greatly simplified. Any number of word processing programs will allow you to design and lay out a newsletter. Many programs have several built-in newsletter templates. All you have to do is insert the graphics and text. One good example of this is the *Corcoran Sun* newsletter Freebird Publishers used to publish.

An eye-catching design will help you win more subscriptions. But, if you do not have a computer, you can still develop a winning newsletter. Simply type up your articles in a clean, easy-to-read format. A good example of this is the "lifer" newsletter *Voices.com* which is free if you send a SASE. If you want, you can use paste-up clip art (or cut some out of magazines) to highlight sections and break up large blocks of text.

Take a look at several of the more widely circulated newsletters already on the market. They have likely been designed by professionals. Copy the design elements that appeal to you. You may also want to look at books that address typography and design. As you study, you will gain new insights into what factors will help your newsletter succeed. You'll pick up a few basic pointers that will help you create a winning, attractive newsletter. The best example of a newsletter that started in a prison cell, and has since turned into a leading magazine, is *Prison Legal News*.

Once you have prepared the basic design of your publication and are gathering information for the first issue, begin your promotion campaign. If you regularly read large, national magazines in a field of interest similar to the topic of your newsletter, place one or more classified ad in them offering a free or low-cost sample issue of your newsletter. When folks respond, send the sample issue along with a sales letter and subscription offer. Some will write simply to get something free. However, if you have advertised in a magazine whose readers are strongly interested in your topic, you will gain a large number of subscriptions.

You will also want to create a direct mail campaign aimed at potential subscribers. You can rent a mailing list of subscribers to the national magazines in your field. In the beginning, when funds are low, you will want to mail to a small number. Since most mailing list brokers require that you rent a minimum of 5,000 names, start there. Always mail by third class bulk rate to keep costs low.

If your first mailing goes out to 5,000 people and you have a 5% response, you will gain 250 new subscribers. If each pays the $80 subscription price, that's $20,000 – enough to pay the cost of printing and mailing your offer to all 5,000 potential subscribers, filling the 250 subscriptions for one year, and still leave you a tidy profit. Roll your profits over and invest in a larger mailing list – and just repeat the process for an even greater payoff!

Testing has shown that your mail solicitation should include five basic elements:

- Outer envelope with teaser copy.
- One-or two-page sales letter.
- Small fold-over note to emphasize the offer.
- A reply card.
- A post-paid reply envelope.

Your outer envelope should be imprinted with some sort of teaser copy that will prompt the recipient to open it and investigate. If you can capture his attention when he first sees the piece, he is more likely to simply throw it in the trash unopened than to investigate further. If possible, print the teaser in a colored ink that will also call attention to your offer.

Your sales letter must directly offer benefits to the potential subscriber. He must be convinced that there is "something in it for him." Whether your newsletter offers to make the reader wealthier, happier, slimmer, smarter, a better cook – whatever – you must stress the direct benefits of the product to the reader. Tell him what you're offering, why he should subscribe, what he can expect in return, how he can profit, what guarantee you offer, etc. If possible, offer an additional "free" bonus along with his subscription. This offer will sway the undecided. It will cost you little, but will make all the difference in the world.

The small fold-over note is simply a short, second sales letter. Often, the outside is printed with a slogan like, "Only open this if you've decided NOT to subscribe" or something similar. It also must capture the reader's attention, giving you a second chance to address any objections the reader might have, breaking down his sales resistance. It is best printed on a colored paper.

The reply card allows the new subscriber to fill in the pertinent information – name, address, method of payment, etc. It also allows you to reiterate your guarantee and the personal benefits the subscriber will receive. The post-paid reply envelope (usually a Business Reply Envelope) allows him to return the card free of charge. It means a small cost to you, but is well worth the expense of gaining a new customer.

I hope I've sparked your interest in newsletter publishing. You can make a great profit if you develop a winning publication. All it takes is a little study, determination, careful consideration of the potential market, and the development of a unique method to meet the needs of potential subscribers. I wish you every success in your endeavor. For more inspiration, read the following story.

Note: Check out the resources in the back of this book to find some prisoner-based newsletters being published today. Some are free, others are subscription based. Order a few so you can see examples of how others are doing them.

WHERE TO GET FREE MATERIAL FOR YOUR BOOKS

Public domain. These two words can be worth millions. Okay, maybe you won't make millions, but you can certainly make a lot of money off of public domain material. What is public domain? Public domain means that the material is not protected by copyright law, and anyone is free to reproduce the material, and in any way they choose. In other words, this is equivalent to free money, if you know how to take advantage of it.

Let me give you a little-known secret that can be worth lots and lots of money. Ready? All government publications are public domain. They are not protected by copyright law. And guess what? All subjects imaginable are covered by publications funded and published by the U.S. government. Anything you can think of that is a popular topic, there are at least a thousand government publications on each of those subjects!

And government publications are prepared at great expense (using tax payers' money). They are top-of-the-line in terms of writing quality. So, the trick to publishing a book using this method Is to get ahold of government publications that are of your topic of choice and interest, put them together however you want, then sell the "collection" at whatever price you want, as your own, under your name. And it's perfectly legal!

One place you can find public domain material right in your prison? The law library! All those government-published books on case law, etc., is in the public domain, and you can do whatever you want with the information. Those big, expensive books you see in *Prison Legal News* full of citations and things? All that information is free to use, however you want.

Another thing to pay attention to is anything published by a website with .gov at the end. If you get printed publications that use that kind of website as the place to get more, it's in the public domain. Anytime you can find something on a website with .gov, it's a government publication and can be used and sold however you want. So, if you think something might be in the public domain, look to see if you can find that kind of web address attached to it. Or, you can have your people go online and find you publications from .gov websites. You should also look for websites with .org. While that doesn't guarantee it's a government-owned/funded website, it usually is. You can contact them and ask if it's okay for you to reprint some of their information. They will usually let you. This along can provide you with unlimited content to use in a book of your own, and it's all perfectly legal.

Other material in the public domain? Classic books whose copyrights have expired, which they usually do-expire-after 50 years. There are a lot of great classic books that are in the public domain, and you can reproduce them however you want, even under your own name. Savvy TV and movie producers have been taking advantage of this opportunity for years. For example, the movie H*eart of the Sea*, that's just the *Moby Dick* story with a fresh look given to it. A few years ago, there was a TV show called *Sleepy Hallow*. *Sleepy Hallow* is a classic book in the public domain. *Lord of the Rings* is another movie made from a story in the public domain. You might be surprised what you can find in the public domain that you can bring back for today's generation and give a fresh, modern look to it.

Another place you might be able to find a lot of free material is on the anarchist websites, like the anarchistlibrary.org, who clearly state they are "anti-copyright." These sites are huge, with all kinds of stuff on politics, prison, war, etc. A savvy hustler will know how to take this material and make it work for them. And being a successful author and publisher is very much about being a savvy hustler.

Again, look for websites with .gov and .org at the end. And check out gutenburg.com, too, as it's a digital library with over 15,000 pieces of literature in the public domain. Also, when using material with expired copyrights, be sure to use the original version. If someone modifies 20 percent or more of a public domain piece, they can copyright that version. You can still use the original version, however, and modify it (or not) however you want. And if you really want to be safe, it might be worth consulting with a copyright lawyer.

HOW TO WRITE LOW-BUDGET HORROR

So, you're dreaming of writing that blockbuster screenplay that Hollywood will pay millions for? Is it going to happen? Not likely. But I'll tell you what realistically can happen. Some indie producer (who makes movies for the "direct-to-DVD" market) might like your script if you're writing screenplays with a low budget in mind. That's a way of increasing your chances of getting your script made into a movie. But what exactly does low budget mean? Here are eight secrets.

1. Few locations. Make the story center around as few locations as possible. A house in the woods. People trapped in a mall. The fewer locations the better.

2. Few characters. Same with the locations – as few as possible. Actors are expensive, so only use the characters absolutely necessary for your story. That means no "Braveheart" scenes with hundreds of people.

3. Present day. Keep the story happening now – in our time. No Sci-fi or period pieces (those are really expensive).

4. No stunts. Stunts are expensive, difficult, and take time (and time is money).

5. Minimal special effects and CGI. Computer graphics and other special effects can be very expensive. So, try to keep explosions and armadas of spaceships to a minimum.

6. No weather. This one is hard, but try to avoid weather effects (rain, snow, etc.) because it's difficult for a low-budget filmmaker to create stuff like that.

7. Not too long. Don't write scripts with 120-130 pages – it's too long. A low-budget filmmaker might not be able to afford to make such a long movie. If you remember the low-budget movies from your video store, you'd find out that they are usually somewhere between 85-100 minutes, so your scripts should be somewhere between 85-100 pages (1 page = 1 minute).

8. Off screen. Everything doesn't have to happen on screen. If you write an end-of-the world script, your heroes can be trapped in a cellar and you can have them hear all the horrifying things happening outside over their radio. You don't have to see a car crash; if we hear the sound of a car crash, we understand what just happened. Or have the characters read about it in the newspaper. You don't have to show it happen.

Try and include some of these things into your script to make it more low-budget friendly. You won't make millions with a low-budget script, but you can realistically make thousands, and finally get your screenplay made into a movie. Many low-budget directors are looking for scripts right now. Start your today!

Power Tips...

Finally, here are some random power tips that I don't want to leave out.

1. Outline. If you don't already do this, it's time to start now. Do a one-or two-page outline of your horror story, where every important plot point is included. This should be a very condensed version of your story, from start to finish. Here you can see what works and what doesn't. Here you make the changes and tweak the story until everything works. Making the outline is crucial; once you've got it just write, all you have to do is fill in the in – betweens.

2. If you're writing a supernatural story, have a skeptic in your gang (remember Scully in "X-files"?) who can be the voice of reason. The skeptical part of the audience needs someone to identify with.

3. Fight against logic. Let's face it, all horror stories are a fight against logic. So, you have a haunted house. Why don't the family just pack their bags and get the hell out? Good question. To make your story appear a little more logical, your family has to at least try to leave – but then you can make sure there's no cell signal so they can't call for help. Or maybe their car breaks down so they can't get away. Be creative.

4. Go easy on the gore. It's not always necessary to use a lot of gore and buckets of blood. Remember that less is more. Sometimes what we can't see is the scariest of all.

5. Sleep on it. Sometimes when you're tired and you're writing, your story can appear scary, but the next day, with a fresh mind, you may realize your idea was lame.

TIPS & TRICKS TO WRITING A HORROR SCRIPT!

This is a very short, no fluff, blueprint of how to write a horror script.

1. The Hook. Start with a bang. Step right into the suspense scene. ("Scream" opens with a terrifying sequence with Drew Barrymore on the phone with a killer)

2. The Flaw. Introduce your hero. Give him a flaw. Before you can put your hero in jeopardy, we must care for him. We must want our hero to succeed. So, make him human. (In "Signs" Mel Gibson plays a priest who has lost his faith after his wife died)

3. The Fear. A variant of The Flaw. The hero has a fear. Maybe a fear of heights, or claustrophobia. (In "Jaws" Roy Scheider has a fear of water. At the end he has to conquer his fear by going out into the ocean to kill the shark)

4. No Escape. Have your hero at an isolated location where he can't escape the horror. (Like the hotel in "The Shining")

5. Foreplay. Tease the audience. Make them jump at scenes that appear scary – but turn out to be completely normal. (Like the cat jumping out of the closet) Give them some more foreplay before bringing in the real monster.

6. Evil Attacks. A couple of times during the middle of the script, show how evil the monster can be – as it attacks its victims.

7. Investigation. The hero investigates, and finds out the truth behind the horror.

8. Showdown. The final confrontation. The hero has to face both his fear and the monster. The hero uses his brain, rather than muscles, to outsmart the monster. (At the end of "The Village" the blind girl tricks the monster to fall into the hole in the ground)

9. Aftermath. Everything's back the way it was in the beginning – but the hero has changed for the better or for the worse. (At the end of "Signs" Mel Gibson puts on his clerical collar again – he got his faith back)

10. Evil lurks. We see evidence that the monster may return somewhere...somehow...in the future. (Almost all "Friday the 13th" Movies end with Jason showing signs of returning for another sequel)

This is very simplified, but gives you the skeleton for your story – the elements. You should, of course, always tweak, twist, and manipulate them so what you end up with is something fresh and new.

Add More Suspense Into Your Horror Script...

Here are some tips and tricks to heighten the tension of your horror scripts.

1. The weaker sex. Have a female heroine instead of a male to create a sense of vulnerability. (Most horror movies from 'Halloween" to "Scream" use this trick)

2. Helpless. A character is injured. Maybe on crutches, or crawling with a wounded leg, when the killer is coming. (In "Rear Window" James Stewart is helpless in a wheelchair when the killer comes from him)

3. The clock is ticking. Something is running out of time. Maybe a bomb, or a kidnapper deadline. (At the end of "Alien" Sigourney Weaver has to escape before the ship explodes)

4. Keep it hidden. Don't show the monster too early. I don't know how many times I've heard people say "The movie was suspenseful until we saw the monster's face...then the tension died." So, keep the monster hidden for as long as possible. (In "Jaws" it takes a long time before we get a close-up look at the terrifying shark)

5. Cramped space. The tighter the space, the harder for the heroine to escape. So, at the end, make sure she's trapped in the cellar, in the elevator, on the boat, or similar. (In "Alien" Sigourney Weaver has to fight the alien creature in the cramped, tight spaces of a spaceship)

6. The almost escape. The heroine escapes, or gets help from a trustworthy outsider. She thinks she got away, but she gets betrayed. (In "Rosemary's Baby" Mia Farrow escapes to a doctor, only to find out he has no intention of helping her. She is forced back home again)

7. The truth. No one believes the hero. He tells the truth, but no one (especially the police) believes him. (In "Jaws" Roy Scheider tries to convince the authorities that a killer shark is lurking in the deep, but no one listens to him)

8. Sickness. A character is sick and needs medication. (In "Panic Room" Jodie Foster's trapped daughter has diabetes and needs her insulin)

9. Keep it real. Horrors from our everyday life can often be scarier than monsters. That your little child is in a car accident is scarier than Dracula. A shark is scarier than the devil. Why? Because in real life you could be eaten by a shark, and you could lose your child – it could really

happen. Of course, you will write about monsters and supernatural events as well, but the more real you make it, the scarier it is.

10. Nail-biting suspense. Let's say we see a killer hiding in the backseat of the hero's car. Don't just let the hero get in the car and be attacked right away. Try to stop him from going to the car. He could come to the car and discover that he forgets his keys, so he has to go back and get them. And when he comes back with the keys and is about to open the car door – his cell phone rings. He answers and stands there chatting for a while. And finally, when he enters the car, maybe the backseat is empty, the killer is not there anymore. You get the picture. Do this and the audience will be on the edge of their seats.

THE MIKE ENEMIGO STORY: HOW ONE PRISONER IS CHANGING THE GAME, ONE BOOK AT A TIME

By Seth Ferranti

"If a person has done even a couple of years in prison and possess even the most basic means to obtain literature, there is a 99 percent chance that they've heard about Mike Enemigo and The Cell Block," says Damaneh Abdolah, who plans to produce a podcast and documentary on Mike's book *Conspiracy Theory*. But, make no mistake about it, things were not always this way. "Getting to this point has been a very long and arduous process," says Mike about his journey to becoming America's #1 incarcerated author. "Everything I've done, I've done from inside my prison cell. No Internet, computer, phone, text, e-mail or other fancy, helpful devices. Just a few pennies for a budget, and a bunch of ink pens, paper, stamps, envelopes, coffee, adversity, failures, determination, dedication, resilience, creativity and hard work. Oh, and a lot of time. In fact, several years."

See, Mike's plan was never to write books, it was to rap. He started rapping back in 1993. Unfortunately, he got caught up in the streets, was arrested in February of 1999, and in 2002 was sentenced to Life Without the Possibility of Parole – LWOP, as it's called – for a 1998 murder. Despite this, in 2004, after he'd been incarcerated for about 5 years, he decided he was going to do what he had to do to record his vocals, even if he had to do it over the prison phone, have his songs produced in the style of mixtapes, and distribute them independently –"maybe have my folks slang 'em out the trunk, put 'em in some local stores, etc. – nothin' too fancy." And though he hoped to make a few bucks, he didn't expect to get rich and famous and become a huge rap star: "My primary objectives were to break my story out of prison, give my brain something to focus on other than my confinement, and at least make the money back I'd spent producing the records," he says.

He contacted some people he knew from the streets who were in the rap game and got the ball rolling. But though progress was made, things moved extremely slow. "Being that my resources were very limited, it took a long time to get the simplest of things done." And by the time he'd accomplish one thing, the music game would change and make what he'd just gotten done less significant. In addition to that, as the years went on, people bought music less and less, due to things like file sharing and illegal downloading, and artists had to start depending more and more on things like live performances to make money; something he obviously couldn't do from his prison cell. With that, the hope of making any profit got smaller and smaller. However, "I didn't want to give up because I figured I could create my own little lane, and I'd use my music to promote it, feel me? I'd give my music away by way of downloads to promote myself, then I'd make my money off of something else that couldn't be illegally downloaded or need to be performed live: maybe I'd learn to draw really well, become a 'famous' prison artist and sell my artwork, start a T-shirt line, or maybe even ghostwrite rhymes – something like that."

He continued on, but so did the problems. In addition to the rapid game changes, coming up on a recorder (something prisoners are not allowed), then recording his vocals and smuggling them out, was a near-impossible task (though he did manage to record and get the vocals to over 100 songs to the streets). And if that wasn't enough, he began having problems with unreliable industry people and producers who didn't put his music together the way he wanted, being that he wasn't able to be present during his studio sessions. In the end, "It got to be too costly for me to do it myself, with my resources, or lack thereof, and I had to pull the plug because it was just to economically foolish to continue," he explains.

So, though it was tough, Mike shut everything down; even to the point of distancing himself from most of the world. "I had to strategize and figure out what my next move was going to be." He began to research. He began to study. He began to learn, and he began to plot...

Welcome to...The Cell Block

In 2010, while in the hole, Mike decided it was time to redirect his efforts from that of the rap game to the book game. He'd been flirting with the idea for nearly two years already, so when he was given his property in the hole, he made sure to grab the *English Grammar for Dummies* book he'd bought for this very reason – so he could tighten up his grammar game. "I was always creative 'cause I'd been writin' raps. But writin' raps and writin' books is a whole different game. I knew if I was gonna do this, I needed to learn to write properly, and I had to master it," he says. "So I began studying *English Grammar for Dummies*, while also working on my first book, which was *Surviving Prison*." (This book wouldn't be published until 2018.)

Eventually Mike got out of the hole, where he was able to buy a typewriter and other supplies, and he began typing the books he'd written by hand, as well as figuring out how he was going to publish them, under the new publishing company he was building, The Cell Block, which he planned to run just like a record label.

"When first trying to figure out how I was going to publish my books, I had no idea what I was gonna do," he says. "My people were taking the Directory [*The BEST Resource Directory for Prisoners*] to Kinkos, trying to have it printed up. I think it cost us around $17 to have one copy printed and bound with one of those plastic strips. And with the leading directory at the time priced at $18, there was no way we were going to be able to sell ours at a profit," he explains. "But one thing I knew for sure, I wasn't gonna quit or give up. So I kept reading everything I could find, and eventually I saw something about CreateSpace. This was a game-changer for me."

Mike launched The Cell Block officially in 2014 with five books – *The BEST Resource Directory For Prisoners*, *The Art & Power of Letter Writing for Prisoners*, *Thee Enemy of the State* and *Conspiracy Theory*, all of which he wrote; and *Loyalty & Betrayal*, a book he did with Armando Ibarra – with a promise of many more to come. And, though things did not go exactly as he hoped (what else is new, right?) in 2014, he learned a lot and built upon his team. In January 2015 he dropped four more books – *BASic Fundamentals of The Game*, by Mac B.A.$.; *Lost Angels*, a book he did with Alex Valentine; and *Money iz the Motive*, a book he did with TCB author Ca$ciou$ Green, plus the revision of his *Directory*.

He continued on, and in 2016 dropped seven books: *How to Hustle & Win; Sex, Money, Murder Edition*, and *Underworld Zilla*, with TCB author King Guru; *Money iz the Motive 2*, *MOBSTAR Money* and *Block Money*, with TCB author Ca$ciou$ Green; *The Millionaire Prisoner: Special TCB Edition*, with incarcerated author Josh Kruger; and *A Guide to Relapse Prevention For Prisoners*, with inmate Charles Hottinger. In 2017 he dropped the newest edition of *The Best Resource Directory for Prisoners*, and *Kitty Kat*, a non-nude adult entertainment resource book he did with Freebird Publishers.

In 2018 he dropped several more books: *Surviving Prison: The Secrets to Surviving the Most Treacherous and Notorious Prisons in America!*; *The Art & Power of Letter Writing for Prisoners, Deluxe Edition;* and the revised edition of *The Best Resource Directory for Prisoners.* He dropped *Pretty Girls Love Bad Boys: An Inmate's Guide to Getting Girls* and *How to Write Urban Books for Money & Fame* with TCB author King Guru. He dropped *Get Out, Get Rich: How To Get Paid Legally When You Get Out of Prison!* (also titled *Hood Millionaire: How to Hustle & Win Legally*); *The CEO Manual: How to Start Your Own Business When You Get Out of Prison!* (also titled *CEO Manual: Start a Business, Be a Boss!);* and *Money Manual: Underground Cash Secrets Exposed*, all with self-made hood millionaire Sav Hu$tle; and he dropped *Prison Legal Guide* with Freebird Publisher. He also completely revamped his website, thecellblock.net.

In 2019, the hustle didn't stop, or even slow down. He tapped in with Wahida Clark, the Official Queen of Street Lit and worked a distribution deal for TCB books *Underworld Zilla*; *How to Hustle & Win: Sex, Money, Murder Edition*; and *Money iz the Motive: Special 2-in-1 Edition.* Then he dropped *The Prison Manual: The Complete Guide to Surviving the American Prison System* and *The Ladies Who Love Prisoners,* both of which he wrote; *Loyalty & Betrayal: Special Deluxe Edition*; *OJ's Life Behind Bars: The Real Story*, a book he did with incarcerated author Vernon Nelson; *Get Out, Stay Out: The Secrets To Getting Out of Prison Early, and Staying Out For Good!* with Shane Bowen; and *Raw Law For Prisoners: Your Rights And How To SUE When They Are Violated!* with TCB author King Guru. He also dropped two e-shorts: *The Mob*, with author PaperBoy; and *Angel* with incarcerated author Tre Cunningham.

As you can see, the hard work, determination, and perseverance has paid off. When asked about his drive: "I've always been a hustler. Above all else, that's what I am – a hustler. My desire's always been to get the bag [money]. Before, I put a lot of effort and drive into negative things – thuggin', basically. So the things I was doin' to get the bag was, essentially, just getting me further into debt, you feel me? I knew I had to transform my hustle if I wanted to truly be successful, and this writing thing is a major part of that. I also knew that if I put the same drive and energy into this as I did the gimy shit I was doin', I'd win.

"So, I went from dope dealer to hope dealer. I dreamed of slangin' birds, but now I'm achieving my dreams slangin' words, you feel me? I'm shippin' boxes of books like I wanted to ship bricks. And not only am I completely legit, I'm making more money now than I ever did with my grimy endeavors.

"I found my lane – my frequency. I want to be the best, and I'm willing to do whatever it takes to ensure that happens."

Not only has Mike been making noise inside prison, the streets are taking notice, too. He's received praise from bestselling authors like JaQuavis Coleman and Kevin Deutsch, and he and/or The Cell Block have been featured in magazines like *Straight Stuntin*, *Kite*, *State V. Us*, *Street Money*, *Prison Legal News*, and others, and on websites like The Huffington Post, Gorilla Convict, Thizzler, Rap Bay, Hood Illustrated, and many more. "I promise you I'm just gettin' started," he says.

What's next? Well, more books, of course. "For years prisoners have written me, asking how to go about doing what I do in regards to publishing books, so I wrote a book on jailhouse publishing that I'ma drop sometime this year [2020]. The book contains everything I've learned over the last ten years the hard and expensive way. I have several more books in the works, including audio books, something I plan to take to the next level. I also have some things in the works with the big homie, Dutch, the OG of the street lit game. I have a bunch of projects going on right now that I'm excited about." But something he's especially proud of? "I launched a new blog on my website where me and other TCB writers provide raw, uncensored news, entertainment and resources on the topics of prison and street-culture. It's connected to all social medias, as well as book platforms like Amazon, Goodreads, etc. It's a game-changer. I'm building The Cell Block's own digital platform so we're not at the mercy of anyone else. This is going to increase our power and presence dramatically. Everyone needs to tap in to our website, thecellblock.net, and follow us on all social medias."

And when asked about the possibility of getting out of prison? "Laws are changing in my favor. In addition to that, I'm not sittin' around waitin' on somebody to just let me out. I'm taking aggressive, proactive measures to earn my freedom. I have a 5-year plan and a 10-year plan. I'd say I'll be out in about eight. It took me a minute to understand how all this works, but if one wants to get out bad enough, and is willing to do what it takes, it can be done. At least in California. And though I'm not certain, probably most everywhere else, too. The secret is to identify what it is you need to do, then do double that."

And Mike's been inspiring prisoners all over the country, as evident by the mass amounts of letters he gets, thanking him for what he's done. "I'm in prison in Tennessee. I'm a huge fan and receive knowledge and wisdom from your teachings," writes one prisoner. "Thank you for all you do to make life easier for us prisoners," writes another, from California. "I have bought every book that you've published and I encourage you to keep serving it like you're doing," says prisoner Ethan McKinney. And Jorge Cabrera from Oregon says, "I have to say, I've been incarcerated for 20-plus years, and this is the first time I've invested money into something that's profitable." Literally, the list goes on and on.

"I'm proud of all that's been accomplished," says Mike. "Not only have the years of hard work paid off for me and the TCB team, I'm proving that, despite our situation, we can still achieve success if we're willing to do what it takes.

"I'm very grateful to the prisoners who've been rockin' with us. It's because of them – their loyalty – that we've been able to get to where we're at. You can be the dopest writer in the world, but if the people don't fuck with you, you ain't ever gonna get anywhere. Fortunately, for me, the people fuck with me. They understand I'm talkin' their language, and for that, they embrace me."

And when asked what kind of advice he'd share to other prisoners? "Stay positive and motivated. When you live inside a box, you must learn to think outside of one. Be creative. Confinement can cause a man to tap into the deepest parts of the mind. Take advantage of that, be dedicated and determined, and you'll be surprised at what you can pull off. This is proof. My story is a testament that you must never give up. You're first idea is rarely your best one, and the road to success is not a straight shot.

"Now get to work and hustle hard."
Indeed.

SETH FERRANTI: GORILLA CONVICT

I first learned about inmate-author Seth Ferranti in 2008. My celly had given me a *Black Men* magazine, and inside was an article on Seth. Ironically, this was the same time I'd began flirting with the idea of trying to write a book, so naturally the article stood out to me and got my attention. I can't remember much about the article, which I believe was more of an interview, but it mentioned his book, *Prison Stories*. I knew I needed to order the book so I could see what type of writing was being done from prison. Shortly after the *Black Men* article I saw a book review in *Smooth* magazine for another one of Seth's books, *Street Legends* volume one. I ended up ordering both books.

I found *Prison Stories* and *Street Legends* to be great books. But what I got most out of them is inspiration. Seth's writing wasn't *perfect*. This gave me confidence. Here was this prisoner, who wrote a couple books – and not only wrote a couple books, but published them – and I had them, across the country, in my prison cell. He was making noise in magazines I respected. And he was doing all this without his writing being *perfect*? Seth masterfully employed the 80/20 publishing principle before I even knew what it was. This made me feel like I could really do it. It taught me that the difference between Seth and the many other, wannabe inmate "authors," wasn't necessarily that he wrote better, but that he actually *did* it. He executed. Rather than sitting around, talking about it, he made it happen.

Seth had been incarcerated since 1993. He'd been sentenced to 304 months in federal prison under the kingpin statue for selling LSD. According to the US Attorney, Seth and his crew distributed more than 100,000 doses of the LSD in the Fairfax, Virginia area.

While in prison, Seth took a correspondence course in creative writing. He began writing short stories about prison, which would later turn into his book, *Prison Stories*. He got the idea for the book after reading other prison-based books, like *The Belly of the Beast*. *The Belly of the Beast* came out in 1981; Seth's idea for *Prison Stories* was to make a 1990's version." However, after publishers wanted him to "tone it down" because it was "too raw and too real," he decided to publish it himself, so he launched his own publishing imprint, Gorilla Convict, with the help of his wife.

To promote his books, and himself as a writer, Seth began writing for more established publications, like *Don Diva* magazine, *F.E.D.S.* magazine, *Vice*, *The Fix*, *Slam*, and others. However, his writing, which was often about prison life, like the drug trade, cigarette trade and cell phones, often landed him in the hole. "The prison staff would come and lock me up, and they told me, 'Ferrenti, we don't care about your writing. But you pissed the warden off, so we're going to lock you up, and you're going to sit back here for 30 to 60 days. Think about what you write so you don't piss our bosses off again.'"

Despite obstacles, Seth continued writing and publishing. He's since been released from prison, where he's continued to write and publish street classics, as well as write and produce the hit documentary *White Boy,* on STARZ.

When I had a cell phone of my own, all during 2018 and half of 2019, I followed Seth on social media – Facebook and Instagram – to see what he was doing and how he was doing it. Many of his books are nonfiction/journalistic, about street legends like Kenneth "Supreme" McGriff, Pistol Pete, and others, many of whom he did time with, and he writes articles on prison-based topics, like gangs, drugs, etc., and this is largely what I write, so Seth was the perfect prisoner-turned-author for me to study. Researching Seth and seeing what he was doing is how I learned about best-selling crime writer Kevin Deutsch and his podcast, *A Dark Turn*, where he interviewed Seth. Seeing that Kevin had interest in the prisoner-turned-writer subject, I contacted him. We eventually became friends, and he gave me my very first live interview, which aired on his podcast. You can find it on my website, thecellblock.net.

After Kevin, I tapped in with Seth. He posted my promo graphic on his Instagram and told his followers to support incarcerated authors, but other than that, he seemed more focused on the vacations he was taking with his wife. Which, after all those years in prison, I can't really blame him.

Seth has been a great example for me. If you want to write on the topic of prison, I suggest you at least read his book *Prison Stories*. If you desire to be a journalist type who writes on gang life, drug lords and other true crime, I suggest you check out his other books, too, which include, among others, *Street Legends* volumes 1 and 2; *The Supreme Team*; *Crack, Rap and Murder*; and *Rayful Edmond*.

Here's an article Seth wrote about incarcerated authors that I found online so you can see his style – or at least his earlier style.

Incarcerated Authors
[By Seth Ferranti, October 22, 2011]

Just like the rap game before it the world of hip-hop fiction is blowing up. Street lit as it's called is now grossing over $50 million annually and a genre that started with self-published authors selling books out the back of their cars has quickly become a legitimate market that has harnessed the talents of writers either fresh out of prison or still in the pen. The books often published under pen names, following the lead of rappers, are in high demand, especially among young people indoctrinated in the hip-hop culture.

You know the publishers – Teri Woods, Triple Crown, Nikki Turner Presents, Relentless Content, Urban Books Amaiya, Hampstead Publishing and Gorilla Convict – but do you know the authors. The best of who are still incarcerated. Real convicts with real time who write real books. These authors were living the life your favorite rapper is rhyming about. Ain't no studio or cardboard gangstas in this group. And Gorilla Convict would like to introduce them to you.

"I'm incarcerated in North Carolina for two counts of murder, kidnapping and armed robbery that I'm fighting to prove my innocence on." says Kwame Teague the 33-year-old native of Newark, New Jersey aka Brick City, who penned the Teri Woods produced *Dutch*, *Dutch II*, and *Adventures of Ghetto Sam*. The author who's been locked up since 1994 is serving 2 life sentences. "My parole date would be after 40 years." He says. And the thing about it is Kwame's name doesn't even appear on his books, *Dutch or Dutch II*. Two of the best street novels ever. Teri Woods is listed as the author.

"*Dutch* is a fictional novel about crime and murder," Kwame says explaining why his name isn't on the books he authored. "And I was trying to fight an unjust murder charge. I didn't want the book to become a factor against me." That's understandable, but how did Kwame first get with Teri Woods.

"Back in like 2000 she had an article in the *Vibe*," he says. "She had just put out *True to the Game*. I had just self-published *Ghetto Sam* through Iuniverse.com then I saw that. So, I had my people contact her and sent her my book, she dug it and it started from there." And now six figure book sales later Kwame is still in jail, writing and fighting to overturn his conviction. But it hasn't all gone smoothly.

"When they truly understood how successful the books were," Kwame says referring to the prison administrators. "They put me in segregation for 60 days on trumped up charges and shipped seven hours from my family. They fear the influence I have over other inmates, their exact words. They also banned the books in every state prison." Harsh measures, but measures any incarcerated author might have to deal with. Kwame Teague is currently incarcerated at Taylorsville Prison in North Carolina working on future projects and fighting for his freedom.

Another noteworthy incarcerated author is Trenton NJ native Wahida Clark who is doing a 125-month sentence at FPC Alderson in West Virginia. "My charges are conspiracy/money laundering, mail and wire fraud," she says. Wahida has three books out – *Thugs and the Women Who Love Them, Every Thug needs a Lady* and *Payback is a Mutha*, which is her current release on Kensington Publishing. Wahida whose release date is next year is an *Essence* Bestselling author whose books have sold over 50K copies. She writes what she calls reality fiction.

"Ghetto/street life from the hood," she relates. "Welfare, food stamps, government cheese, weed, boosting and partying." She started writing books after seeing black authors in magazines and reading their interviews. She told herself she could do that, took a creative writing class at the prison and boom – three books later she is among the leaders of the genre with an imprint at Kensington and a new series, *Ghetto Stories* coming out.

"A sista had to do what a sista had to do," Wahida says. "And writing a hotty novel on lock makes it feel that much better." She relates that there are advantages and disadvantages to being an incarcerated writer. Pros – "You have time to write. You have three pots and a cot, no worrying about lights, gas, car note, food." Cons – "On the business tip you can't really spread your wings and soar. You're forced to crawl. So, like my friend Relentless Aaron said, while you're locked up, pump out as many novels as you can." Wahida who was recently profiled in *King* magazine is currently getting her *Ghetto Stories* series ready for release.

Joe Black's name has been ringing bells in the feds for the last decade due to his various photocopied legal writing paper manuscripts, which have been sweeping the underground prison nation causing a stir like the mixtapes of the prison system. The 38-year-old Bronx native whose been down since 1994 is doing 19 1/2 years for a drug conspiracy. After finally self-publishing his first novel *Street Team* on illstreetz.com he inked a deal from the pen with Hampstead Publishing who took *Street Team* national and plans to put out Joes second novel *Squeeze* next. The author who's been profiled in *Don Diva* and *King* gets out in 2008.

"It's an autobiography of everyone who ever played the game," Joe says of his novel. And he admits to admiring, "Donald Goines and Iceberg Slim, because they didn't have to interview gangstas to bring me their stories. They were gangstas and when I read their books it was like they were in the cell kicking it with me." And readers of *Street Team* have come to the same conclusion. Real recognizes real.

"It's the closest you gonna come to being in the game without being indicted," Joe says of his book and concerning life in the streets he has this jewel to offer. "There's no pot of gold at the end of the rainbow. There's only a pot of cream of wheat in the morning at the mess hall or your casket in a plot with your name over it." Incarcerated authors like Joe have spent decades of their lives inside, but with his novel he tries to show the consequences of the drug game. And it isn't pretty. Look out for *Movin Violation* by Joe Black on Gorilla Convict Publications which comes out soon. Check out hampsteadpub.com.

Robert Booker, Sr. out of Detroit, Michigan is another incarcerated author whose work has the streets talking. The 40-year-old who's been in since 1994 is doing a natural life sentence in the feds for a cocaine conspiracy. His novel, *Push* available on Sims and Sims Productions is a story of crime, sex, loyalty and murder on the streets of Detroit.

"I started writing in 2000 after I read Teri Woods *True to the Game*," Booker who's incarcerated at FCI Gilmer in West Virginia says. "I knew my stories was way better then hers because I was living in the streets. I write what I know. You change the name to get the fame." And the streets, prisons plus the industry has recognized. Off the strength of *Push* Booker has signed to do *Deep in the Game* with Hampstead Publishing and *Keep it Gangsta* with Gorilla Convict. Expect both books out by 2007.

And about having a book out while in prison Booker says, "Everybody act like you a star but it ain't nothing. I'm just another prisoner." But with acclaim coming from the streets and the prisons and with more books coming out Booker is a writer on the come up.

"My writing skills is raw, straight from my mind onto paper like a rapper doing freestyle on BET's Freestyle Friday," says the author who was profiled in *The Ave* magazine. And in his novels Booker keeps it all the way real.

"I understand street life. I understand the struggles in the streets." He says. "I'm a real nigga, I got served life. I know what gangstas do and what they don't do." And Booker who's at FCI Gilmer in the feds right now is cranking out more books and stories for his audience.

From the west coast out in the California prison system is blood gang member and convict writer, Terrell C. Wright aka Loko, author of *Home of the Body Bags*, a tome that tells the tale of a blood soldier, which is out on Senegal Press now.

"I've always wanted to tell my story as a blood soldier." Loko says. "The Neighborhood bloods in particular." And the 38-year-old Loko, who is at Corcoran State prison in Cali is serving time for a jewelry store robbery.

"I was born and raised in South Sintral Los Scandalous," Loko says. "By 1982 I was a full-fledged LA gangsta and the rest is history as my book expresses in vivid details." And Loko has always wanted to write a book, but prison finally gave him the time to do it.

"I've always had an innate desire of wanting to share the blood experience with the world at large," he says. "I've always felt I had an author dwelling inside me. But it was the addictive high of being in the streets which kept me from taking out some quality time for myself to sit and write." And with the success of *Home of the Body Bags* Loko has penned another book, *Thugs*, which will be out on streetgangs.com shortly. Check it out.

Another convict author straight out of the Chocolate City is 29-year-old Eyone Williams who is serving 15 to life on a second-degree murder charge. His novel *Fastlane* "is a tale of the streets mixed with events of my youth and what I saw around me." The Northwest DC native says. And the book has sold several thousand copies to date without any distribution or major promotion.

"My wife and I were inspired to start our own publishing company when we saw how many big companies reject manuscripts from unknown authors." Eyone says. So, they started Fast Lane Publications and put out *Fastlane*, which takes a look at the lives of DC street hustlers. "My wife, Aisha Bailey, keeps everything together while I'm in prison by keeping up with the business side of running the company." Eyone says and they have plans to put out books by other prisoners also.

"I've been pleased to see that the streets and the prisons have been feeling Fastlane," Eyone says. "All of my support has come from those places." And Eyone who's been locked up for 13 years is only beginning. He's been penning *Lorton Legends*, which takes a look at the notorious DC prison. Look for it soon at fastlanepub.com.

Cuban-American author Michael Santos has been in the feds since 1987 serving a 45-year sentence for a continuing criminal enterprise conviction. And although his work isn't considered hip-hop fiction, he has still made tracks in the genre. His current book *Inside: Life behind Bars in America* is out on St. Martins press and has been compared to prison classics, *Hot House, Soledad Brother* and *In the Belly of the Beast*.

"As a long-term prisoner," says the 42-year-old Santos who is eligible for parole in 2013. "I recognize that writing provides the only opportunity to reach beyond these boundaries that hold us physically. I want to connect with the world." And he has. With three other books – *About Prison, Profiles from Prison*, and *What if I go to Prison* along with his website, Michaelsantos.net. Santos has made himself an authority on life in prison.

"I am not a fan of the prison system," he says. "I am convinced that if one were charged with the responsibility of designing a system that conditions men to fail in society that person could not do better than the concept of imprisonment. In learning how-to live-in prison, the individual simultaneously learns how to fail in society. But I've always believed that the pen is mightier than the sword, so I write." And the world has taken notice of the author who is currently confined in the camp at FCI Lompoc.

As Y2k moves on jailhouse writers are becoming more prolific. The flood of prison writing is a result of the alarming numbers of incarcerated African-Americans and Latinos, many of them casualties of the war on drugs and the draconian sentencing guidelines now in place in most states and the feds. Like street fiction fathers Iceberg Slim and Goines, who both served time, the new writers are capturing the life they know. The authors profiled here are only a few of the most prominent and successful, but still there are many more. In many prisons, men and women on lockdown are spending their hours putting pens to paper and finding words to describe their prior or current lives. Like they say the streets are watching and the next big hip-hop fiction author might be composing his novel right now in some prison somewhere. Dreaming of success, notoriety and freedom.

MICHAEL SANTOS: WRITE TO FREEDOM

One of the best examples of a prisoner who wrote books successfully while inside the belly of the beast is Michael Santos, who, in 1987, at the age of 23, was convicted of trafficking cocaine and sentenced to 45 years in federal prison.

Michael's first venture with writing was early on in his sentence when he was trying to atone for his crimes and earn support for an upcoming hearing. He did this despite having "never taken a writing course or even written anything more substantial than short letters." He decided to write a book titled *Drugs and Money* to show how he was seduced by the romantic images of the drug trade, which ultimately landed him in prison. It was his hope that, by reading his story, people would by inspired to avoid the choices and mistakes he made. With the help of his sister, he was able to secure a grant for 20k to publish and distribute 2,000 books to schools, jails and other organizations for at-risk youth.

After writing his book, Michael began to focus on education. He wanted to earn a college degree and become more than "just a prisoner." Through these educational endeavors, however, Michael began to correspond with many university professors on the outside who became his mentors. One of these mentors was Dr. George Cole, author of *American Corrections*, the leading textbook at the time used in universities to teach students about the American prison system. In 1999, after reading the articles on prison life Michael had been writing and posting on his website, MichaelSantos.net, Dr. Cole suggested Michael write a book about his prison experience that they could present to Dr. Cole's publisher as a supplement text to sell alongside his textbook. Michael describes how this came about in his book *Earning Freedom*.

"It's the most exciting proposition I've had since I began in the stock market and I ask George to advise me on how I can start. He tells me to write a proposal for Wadsworth-Thompson Publishers to consider. The suggestion presents me with a new opportunity to turn the page, inspiring me with the confidence to launch the next chapter of my life. With my responsibilities to write for the Internet project that Zach coordinates, and the hours I invest to write the new book proposal, the outline, and the sample chapters, I have new reasons to wake before dawn and work 12-hour days.

"Unlike studying towards advanced degrees, writing doesn't require me to seek permission from small-minded administrators. The activity is like a respite, freeing me from spending time with inmates who whine about the injustice of 12-month prison sentences. Further, it doesn't require me to read a dozen financial publications, it cuts my CNBC ticker addiction, and it provides a new challenge of learning how to express myself more fluently.

"To write, all I need is a pen, blank pages of paper, and a dictionary. Still, I know where I am, and I ask for written clarification from the BOP legal department on the rules that govern prisoners who write for publication. That inquiry brings confirmation from a BOP staff attorney who says that as long as I'm not inciting others or being compensated for my writing, I'm within my rights to continue.

"Working to write for publication becomes a goal I can pursue with gusto, and I welcome the challenge of persuading publishers to work with me. To succeed, I must work to become a better writer, and by doing so, I'll transcend prison boundaries, connect with readers everywhere, and build support. I go to the library in search of more information.

"'Do you have any books on the shelves about the publishing business?' I'm hopeful that the librarian can steer me in the right direction.

"'All we've got is an old edition of *The Writer's Market.*'

"'I'll take it,' I say.

"The reference book shows the difficult odds that beginning writers face. Fewer than one in 1,000 authors sign publishing agreements. Those who succeed frequently toil for years, writing many manuscripts before they see one of their books in print. I perceive an edge because of the mentor relationships I've nurtured over the years, and because I'm writing about a unique subject matter.

"After I write my proposal for *About Prison*, George advises me to send it to Sabra Home, a senior acquisition editor at Wadsworth-Thompson. She responds with a publishing agreement, and I write the manuscript that described my first decade as a prisoner. The academic publisher will package the books as a supplementary text for university professors who teach courses in criminal justice.

"With that project behind me, I write to Dr. Marilyn McShane, another mentor who, in addition to teaching criminal justice and authoring books, is a senior editor for Greenwood-Praeger Publishing.

She offers to publish *Profiles From Prison*, my second book, which describes backgrounds, adjustment patterns, and future expectations of 20 prisoners.

"The thousands of hours I spend writing, typing, and editing the manuscripts gives me the feeling that I'm doing something more than simply serving time. It's as if I'm making a societal contribution, living a life a meaning and relevance. If readers find value in the books once they're published, perhaps more people will see the need to think smarter rather than tougher about America's dysfunctional prison system."

In 2002, Michael received a letter from a childhood friend named Carole, who he would eventually marry. Carole began helping Michael with his manuscripts by typing what he would handwrite and mail her. These book endeavors give Michael the idea that he can earn money when he gets out of prison by writing about his prison experience, and consulting people who face challenges with the criminal justice system. However, rather than wait until he gets out to start, he wanted to start now, while still in prison, so he can earn money that can be set aside for his release. He asked Carole to help him start a publishing company, and she agreed. Michael than committed to writing 15 pages of content every day, which he would then mail to Carole each evening so she could type and return them double-spaced, ready for editing.

Towards the end of 2003, however, prison officials become aware of Michael's Internet writing, and they don't like it. They are unhappy that he writes and publishes the inside, goings-on of prison life for all the world to see, claiming it's a threat to the safety and security of the institution. They throw Michael in the hole, then transfer him a total of three times over the next 18 months. Michael does not let this stop him, however, and he continues to work on his books.

By 2004, Michael settles into a new prison and began working on a new project. Here's how he explains it in *Earning Freedom*.

"Other than work in the Supermax laundry, exercise, and visiting with Carole, I devote all my energy to writing a book proposal and three sample chapters for a new manuscript. I'm titling it *Inside: Life Behind Bars in America*. It's my first attempt to reach a general, non-fiction audience, and I invest more than three months with a Bic pen and a dictionary to put the book proposal together. Carole types the document and sends copies to 90 literary agents I culled from an annotated list published in *Writer's Market*. I'm hopeful they'll have an interest in my work.

"Our effort to find a literary agent makes me a hit at mail call. The guard has been calling my name over and over, passing me no fewer than 73 rejections from literary agents who've declined to represent me. But I've also received letters from four agents who express interest. I hold one in my hand now from James Schiavone, a Florida agent who has a doctorate in education.

"Educators guided me through my first 17 years of confinement and they served as role models for me. I admire their devotion to improving society through teaching and I respect them for the energy they invest in helping others reach their potential.

"I respond to Dr. Schiavone's letter, letting him know that I'd welcome an opportunity to work with him. That response leads to more correspondence. I amend my proposal according to his suggestions and sign a contract giving Schiavone Literary Agency authorization to present my manuscript to mainstream publishing houses. It thrills me to have a valid contract with a literary agent Carole and I found through our own work."

Prison officials, however, don't share Michael's elation. They don't want him writing about what truly goes on inside prison. They claim his writing is a threat to the safety and security of the institution. He tries to show them what he's doing by presenting them with copies of his books to look at, as well as letters from numerous professors who use his writings as a resource to teach students in their criminal justice and corrections courses.

The prison officials are unmoved and they place Michael on mail monitoring status. Despite this, Michael refuses to stop.

"I owe no allegiance to Mr. Jimenez, Ms. Otero, or the prison system," he says. "By writing about prisons from the inside, I hope to influence support for reforms to our costly prison system that perpetuates so much failure. I feel a duty to write about America's most flawed institutions, especially a federal prison system hidden from public view and squandering billions in taxpayer resources each year."

Not long after this, Michael received a visit from Carole with some exciting news.

"I'm so proud of you," she says.

"Tell me why."

JAILHOUSE PUBLISHING

"Jim called. He got a publishing deal for your book."

"With who?" he asked her.

"St. Martin's Press. They're giving us an advance. You'll have distribution all over the world."

Michael is thrilled by the news. His first two books were with academic publishers, but this one is with a mainstream publisher – a whole other level of the game. His writing is paying off, and he's doing it all with pens and paper the he buys from the commissary.

"Do I need to talk with anyone, with Jim or someone from St. Martin's?" he asks Carole.

"Everyone understands your situation. You can send everything through me, like always," she says. "I'll type it and forward the manuscript through email. The only question is edits. How will you meet the timeline if the staff keeps holding your mail?"

"Let's send the manuscript pages to Rick," he suggests, referring to his roommate. "No one's checking his mail."

"I can't do that. They probably have some rule about my writing to another inmate."

"Honey, you're free. You can send mail to anyone you want. We can't let these mini-minds in prison block us from success."

"No way," Carole says adamantly. "I'm not going to do anything that might create a problem with our visits. I'll forward the manuscript pages I type to Jennifer. She can send them to her husband, and when he gets them, he can give them to you."

"I'll meet the timeline."

"No one has any doubt about that," Carole assures him.

Michael worked hard on his manuscripts, and on June 1, 2005, after the 5:00 a.m. count cleared, he sealed the envelope that held the prologue for *Inside* and put it in the outgoing mailbox. Except for the final editing, he's finished with the project and looks forward to its publication.

Two hours later, he's thrown in the hole again and transferred, eventually landing in Lompoc Camp.

Michael explained to Carole he wants to start another book. Carole wasn't so sure it was a good idea, though, exhausted by all the prison shenanigans they've had to endure as a result of his writing. She was worried about what might happen when Inside was released in August of 2006, just a few months away.

Michael explains to her that he doesn't care what the prison officials do, his concern is to build something for him to come home to. Plus, he can write from the SHU is necessary.

"What do you want to write?" Carole asked him.

"I've met so many businessmen here. I could start interviewing guys who serve time for fraud, securities violations, or tax problems. I'm thinking of writing their stories for a book we could call *White Collar*. Instead of writing about prison, I'd write to describe how educated people unknowingly make decisions that lead them to prison. I think there's a market for it and I don't see how anyone could accuse me of threatening security. But I promised you I wouldn't do anything that might bring problems unless you agreed. What do you think?"

"I'm afraid they'll take you away."

"Do you trust me?"

"Of course."

"Would you still love me, stay married to me if they took me away and if we couldn't visit?"

"I'll always love you, and I'll always stay married to you, but please don't talk about being taken away."

"We both know that could happen at any time. We need to base our decisions on our future, not our visiting. Writing is the only way I can earn money for us, but I want your agreement, I need you to buy in to this plan."

Carole shook her head, but agreed. "Whatever you think is best," she said to him.

In July of 2006, a man named Lee Nobmann surrendered to Lompoc Camp. Lee fit the profile of the type of man Michael wanted to write about in *White Collar*, so he introduced himself to him. Come to find out, Michael was right. Lee sells lumber, employees close to 500 people, and is expected to do 450 million this year (2006). Lee had to serve a year to serve on a tax case.

Michael explained to Lee that he writes books. This impressed Lee. Michael explained to him that he's working on a new book for white-collar offenders, to help them and other professionals understand more about the system. Lee explained he could have used something like that and agrees to let Michael interview him.

On Monday, August 6, 2006, *Inside* hit bookstores across America. Michael had written the proposal and sample chapters more than two years earlier, and in one way or another, worked on the book every day since. When Michael went to work that morning, his boss handed him an Internet printout from *The Los Angeles Times* Sunday Book Review. It was written by Pulitzer Prize-winning author Ed Humes, and the full-page review has Michael photograph on it.

A little over a month later, Jeff, a recent Lompoc arrival from Seattle who's in the beginning months of a 10-year sentence for selling cocaine, hands Michael the magazine section from *The Seattle Times*. Michael's picture is on the cover and the article is written by Stewart Eskenazi, the same journalist who covered Michael's trial for the newspaper. Jeff allows Michael to keep the magazine and he shows it to Lee, who's thoroughly impressed. Lee wonders why more prisoners don't try and apply themselves the way Michael does, and Michael explains to Lee that the system is not set up for this type of thing to happen. Lee wants to do something to change that.

"That's what my work is about. One advantage of having served this much time is that I have credibility with other prisoners. I hope to show them by example that with discipline they can develop skills that will prepare them to reenter society and have meaningful lives. Few want to live as criminals, but when they don't believe in themselves, they give up. That failure pattern starts when they're young. Without understanding the consequences, kids drop out of school, join gangs, sell drugs, and when they come to prison, they fall further into failure. Through example, I hope to show how they can climb out."

"But how? The people who need the message most don't buy books. Many don't even read," Lee said.

"They only read about what interests them, and you're right, they don't buy books. But if I write about people they identify with, experiences and lifestyles they identify with, I can help. What I need is sponsorship. I need to find businesses and organizations with a social conscience that will buy and distribute the books to those who need them. When I'm out, I'll find those sponsors. I hope you'll help."

"Why wait until you get out?" Lee asked Michael. "I'll sponsor you right now. What would you like to do?"

As they sat at the picnic table, Lee listened as Michael pitched two books ideas. Michael proposed interviewing prisoners who would talk about their criminal histories. Specifically, he wants to write about people who quit school, joined gangs, and became involved in drugs or crime. He suggested a book that would profile prisoners and be followed by a series of open-ended discussion questions for the readers to consider. With Lee's sponsorship, Michael would be able to produce and distribute the books free to schools with a large number of at-risk kids. Teachers and counselors would be able to use the books to show actual stories of the consequences that follow criminal decisions.

The second book would be for adults who are just beginning their terms in prison. This book would also tell prisoner's stories, but the stories would highlight the steps they took to turn their lives around and live responsibly. The book would show how anyone could use discipline and readily available prison resources to prepare for a successful life upon release.

"What would you call that one," Lee asked Michael.

"I haven't thought it through yet, but I'd base it on what I've learned."

"I'll sponsor those projects right now. Count on me for $75,000. That should give you enough to write and print both books, distribute them at no charge, and take the pressure off Carole while she finishes school."

"Are you serious?"

"Believe me, my family's been blessed in many ways," he said. "I'm completely serious. One lesson I've learned is that supporting worthwhile projects for society comes back a hundred-fold. Besides, after all the work you've done in here, you deserve it."

On April 18, 2007, Michael is working diligently on the writing projects Lee sponsored when an officer cuffs him and throws him in the hole. He is investigated for running a business. He didn't know if it was because of Inside, his website, or the projects he was doing that Lee sponsored. Carole goes to work, fighting to get him out. Mike spends his time working out and writing a daily journal that Carole posts on his website about all that's going on. Ultimately, Michael is cleared of all charges, but transferred to Taft Camp. When Carole visits him, she wants him to stop writing, at least for a while.

"Please, Michael. No writing about prison or prisoners."

"Nothing?" he said as he shook his head.

"Nothing."

Writing enables Michael to transcend boundaries and connect with the society he longs to join. By writing about what he's learned from others, observed, and experienced, he's able to take meaningful steps to reform the system and show tax payers what the prison officials don't want them to see. As a writer, Michael feels relevant, more than a prisoner, and part of something bigger than himself. Despite this, he doesn't want to give the prison administration reason to uproot his wife's life again.

"Okay. I promise," he told her.

Michael spends his time educating himself and others. He still writes and interviews prisoners, but he plans to hold off on publishing any material until he and Carole are in a better position to do so. He mentors prisoners on how they can do their time better, and one person he takes a special liking to is a fellow inmate named Justin Paperny, a former Wall Street investment broker. Michael suggests steps that Justin can work to position himself for a new career as a speaker and consultant upon release and Justin is interested.

Michael shows Justin how he – Michael – reaches beyond prison boundaries to connect with the world by writing for his website. Justin starts his own website, JustinPaperny.com, and Michael suggests he write a manuscript. Justin writes an outline for a book titled, *Lessons From Prison*. He also tells his friend Brad Fullmer, a former pro baseball player, about Michael, and they want to invest in his career. Michael thinks about the offer, considering that his writing has earned more than $200,000 in after-tax earnings for his wife. Michael eventually negotiates a number and sells them ten percent of the Michael Santos brand's future earnings.

Justin is released on May 20, 2009, and as Michael has suggested, starts his own consulting company, where he will consult with and advise soon-to-be prisoners on what to expect when they enter the prison system. By January of 2010, Justin helps Michael secure a $150,000 grant for The Michael G. Santos Foundation so he could write a program for at-risk youth on how they can change and build a better future for themselves.

On September 11, 2010, Michael meets fellow prisoner Greg Reyes, CEO of Brocade Communications, a company worth billions. Greg is familiar with Michael because his family had been reading his website. Greg expresses to Michael how angry he is to be serving 18 months in prison over an honest mistake, and having his name dragged through the mud because of it.

"Why don't you use this time to write your story," Michael suggested. "Set the record straight, explaining in your own words exactly what happened. If you don't do it, the only record out there is going to be the government allegations."

"Writing isn't my strong suit," Greg explained to Michael.

"I'll help you," Michael urged. "This is an important project. You have to tell your story. If you can talk about it, I can help you write it in your own words. It would be a great project, carrying both of us through the next year."

"How would you see the project unfolding?" Greg asked, churning over the idea.

"It's simple. I'll ask you questions. Some of the questions may seem foolish and irrelevant, but I'll ask because I want to understand as much as you'll share. We'll talk every day for several hours. Early each morning, I'll write out notes of what I learned. After you've told me everything, I'll outline the story, try to put some structure around it. If I can tell it back to you, then we'll move forward with a more formal, chapter-by-chapter interview. I'll write a chapter, then read it to you. If you approve it, we'll move on to the next one and repeat the sequence until we've told the entire story."

"Let's do it," Greg said as he reached over and shook Michael's hand. That Christmas, Michael gave Carole a check for $45,000.

On Monday, August 13, 2012, Michael paroled from prison, and with over $100,000 in the bank, largely for the writing he did while in prison. Today he is a speaker, consultant, CEO of Prison Professor, real estate investor, and more. He continues to write books and is worth over a couple million dollars.

SHAKA SENGHOR: WRITING MY WRONGS

Shaka grew up on the east side of Detroit in the same neighborhood as street legends The Best Friends, Chambers Brothers, and White Boy Rick, where he sold crack during the 80s. After getting shot on March 8, 1990, Shaka became paranoid and vowed to never leave home without his gun. He ran the streets fuming with anger and despair.

"I had become obsessed with carrying a gun, treating my 9-millimeter Taurus like a crackhead treats his pipe," Shaka recalls. "I went to bed with my gun, woke up with it, and wouldn't so much as take a dump without it being in arm's reach. At the first sign of confrontation, I was ready to shoot."

And fourteen months after being shot, he would do just that –shoot a man to death.

Shaka was ultimately sentenced to "17 to 40 years" in prison. He went to prison angry at the world. One day, a fellow prisoner named O'Neal-El introduced Shaka to street lit. "He told me he was trying to finish a book he'd been writing about his old neighborhood. O'Neal-El was a member of the infamous drug crew Young Boys Incorporated, and his book was a collection of stories loosely based on his experience in the streets. He asked me if I wanted to read one of his stories, and I laughed at the idea of an inmate writing a book. But I didn't have anything else to do, so I said yes.

"When I started reading O'Neal-El's stories, I couldn't put them down. The stories were only 80 or 90 pages long, but they were detailed and vivid. When I finished, I felt like I had grown up alongside O'Neal-El and his crew, wearing Adidas Top Tens, fur-lined Max Julien coats, and wide-brimmed campaign hats."

When Shaka explained to O'Neal-El how much he enjoyed his book, O'Neal-El suggested Shaka check out the books by Donald Goines, also from Detroit. Shaka went to the prison library and checked out Goins's book Eldorado Red. When he got back to his cell and began to read, he was hooked from the first page. "Goines's vivid tale of inner-city life and the underground lottery had me in its spell, and his ability to articulate the pain of the streets validated the anger, frustration, and disappointment I felt toward life in the hood," Shaka said. "Goines placed me back on the streets of Detroit; he made me feel alive again. I read the whole thing that night.

"By the time my next callout came, I nearly ran to the library, and when I got there, it was as though the clerks had known I was coming. They had watched other inmates become intoxicated by Donald's work, and they knew I would be back. They smiled as they handed over *Dopefiend* and *Whoreson*, the books they had reserved for me. I took the books in my hand as though they were the Holy Grail and rushed back to my cell, where I proceeded to read through the day and late into the night. By the time I lay down at three in the morning, my eyes burned with strain. But I couldn't wait for sunlight so that I could keep indulging what was fast becoming my deepest passion."

Goines's books were not the only books Shaka read. He also read books by other prolific Black authors like Malcolm X, George Jackson, Angela Davis and more.

Eventually, while in the hole, Shaka discovered the magic of writing, first with letters. "It was through these letters that I realized writing could serve as a means of escape. With a pencil and a piece of paper, it was almost like I could travel outside of prison and go wherever I desired. I could stand on the corner in my neighborhood, and no one could stop me. I could drive down the freeway to see my ex-girlfriend in Ohio, and the bars and wired fences couldn't hold me back. Writing was freedom, so I wrote till my fingers were sore," Shaka says.

In 1994, while in Michigan Reformatory, Shaka decided to write an article for the prison newspaper about his sister's battle with crack addiction and how it made him feel. "I didn't give it much thought, but a month or so later, the article prompted a conversation that would change the course of my life."

When Shaka went to his work assignment the next day, his supervisor was reading the newspaper. "He kept looking up from the newspaper and then at me, with a curiosity that I hadn't recognized before."

"Shaka, did you really write this?" his supervisor asked.

"Yeah, I wrote it, Tom," he said with a chuckle.

"This is really good, Shaka. I want to take it home and share it with my wife."

"The next day he told me that his wife, who was a magazine editor, thought I had a future as a writer. I had never thought of writing as something to be taken seriously. I was serious about reading, of course, but the only future I could dream of was one where I simply got out of prison and went on with my life. I had never thought of becoming anything other than free.

"But Tom's words stayed with me. It had been a long time since someone had said something affirming about me that wasn't connected to violence. It made me feel like I could be good at something other than hustling drugs and hurting people."

Unfortunately, Shaka would end up in the hole again for hurting someone – a guard. But while there, he began a transformation, and in no small part due to another form of writing – journaling. "Each time I filled a page of my journal, I felt as if a great weight had been lifted. No longer did I feel the old familiar bitterness; I was learning a new way to get it out. No longer did I need to carry my anger around inside of me in a tight little ball, keeping me one provocation away from explosion."

Shaka also began to write books. The first one was a novel called *Shadowatchers*, which was about a group of young men and women who vow to make their neighborhood a better place after speaking to the ghosts of famous civil rights figures like Rosa Parks and Malcolm X. He also penned a novel called *Flagrant Foul*, which followed the story of a young woman who is sent to prison after getting into her boyfriend's car that turned out to be loaded with drugs.

By April 2004, Shaka was finally released from the hole, back into general population. "Once I got into general population, one of the first things I did was get a word processor and go straight to work typing out the books I had written on prison stationary while I was in the hole. By the time I was released, I was on my third novel, a detective story called *Crack*. It was my favorite of the three because it allowed me to take readers on a journey through the underbelly of street life.

"Day after day, I pecked away on my five-year-old word processor. Every thirteen pages, the memory would fill up, and I would have to print out all the pages, clear the memory, and start typing again. I was in a cell by myself, so I was able to sit for eight hours at a time typing. Still, it took several days of working from breakfast to lights-out for me to finish a manuscript."

Shortly after, Shaka was transferred to a lower-level prison. As he settled into his routine, he met a guy named Anthony Moorer who knew a lot about urban literature and had started a publishing company on the outside. "Anthony gave me a lot of pointers. He told me that if I saved up enough money, I could hire an editor and a graphic designer to publish the books I had written. He and I would walk to chow every day, talking about the future and how we would work together in the publishing business when we were released. Those conversations kept me inspired and motivated."Shaka began to read everything he could on self-publishing, the publishing business, etc.

Eventually, Shaka met a woman named Ebony who held him down and supported his writing dreams. They became romantically involved, and together started a publishing company called Drop a Gem Publishing, to print and release their first novel. In addition, they also partnered with HOPE to publish a book for children with incarcerated parents. Shaka also began to write for anthologies and national magazines.

Finally, after 19 years in the belly of the beast, Shaka was released on June 22, 2010. After getting reacquainted with family and friends, Shaka went to work trying to gain traction with his writing career.

This did not come easy. He was met be several challenges as he tried to hustle his books at local bookstores, and hoods that were not the safest places to be. Passionate about mentoring at-risk youth, he applied for a grant being offered by BMe (Black Male Engagement). "Ebony and I submitted a proposal for a twelve-week mentoring program that would teach at-risk youth to use writing to process their emotions and get at the root of their anger and frustration – an idea I had gotten after seeing two of my nephews and one of my childhood friends get shot the previous summer. My hope was that, with the guidance of a mentor and the self-examination I had discovered through literature, children in our community could begin making sense of their environment and receive the love, acceptance, and guidance that they needed to thrive.

"A month after submitting my proposal, I got the news that I was one of the winners of the BMe Challenge. I couldn't wait to implement the project at the schools where I had been mentoring."

In 2013, Shaka published his memoir, *Writing My Wrongs: Life, Death, and Redemption in an American Prison*, under his publishing company, Drop a Gem Publishing. It's a "page-turning portrait of life in the shadow of poverty, violence, and fear; an unforgettable story of redemption, reminding us that our worst deeds don't define us." The book was so successful, it was picked up by Convergent Books, an imprint of

Crown Publishing Group, who would republish it in 2016. The book would go on to become a *New York Times* Bestseller, and also in 2016, Oprah would name Shaka as one of her Super Soul 100 lists of visionaries and influential leaders. Because of Shaka's work in the community and courage to share his story, he's received fellowships at the MIT Media Lab and the Kellogg Foundation, and he's been invited to speak at events like TED and the Aspen Ideas Festival. He lectures regularly at universities, is a leading voice on criminal justice reform, and is working on his next book.

STANLEY "TOOKIE" WILLIAMS: THE WRITE TO REDEMPTION

Stanley "Tookie" Williams cofounded the notorious Crips street gang in 1971, at the age of 17, with fellow teenager Raymond Washington. By 1981, Tookie was on California's death row at San Quentin State Prison after being convicted or two robberies and four murders.

While doing a seven-year stint in the "hole" after confidential informants said he was plotting a gang war, Tookie began to reflect on life and the path he'd taken that landed him on death row. He decided he wanted to warn kids about the dangers and consequences of gang life, and he began to write a series of books directed toward the youth titled *Tookie Speaks Out Against Gangs*.

In 1993, Tookie was contacted by Barbara Becnel, a full-time writer of books and magazine articles, who was researching a book about the Crips street gang. She wanted to meet with Tookie to get a better understanding on how the Crips had gotten started. But Tookie had a request: He wanted to know if she could get his children's books published; books that would help them avoid gangs and make better choices than he did. He didn't want to die and leave the Crips street gang as his only legacy.

Tookie and Barbara became great friends. She got her interview and Tookie ultimately got his children's books published. He published ten anti-gang books under the title *Tookie Speaks Out Against Gangs*. Tookie was contacted by several major New York publishers asking him to write books for adults that depicted in coarse language and graphic scenes, stories about gang shootings, murder, and the culture of gangsters, but he refused, instead wanting to focus on his books for children and desire to end gang violence. He wrote a 25-page booklet providing sample peace treaties along with a step-by-step process for how to gain the support of gang leaders so they can stop street violence in his "Tookie's Protocol for Street Peace" endeavor.

Tookie's writing did not stop there. He also wrote *Life in Prison*, a book that teaches kids that real prison life is a brutal, lonely, and life-threatening place. "It's nothing like the movies," he wrote. Tookie's work to create street peace despite being on death row won him many honors, including five nominations for the Nobel Peace Prize, and four nominations for the Nobel Prize for Literature. Tookie also wrote his memoir, *Blue Rage, Black Redemption*, which was turned into a television movie starring Jaime Foxx titled *Redemption: The Stan Tookie Williams Story*.

Tookie was eventually put to death on December 13, 2005, but today his legacy lives on, not only because he cofounded the Crips, but because of the writing he did in prison. Though originally published in 1996, his books for children are still used in libraries and classrooms throughout the United States, even to this day.

DONALD GOINES: THE BLACK GANGSTER

Donald Goines is considered by many to be the Godfather of street lit. Many of today's street lit stars including Kwame "Dutch" Teague, have been inspired by him. Born in Detroit to a relatively comfortable family, he attended Catholic elementary school and was expected to go into his family's dry-cleaning business. Instead, after lying about his age, he enlisted in the U.S. Air Force. He served between 1952 and 1955, and during this time got hooked on heroin. When he returned home to Detroit, from Japan, he was a full-blown heroin addict. For the next 15 years, as a result of his addiction, he would spend his time pimping, robbing, stealing, bootlegging, and doing time. His seven prison sentences totaled 6.5 years.

While in jail in the 60s, Donald decided he was going to pick up the pen and start writing books. A huge fan of cowboy movies, he tried penning western novels, but was unable to find much success. A few years later, however, while in prison again, he was introduced to the work of Iceberg Slim. Iceberg Slim, another convict and pimp turned author, had decided he was too old for the pimp game, and with encouragement from his wife, wrote his autobiography, *Pimp: The Story of My Life*, which was published by Holloway House in 1967. This inspired Goines to write his semi-autobiographical novel, *Whoreson*, which he would eventually get Iceberg Slim's publisher to publish in 1972.

When Goines was released in 1970, he went hard on the writing tip. His pace was remarkable, sometimes producing a book a month. He worked on a strict schedule where he would write every morning, then devote the rest of the day to heroin. Hoping to go straight and avoid the dilemmas he faced in Detroit, he moved with his family to the Los Angeles ghetto of Watts. Though Goines's books sold well, he did not receive much critical attention, and after two years of being in Los Angeles, he moved back to Detroit. Unfortunately, after only a couple years back in Detroit, on October 21, 1974, he and his wife were shot to death in a scene straight from one of his novels. The identity of the killers is unknown, but it's rumored that Donald and his wife were murdered over a drug debt.

JAILHOUSE PUBLISHING

Over the course of his career, Donald Goines would go on to write sixteen novels, all of which gave vivid details about crime, the ghetto, prostitution, gang lords, sex, drugs, murder, and other elements of the underworld, all of which he knew from firsthand experience. Some of his books have even been made into movies, such as *Never Die Alone*, which stars DMX. Though he was never able to shake the hold heroin had on him, he's regarded today as one of America's best and most influential Black writers, most certainly in the genre of street lit, and it all started when he decided to put pen to paper while in prison.

PAUL WRIGHT: PRISON LEGAL NEWS

Once a year, Paul Wright leaves his offices in Lake Worth and heads to a classroom at Yale University to talk about prison law. He's a national authority, yet he's not a lawyer.

He's the founder, editor and publisher of *Prison Legal News*, a national trade publication for people behind bars, their families and their lawyers. He began it in 1990 when he was in prison himself – for murder.

Back in 1982, Wright's future had been bright. He graduated Lake Worth High in a speedy three years. The young man set his sights on a career in law enforcement and eventually became a military police officer stationed in Washington.

But the pay wasn't great and in a rash moment he decided it'd be quick money to rob a drug dealer.

The drug dealer pulled a gun and Wright fired his.

The worst phone call in his life soon followed, when he had to dial up his parents to tell them he was sitting in jail charged with killing a man. "Your son's a cop," Wright recalled. "You don't expect him to be calling from jail."

He was sentenced to 25 years.

Who knows how it would have turned out if not for a box of cereal?

"I'd been inside about two years; a guard dumped a box of Cap'n Crunch on the floor of my cell. I'm making like $50 a month in the kitchen. The box is 10 percent of your salary," Wright recalled. He was outraged. "That sent me to the law library."

It turns out, he didn't have a lot of options. "I was pretty much screwed. But that's what got me asking, 'What are prisoner rights and what can be done?'"

Finding his voice behind bars...

Paul Wright, 51, grew up in Lake Worth. His dad, Rollin Wright, was a U.S. postal worker and along with Paul's mom Zuraya ran the Aztec Stamp and Coin shop downtown until it closed in the early 2000s. They subscribed to their hometown paper, The Palm Beach Post. Wright figures he started reading it when he was in sixth grade. Both parents and son landed in its feature pages for their hobbies.

But newspapering wasn't in Paul Wright's plan. Nor was being prisoner No. 930783 at the Clallam Bay Corrections Center in Washington state.

"In some respects, I was fortunate. I've never been beaten, never been raped or stabbed. But I've seen it happen to others," Wright said.

When he first saw it happen, a prisoner beaten by guards, Wright alerted the media – and was ignored. If they weren't going to write it up, he decided he would – with a typewriter, some 8 1/2 x 11 paper and a volunteer to run off copies at Kinkos.

Co-founded with fellow prisoner Ed Mead, the first *Prison Legal News* issue ran 10 pages and contained more than 20 articles, including an explainer of a court ruling that eased a path to inmates' legal research, and another that rallied readers to come together in class action suit over how parole hearings were conducted. A convicted rapist penned poem title *The Terror*. And at the top corner of page 7: A letter from the editors.

"Welcome to the first edition of *Prisoners' Legal News*." (The title later got an edit.)

Don't want to be on the mailing list? "Write to our outside address and say so." Wright's dad, with his postal experience, agreed to be the mail clerk.

They asked readers to help them build a long-term agenda – things to fight for, perhaps the right to vote. "By working to extend democracy to prisoners we can change from being mere criminals to the defenders of democracy."

The founders eventually parted ways – once released, the terms of Mead's parole barred him from associating with felons like Wright. His appeal on the matter failed and Wright was left to carry on with the cadre of other confined contributors.

"I never really thought about writing until I went to prison," said Wright, who likes to note that his degree in Soviet History became obsolete when the Soviet Union collapsed three years after he got it. "Like most Americans, I didn't think I had a lot to say."

Not only did he find his voice behind bars, he was the voice for others, said David C. Fathi, director of the American Civil Liberties Union's National Prison Project. Fathi was working for another advocacy organization in Washington when he met Wright.

"He took it upon himself to help prisoners," Fathi said. "Paul put himself at significant risk of retaliation to stand up for fellow prisoners. His courage is astounding."

Standing up has sometimes meant exposing the system and its flaws in print. "We've broken a lot of stories," Wright said.

Creative thinker, strategist...

A favorite example: In 1994, *Prison Legal News* readers learned that in his run for office, then-Washington congressman Jack Metcalf used prison telemarketers to conduct a phony poll that painted his opponent as soft on crime. "He was using convicted rapists and child molesters to do this for him," Wright said.

The congressman wasn't alone. *PLN,* as it is sometimes called, also has outed Nintendo, Starbucks, Boeing and Microsoft for tapping prison labor at one time or another.

The magazine exposed price gouging in the lucrative prison phone industry. Beginning in 1992, the magazine revealed how prison phone company rates took a financial toll on the families of those incarcerated. The stories were influential in prompting federal rate caps and other reforms in 2013 and 2015.

At other times, standing up meant filing a lawsuit.

A lot of work is done through the non-profit organization to publish PLN and advocate on other fronts, the Human Rights Defense Center, with Wright as its executive director.

"Deaf prisoners get interpreters because of a lawsuit I filed," he said.

And the only lawsuit to successfully challenge those phone company practices was filed by Wright's ex-wife, a HRDC board member, and his mother in Seattle in 2000. Notes Wright: "It settled in 2013 for $46 million." And sometimes, he took another route altogether.

"Paul is one of the most creative thinkers and strategists," the ACLU's Fathi said, recalling the time when Wright foiled his prison guards using the U.S. Fish and Wildlife Service.

The guards at Clallam Bay Corrections Center were beating prisoners, said Wright.

"No one would do anything about that, but then one day guards went around with sticks and were destroying the nests and eggs of birds in the eaves of the prison," Wright said. The birds, however, were a protected species. "So, I complained to the federal Fish and Wildlife Service and they were at the prison within two days telling the staff they would be arrested if they destroyed any nests or harmed any birds. No such luck on the prisoner beatings."

For his efforts, Wright said he was retaliated against "on pretty much every level" for the bulk of the time he was in prison.

"I filed four retaliation lawsuits and only won one of them so I figured it goes with the territory... I was subjected to retaliatory transfers, placed in segregation, denied visits with my family, subjected to bogus write-ups, etc. And that is kind of how I got to be good at litigation, especially around the First Amendment and discipline hearing issues."

He found his life's work...

His career in law enforcement was forever derailed, but Wright had found a calling.

That calling incidentally fanned his love life as well. One of his subscribers was on the outside and wanted to write a book. She came to visit Wright. The two eventually married and had two boys courtesy of conjugal visits.

His oldest son, Carl, was 10 days old when he first set eyes on dad. His second son, Felix, came for a visit earlier – day 4.

Retelling this information, Wright ticks off numbers to attest that his family wasn't alone. "Eighty percent of prisoners in this country are also a parent. That's several million kids."

Wright got out in 2003, after serving 17 years of his sentence. He could've given up advocacy and writing.

His cousin had an 'in' at General Motors selling cars to dealerships. Another relative was an investment banker, who said, "You know Paul, you need to get a real job," Wright recalled.

Wright wasn't interested. He'd found the job. He just didn't know if he could earn a living.

"My target audience is among the poorest in the nation and in some areas the least literate," said Wright.

But his potential audience has done nothing but multiply. In 1990, the number of people in jail, state of federal prison hit 1 million. On the eve of Wright's release, the number had surpassed 2 million.

And fear that he could not make a go of a bare bone's magazine printed on gray newsprint with nary a photograph proved unfounded.

The magazine's home base has moved around a bit from a cell in Washington with a P.O. box in Lake Worth, to a home in Vermont and back to Lake Worth in 2013 after Wright's divorce from both his wife and northern winters. (His father died in 2012, but his mother still lives here.)

Not only does the magazine support Wright full time, its payroll now boasts 15 full-time employees, 13 of whom work out of offices on Lucerne Avenue.

Wright and his staff have produced 306 issues and counting – 26 years of monthly magazines.

PLN regularly tops 70 pages. They print and mail some 12,000 copies to subscribers who then pass it around. The readership is estimated at 70,000 – about 65 percent of whom live in federal or state prison. (Subscribe from the inside? Your rate is $30 a year. A lawyer or other professional or institution? That will be $90.)

Another 120,000 to 150,000 read *PLN* online each month.

"By the mid-2000s our subscribers pretty much mirrored prison populations," he said. States with more prisoners are states with more subscribers. But while *PLN* has thrived, other publications folded. Where once, each state had a publication to two – or six in California – only *PLN* is left.

"Pretty much, we're it, which I think is pretty sad. I think having a monopoly is pretty sad."

Still fighting the state of Florida...

Tom Julin, a Miami attorney whose specialty is first amendment rights, calls Wright's work incredible.

"His organization is really the only organization in the country that tries to make sure prisoners have the kind of information he gets to them," said Julin. "He's fought battle after battle across the country and won."

By one count in the *American Bar Association Journal*, Wright and his team have fought prison and jail officials in at least 30 states who have tried to ban *Prison Legal News*. Their reasons are what lawyers including Julin like to call "spurious."

The ACLU's Fathi recalled, "In one case in which we represented *PLN*, the institution claimed the magazine had to be excluded because it's held together with staples." The staples, the argument went, were problematic. "We pointed out that the jail also sold legal pads that also had staples."

PLN and its lawyers have obtained consent decrees in 10 states that prevent prison officials from failing to deliver the newsletter to inmate subscribers, the Journal reported.

The one case it continues to fight? The one in its home state, where Florida's Department of Corrections refuses to deliver *PLN* to subscribers on the inside.

It is a case that dates back to 2003, when corrections authorities put an end to a history of inmates receiving the magazine in the mail. They argued that *PLN's* ads for pen pals, three-way calling services and postage stamps posed a security threat. The DOC then relented in 2005, telling a judge it would cease censoring based on ad content, only to halt delivery again.

The case is now awaiting a ruling from the Eleventh Circuit Court of Appeals and has attracted the attention of former U.S. Solicitor General Paul Clement, a high-profile attorney.

"That tells you about the importance of the issue in the case that Clement would take it," said Julin, whose former firm attempted to file a friend of the court brief in the case. "Clement is hugely in demand. That's a real signal that it's a Supreme Court-worthy case."

Wright isn't measuring his success by court rulings.

In fact, when he looks at the landscape as a whole for prisoners and prison rights the picture looks bleaker than the day, he went in.

"Brutality and beatings remain our biggest subjects. Medical and mental health care takes up more than 50 percent of our coverage. Every three years for the past 15 years or so, it's time for a story about prisoners being raped by guards. There's the notion it's just a few bad apples, but when you come to the conclusion the whole orchard is rotten? Then there's child support. It's one thing to lock up criminals, it's another thing to lock up someone whose crime is not paying."

Still, Wright remains proud of the work.

He counts the changes in prison phone rate rules as one of *PLN's* biggest accomplishments. "One of our goals is making sure we're relevant to our readers and their lives."

Said Julin: "Most people who leave prison don't look back. He's remembered all those left behind and really tried to improve their fate. It's so important for their mental health to know someone still cares for them and is looking out for them."

[Originally published by *Palm Beach Post*, Friday, Dec. 9, 2016]

ALARIC HUNT: CUTS THROUGH BONE

In 2011, a St. Martin's Press subsidiary called Minotaur Books held a private-eye novel writing contest with a $10,000 prize and a guaranteed publishing contract. The winner was Alaric Hunt, 44 at the time, a literary phenom, and unbeknownst to Minotaur, a prisoner in a maximum-security facility in Bishop, South Carolina. He'd been serving a life sentence for murder since 1988, but he was also a really good writer; good enough that Minotaur overlooked his... "situation."

Hunt wrote his book, *Cuts Through Bone*, in two longhand drafts, then typed it on a typewriter. Three years later, it was released, and is now available on Amazon. (Note: South Carolina has repealed its own Son of Sam law and allows prisoners to profit from their work, so there were no legal complications.)

Here's an excerpt from *Cuts Through Bone* so you can see what type of thing was successful for Hunt. Can you do something like this, or maybe even better?

CUTS THROUGH BONE

The blare of car horns from Thirty-fourth Street in midtown Manhattan leaked through two tall windows on the far end of the rectangular office. Rachel Vasquez was annoyed, but she only glanced across her jumbled desk at her boss, Clayton Guthrie, before turning back to her computer monitor. In the three months that the young Puerto Rican woman had worked for the little detective, he hadn't done much detecting. The job that started the spring as a godsend was becoming a curse. Clayton Guthrie was crazy. Three days before, Vasquez had gone home intending to quit, but intention was as close as she came.

That morning had started easily. Vasquez drove Guthrie's old blue Ford while they followed a couple around downtown Manhattan. The man was a short, muscular Italian, with gold chains glinting on his dark, hairy neck. He had a prize-winning glare that moved people around him like chess pieces. Vasquez found him easy to dislike. The woman was taller, with light brown hair that glowed like butter when the morning sunshine touched it. She dangled her rounded curves before the Italian like presents, gift-wrapped in a short white skirt and a clinging blue top, but her pinched expression changed to a smile only when he was looking.

Vasquez thought the couple was gangster-movie comic, but Guthrie watched and filmed with the soberness of a government employee. The detectives wore walkie-talkie earpieces like Secret Service agents, and Vasquez had a second camera tucked into her jacket pocket while she drove.

After a morning spent slowly shopping boutiques in SoHo and TriBeCa, the couple stopped for lunch at an upscale grill on a corner of Broome Street. Their table was on the outside corner, and visible through front windows on both streets. Guthrie left Vasquez to film from the front of a shoe store on Broome, and he hurried around the corner to shoot from the other side. The angry Italian and his simpering mistress settled at their table and ordered. Vasquez filmed. Her view was so clear, she could see every gold tooth in the man's busy mouth.

Partway through lunch, the Italian made a phone call. The street traffic was light, mostly Yuppies taking their cell phones for a walk. Vasquez filled her time by guessing whether passersby would enter the grill, and counting the number of taxis that passed without a fare. She despised surveillance. Guthrie tired of her monologue, and reminded her she was on a mike by asking if she would rather be driving a taxi. Several more minutes passed before Vasquez understood that the Italian in the restaurant had spotted her. He started laughing and pointed at her. His mistress turned around to look; the last thing Vasquez caught on video was the woman's terrified smile.

A heavyset young Italian gripped Vasquez's right arm and whipped her around. "Hey there!" he exclaimed, a happy note in his voice. "Whatcha doing?" A drooping mustache concealed most of his mouth. His face was rough like a concrete block, and his shoulders had layers like a vault door. Another young Italian in a jogging suit stood beside him. He wasn't as big, but he looked equally amused.

"Let me go!" Vasquez demanded. After a moment, she emphasized with a knee aimed at his crotch, but he turned it aside with his thigh.

"We got a fighter here," he rumbled. As always, some pedestrians hunched their shoulders and hurried away, while the others craned for a better view. The scuffle was brief. A skinny teenaged Puerto Rican girl with a long black ponytail didn't burn much time on the fight cards of two Italian heavyweights. They wanted the camera; they took it. Vasquez's ears were ringing before Guthrie arrived, but she held a grip on the bigger thug's wrist, trying to reach past his long arm with a punch.

The big Italian with the mustache tossed Vasquez against the window of the shoe store, but he stumbled as he rushed Guthrie. Vasquez watched as the little detective drew back an open hand. After a thunderclap, the big Italian slid to his hands and knees.

"Yo, Dave, what happened?" he muttered.

Guthrie stepped over to the other thug and snatched Vasquez's camera from his hand before bending to pluck his crumpled brown fedora from the man's face. Vasquez pushed herself away from the storefront window as the Italians struggled to their feet. She could hear the sounds of traffic again. She aimed a few cheap kicks at them as they scrambled down the sidewalk. Bystanders hooted and catcalled, and a clerk rushed out of the shoe store.

Across the street, the couple was watching from the window of the grill. The Italian was livid, pointing at them while he shouted into his phone. Standing on the sidewalk, just inside the edge of shade from the strong July sunshine running down the middle of Broome Street, Guthrie dusted off his fedora and punched it back into shape. His face twisted in disgust when he glanced inside—fresh speckles of blood decorated the silk. He flapped it against his leg instead of putting it on his head.

Once they were back in the old Ford, the little man caught Vasquez's chin and held it while he scowled and inspected her face. "You ain't too bad," he said.

She shook him off and started the car, pulling out just before a patrol car turned into the intersection at the corner of Broome Street. She wiped her stinging nose with the back of her hand and checked for blood.

"How in hell did they sneak up on you anyway?" Guthrie asked. "I thought you grew up on the Lower East."

"You're *loco, viejo*." Vasquez barked. "They got up on me since you didn't warn me I should be looking! Who the hell was that?" "Or maybe you were too busy counting taxis?"

"Screw that. You should've told me he was connected. Why are you watching him anyway?" "We were watching *her*."

Vasquez pounded the steering wheel and poured out some rapid curses in Spanish. The detective laughed at her, and fired some more that she hadn't used. Discovering that he spoke Spanish startled her into quiet.

"Maybe I should have warned you about my suspicions," he said after a minute. The old Ford rolled past Washington Square. "And maybe you should've just paid attention. He spotted you, so you blew it—hugs and kisses won't make it sound better. You gotta see that, Rachel. This's a tough job, but I got faith in you. You're a smart girl. You'll figure it out."

Vasquez went home angry, intending to quit after her next check, but she had forgotten about the marks on her face. Billboard advertisements would've drawn less attention in her parents' tenement apartment that night. Even her brothers kept quiet, staring at her face with shocked and angry looks. Papi recounted his top twenty-seven reasons she should be applying for college, finishing with a final silent finger gesture at her face. At that point, she discovered she was determined to keep working for Clayton Guthrie. Late that night, after the apartment was quiet, Vasquez's mother came to the open door of her bedroom. She stood silently, as if thinking of something to say, but only sighed and walked quietly away.

So, Rachel Vasquez didn't quit, and her immediate reward was returning to the study of video-surveillance tapes. After which the little man grilled her like a sandwich to see if she had noticed everything, he wanted her to notice – *without* telling her in advance what he meant her to notice. Clayton Guthrie was crazy. The quiet in his office was driving Vasquez crazy. At least the blare of horns on Thirty-fourth Street below them meant something was happening – kids were pushing racks of clothes on the street and slowing the traffic. That was an everyday occurrence in the Garment District. She glanced across the jumbled desk at Guthrie again. Then someone knocked on the office door.

Beyond a square of mismatched furniture, a shape behind the frosted glass window filled it almost completely. The door swung open after one brief knock. A tall silver-haired man in an ash gray suit stepped inside, followed by a young woman in a navy dress. Guthrie dropped his magazine onto his desk blotter. "Good afternoon, Mr. Whitridge," he said.

The office was well-lit. The desks each faced a couch, squared across a low coffee table littered with books and magazines. Vasquez's desk faced a wall of green paint over plasterwork, split by the frosted outer door, and an oxblood leather couch that belonged to a bygone era, when the entire room had been better dressed. The other couch, overlooked by the tall windows, was ratty brown faux fur. Another remnant of the previous aristocratic era was dark wooden wainscoting on the walls, interrupted by the outer door, and a pair of dark wooden doors behind Guthrie's desk – a supply closet and a bathroom.

The tall silver-haired man, Mr. Whitridge, seemed about the same age as Clayton Guthrie – in his middle years – but he was tailored and distinguished. His gray suit fit him as neatly as a general's dress uniform. A similar number of years left Guthrie rumpled. He was short and slight, and though his soldier-length hair was mostly dark, a dusting of gray seemed to load him down. A dark brown fedora rested on his desktop, and he wore a long-sleeved white shirt tucked into dark trousers. Whitridge stepped around and sat down on the oxblood couch. Moving and seated, the tall man had the perfect carriage of an aristocrat; Guthrie was his workingman opposite, down to the final detail of a relaxed slouch.

Vasquez wore a Yankees cap set crooked on her head, blue jeans, and a red windbreaker with the cuffs pushed up to her elbows. Her ears jutted like open car doors, because her long black hair was tied in a ponytail. The young woman with Whitridge was wearing a loose navy tea dress that couldn't hide rolling curves that had gone out of fashion after Marilyn Monroe. She was pale and blue-eyed, with chocolate brown hair pulled into a short tail with a navy ribbon, like a bloom behind her ear. Despite the curves and clothes, she was plain. Vasquez was dressed like a boy, and slim as a whip, but her dark eyebrows and sharp jaw took her long steps past merely pretty, into the realm of beautiful. The fading marks on her face only made her seem determined, not breakable. The young woman hesitated, then sat down on the brown faux-fur couch.

"Where's Weitz?" the tall man asked after glancing around the office

"She had enough, I reckon," Guthrie said. "This's Rachel Vasquez, my new operative."

Whitridge measured the young Puerto Rican with a glance, then tipped her a diplomat's smile. "I think Michelle may explain this situation better than I would," he said.

Guthrie nodded.

"You're a private detective, right?" the young woman demanded.

"Sort of," Guthrie replied.

Michelle frowned, thinking about it. Her face came to life suddenly became more than ordinary, while deciding that "sort of" was good enough. "I need you to find out who killed my cousin," she said. "The police think they know who did it, but they're wrong."

The videotape on Vasquez's monitor continued running, but she paid no attention. She was listening hard. The job she had taken that spring started with her expecting something serious. Clayton Guthrie was a private detective, and somewhere he found enough power to break laws – enough to buy a teenager a gun and supply her with a carry permit. The first month, she spent six hours a day at an indoor pistol range. The little detective drank coffee, loaded bullets into clips, and timed her with a stopwatch as he flipped targets and shouted "Draw!" Vasquez fired the Smith & Wesson Chiefs Special until both of her wrists ached, because he made her switch hands. The practice suggested something serious in the future, with the same kind of unspoken language as the revolver Guthrie kept hidden in the bottom drawer of his desk.

Then more months passed watching surveillance videos, or sitting in a park or on the street watching passersby do nothing. They ran background checks, which meant finding people and asking them what they thought of someone else, investigating references on résumés to see if they were real people and real companies, and determining whether people paid taxes or had criminal records. Vasquez supposed that was detective work. Maybe people could earn a living doing that. But that wasn't the job she'd expected when Guthrie had handed her the pistol and said, "Hitting what you fire at should be as easy as drawing breath." Now two office visitors and one asked-aloud question were enough to erase Vasquez's boredom and awaken her expectation.

Guthrie gave the young brunette a surprised look. He glanced at Whitridge, then asked, "You mean the Bowman murder?"

"That's right. No *way* Greg kill her, but they arrested him last night...." She trailed to a stop, puzzle.

Before she could ask another question, Guthrie said, "It's a society murder – your society." The detective threw another incredulous glance at Whitridge.

"Oh. I asked Uncle Harry for help, and you're the help. I suppose you'd better be good." She gave Guthrie the once-over, measuring the small man against his advance billing. "Well?"

Guthrie nodded. "I hear you, miss," he said, "but I wonder if you're reading the papers. This guy, they took him in on the Bowman murder, but I shouldn't need to say they're looking at him for all of it.

"But he *didn't!*" she insisted.

Camille Bowman's murder had been the lead headline in every city paper for a week, the latest in a dead cast of characters. She was eye-catchingly blond and beautiful, another young woman murdered and dumped, without an obvious suspect. The newshounds called them "Barbie doll murders," because the victims had been beautiful. For the media, the killings were a carnival, complete with lurking villain, the smell of sex, and a paper chase. New developments were impossible to miss.

"I have sent the young man a lawyer," Whitridge volunteered.

"The lawyer doesn't have a guy? What about him?"

Whitridge smiled. "The law firm doesn't specialize in criminal matters, I'm afraid. That isn't ordinarily useful to me. Then the police found a gun."

"A gun?" Guthrie asked, settling back into his chair.

"See, you think he's guilty," the young woman said. "The police are wrong, too! Greg didn't do it! He loved her!" She dropped back onto the furry brown couch when Whitridge patted her shoulder a few times.

The silver-haired man's face was grim, his thoughts unvoiced. "Can you take care of this?" he asked.

Guthrie nodded. "I'll be all over it."

"Thank you," Whitridge said.

Vasquez went to the office window and looked down at Thirty-fourth Street in time to see Whitridge and his niece climb into a chauffeured Town Car. For once, the street hadn't been blocked by kids trucking racks of clothes. The horns stopped blaring when the Town Car pulled away. "Who the hell is he?" she asked.

"HP Whitridge" Guthrie said. "Harry Edward Whitridge."

CURTIS DAWKINS: THE GRAYBAR HOTEL

In 2004, Curtis Dawkins dressed up in a gangster costume, smoked some crack, then went on a rampage in Kalamazoo, Michigan and shot Thomas Brown to death. After a stand-off with SWAT, he was taken into custody. He confessed, and was eventually sentenced to life in prison without parole.

After his arrest, he felt suicidal. But after about a year, he began writing fiction, which took his mind off his problems. His parents sent him a typewriter, so he started typing his stories and sending them to his sister. His sister began submitting them, many of which took place in jails or prisons, to small journals. Eventually, Jarrett Haley, the founder of *Bull*, a small literary magazine which published Dawkins, helped him gather and edit a collection of 14 short prison stories, as well as an agent, to represent him. The agent later sold the collection/book, which they titled *The Graybar Hotel*, to Scribner, a major publishing house, in 2016, for $150,000. Yes: 150 thousand dollars. When the book was published, critics said Dawkins was "a gifted stylist."

In my research for this book, I bought *The Graybar Hotel* to get an idea for what kind of writing and stories Scribner was willing to pay $150,000 for. The book is 5.25" x 8", 206 pages, and I'd say, roughly 70,000 words. After reading the book I found the Dawkins is indeed a great writer, style wise; however, if I'm totally honest, I found most of the stories to be "basic," and boring. When I think "prison stories," I think of gang activity, violence, drugs, plottin', plannin', schemin' and scammin', but maybe that's because I'm from California, and I've done all my time on level 4s, where that's what prison life is like. *The Graybar Hotel* is not at all like that. However, he got $150,000 for it, the biggest deal I personally know of a prisoner ever getting for a book, so if that's what the big dogs want to cut the check for, as a writer, this is something we need to pay attention to.

Here's an excerpt of *The Graybar Hotel* (what I found to be the most interesting part) so you can get an idea of Dawkins' style, and what Scribner was willing to pay all that money for. Can you do something like this, or, perhaps, better?

DEPAKOTE MO

His name was Maurice. A new guy in the cell next to mine. We could still smoke when I met him.

This was during the Great Tobacco Fiasco of 2009, after the state issued a mandate to phase out smoking in Michigan prisons. The amount of tobacco we could buy from the commissary was slowly dwindling down to none by the end of the year. In theory, stepping down was the way to stop, but addiction and theory work together about as well as children and fireworks.

Our block had seen an ever-increasing list of casualties and vanishings due to the rationing. Maurice replaced a thin, white man named Doo Wop, a lifelong smoker who by November found himself deep in debt. By then we could buy just a single two-ounce pouch of Bugler a week. But Doo-Wop hadn't cut back his smoking at all, buying pouches inflated at ten times the normal $2.50. The nonsmokers had banded together to form a brutal black market. Debt-laden addicts were regularly beaten up by clean-lunged thugs.

The nonsmokers let Doo-Wop run up his bill because they knew he was good for it. He'd been in the same cell, at the same kitchen job for a decade. You could ask anybody and they'd tell you, Doo-Wop is an old-school convict – a stand-up guy, his word gold. But two nights ago he locked up, which means he walked up to a CO and said, I owe a bunch of money and I'm afraid. After that they have to protect you. They put you in the hole until a bed is found at another prison. Slim said, "At least he's stopped smoking now." It was true, but inside I shuddered to think about quitting cold turkey down in segregation.

As for me, I owed $150 was paying it down steady with my hustle: tattoos and hand-painted cards. This was the boom time of year too – Christmas cards. My most popular card this year sold for $2. It was Snoopy wearing a glittery Santa suit with an armful of gifts and Woodstock perched on his shoulder. I'd been drawing Peanuts characters since grade school.

I'd invested twenty dollars in supplies from a mail-order catalog: card stock, glitter, paint, and glue. I figured I could triple that easily over the season, then buy some more Badger calligraphy ink for tattoos and be out of debt by spring. Badger was the only ink we could get, and it was decent but expensive. I'd tried other options on myself – ink from a Bic, a needle through typewriter ribbon, and acrylic paint that my skin rejected in painful, itchy welts. I had been out of Badger for a month, and the best thing I'd come up with since was burning bergamot hair grease inside my locker, letting the threads of black smoke rise and collect into a thick, oily

soot that I mixed with spit until it was the consistency of used motor oil.

I had made enough of this for Homer's tattoo when Slim – my bunkie and lookout – said someone was coming down the hail with his duffel bag. "And his head's wrapped in something," he said.

"Like a turban?" Homer asked. He'd just told me he wanted "13 ½" on his left arm. The "13 ½" code for an inmate who had twelve fuckhead jurors, one shithead judge, and a half assed defense attorney, adding up to a life sentence. I know for a taken a plea deal for operating a meth lab. But I'm not in a tattoo. I owed Homer twenty-five dollars for one pouch of Bugler and the "12 ½" was going to wipe my slate clean. With him, anyway.

Slim didn't answer. He just told us to be quiet and I shut off the cassette motor that powered my needle. The man who passed looked like just another inmate to me. I noticed his head, though. It was wrapped in white gauze with a few inches of afro sticking out of the gaps. "Hey," Slim said. "What happened to your head?'

"Burned." His cell door opened electronically.

"How do you burn your own head?"

I had seen a lot of men come to prison wrapped in gauze, but it was usually the hands wrapped up in thick white mittens, a mistake in a meth lab.

The new neighbor walked into his cell and didn't say anything. "Chatty guy, ain't he?" said Slim, before he walked next door. Our cells were open from two a.m. until ten p.m., a sort of pseudofreedom to make up for our lack of access to the yard outside.

The thing about homemade tattoo ink was that it kept clogging the Bic barrel. I had the standard setup: a motor stripped from a Walkman, cradled in a bent-up chow spork, connected to a guitar string threaded through the empty Bic. Just as good as anything on the outside. It only takes more time. We may not have much in here, but we've got plenty of time.

I had to blow out the clogged Bic barrel four times before I'd even finished the outline of Homer's bogus number. Slim had come back by then and we all smoked. He told me the new guy's name. Ten months ago, Maurice and a friend had been in a '78 Lincoln Continental transformed into a mobile drug lab cooking small batches of some new shit Slim could barely pronounce. It was flammable, of course, and between that and the propane stove they used, soon enough that Lincoln turned into an inferno. Mo had been taking a piss outside the door. His friend was in the backseat, dead.

"Burned while pissing," I said, watching smoke rise from the end of my cigarette. Every time I smoke now, I felt a pang of sadness. I tried to memorize every part of the experience, like a loved one I knew was going away. I focused on those thin, silky gray curves I'd never see again.

"Yeah. His forehead nearly melted off. And now he has seizures." Slim took a deep drag then blew the smoke toward the exhaust vent above the stainless-steel toilet. "He said the blast cooked part of his brain."

"What?"

"He takes some drug." Slim yelled out into the hall, "Yo, Maurice, what's that stuff you take?"

"Depakote," came the answer.

The world of prison is upside down. Someone who had blown up his car while cooking drugs would probably be an outcast even in today's shallow, do-nothing-and-become-famous culture, but in prison that guy will be someone of stature. Especially a high-profile case like Maurice's. If your case makes the news, you're a minor celebrity in here, an Arsenio Hall or Jon Levitz.

It was nearly dinner and I had already smoked the 10 cigarettes I allowed myself I rolled two more for the night along with the ten for the next day. Maybe tomorrow I'd do better.

$$$$$

I'd been sleeping in later and later – mostly because it was a good way to keep from smoking. I woke from a dream where I was in the backseat of an old car, and in the front two men kept cooking something, filling bag after bag of tobacco, handing them back to me, where I hid them in my pants. I was only half awake when our cell door suddenly rolled shut, then all forty-four down the rock clanged shut too. Slim got up and held his mirror outside the bars to see what happened. "Something's going on," he said. "A fight or something."

It was an art, the way he used that mirror. An average person couldn't possibly do it – the slightest flick of the wrist moved the view out of the frame. You have to have a very steady hand, and even then, it's still tricky, like bringing in a distant TV station with the old rabbit ears antenna; it never came in perfectly, except by accident.

It was more than a fight, though, more than some smoker's debt catching up to him. We didn't know it until Pete, Maurice's bunkie, was sent back early from his maintenance job. A gray-haired white man named Butch had apparently "beaten the brakes off a CO named Lodge. It seemed strange to me – Lodge was smart and quiet, unlike the typical COs, who tended to be loud rednecks, unemployable anywhere else. When I thought of Lodge, I thought only of the dry skin condition he had – flakes of dandruff coated the shoulders of his uniform like light dust. Butch had not only beaten him up, but was in the process of cracking his skull on the concrete floor like a hard-boiled egg when he was Tasered. "The whole place is locked down," said Pete. "There's blood all over the telephone room floor."

The doors didn't open again for two days. No one went anywhere, except kitchen workers who brought us our food in paper bags. Lodge didn't die, but Channel 8 out of Grand Rapids said he had head injuries and would remain in the hospital under observation for at least another day. As further punishment, we all knew what was coming: our cells would be tossed, we just didn't know when. I took apart my tattoo gun and stuck the motor back in the shell of the cassette player. I flushed the guitar-string needles and the ink-stained barrel of the Bic. And then we waited.

I expected the television to be turned off next. Though we pay for luxuries like cable through the Prisoner Benefit Fund, in the end it's all controlled by the warden. Sure enough, that afternoon during a Sanford and Son marathon, the screen went blank. I turned it off and leafed through a tattoo magazine. On the bunk below me, I heard Slim unscrew the cable on his television to maybe pick up a local station via his antenna made from a headphone wire. "PBS," he said after a few minutes. "That's something, anyway."

Slim liked to talk about which era he would live in if given the choice. It was his go-to subject when he thought something needed to be said. Some people see silence as a space they're responsible for filling, and Slim was one of those people. He had a salesman's gift for talking, probably could have been a hell of a car salesman, had he not trained his talent on selling heroin.

His favorite era, I think, the one he talked about most anyway, was the prehistoric era, when dinosaurs ruled the Earth. He wasn't bothered by any logic in these daydreams – it made no difference that humans didn't actually walk the planet back then, but he talked a lot about training the dinosaurs like horses and oxen, making the planet into his personal Eden, where he would grow crops and work on populating the world with a vast stable of Cro-Magnon wives.

This time he was talking about Bonnie and Clyde. "You know anything about them?" he said. "A little,"

I said. "I've seen the movie."

"It was on last night," he said. "I'd like to live when they lived, but not for the reason you'd think – not robbing banks and road trips and not getting caught or nothing. You know why?"

I didn't.

"Because bras hadn't been invented yet. All those women back then, they just flopped around. You think back then the women were all straitlaced, you know? But they were braless. And that Bonnie, she was a hot little number. Crazy."

I knew he was thinking of Faye Dunaway. I couldn't remember seeing a picture of the real Bonnie Parker, but I was certain she was no braless Faye Dunaway. It was a waste of breath to point out the problems in his fantasies, so I mostly tuned him out, went to my own dreams of the time I'd like to live in: the future. It was the only era that made sense to me. I knew all too much about the past. The past was the past, and all of it, as far as I was concerned, was a nightmare, nothing worth thinking about. But the future – there was hope in the future, there was the chance that things could be new and different.

A whole platoon of COs walked to the end of our hall, walkie-talkies squawking and chirping like robot birds. They emptied the last ten cells, led the inmates off somewhere, and began searching. They carried portable metal detectors and long sticks with mirrors on the end to look under and above everything. After fifteen minutes the first inmates were brought back, and the next ten, us, were led to B-Ward – an indoor gym area with tables and weight-lifting equipment.

It was my first real look at Maurice. The four of us sat around a table. He'd had a previous year most people couldn't even imagine, thinking he was probably dead, hearing his friend burn to death, finding himself in prison for forty to sixty, essentially the rest of his life. I thought I could feel sedate pain permeating his every movement He didn't shift a hand from one spot of the table to another without thinking about it, as if he was afraid any move he made might lead to tragedy. He listened and smiled at Slim, holding forth on the braless women of the 1920s. Pete, Maurice's bunkie, said Slim was full of shit. He said women had been wearing bras since the time of Columbus. "Isn't that right, Mo?"

"I never gave it much thought," he said.

"He's no expert on the history of bras – and you sure as hell ain't either," said Slim. "I doubt you've even seen a bra."

A couple of COs came through the door and one of them said, "Jenkins." Mo stood up and walked over to them, showed them his ID, and then they put the cuffs on behind his back, leading him off.

"What the hell?" Pete asked us. "He never did anything but write some letters."

I figured that was the last time I would ever see Mo. In my twenty years I had seen men, here one minute and gone an instant later, moved to one of Michigan's forty different prisons. Some of those men I was happy never to see again, but not Mo. I had felt something around him – he was so fresh out of the oven of tragedy that he had something indefinable about him, some knowledge of another world. He was led out, and I silently wished him well.

When we returned to our cells, our thin blue-green mattresses were on the floor and there were papers everywhere. The Walkman where I kept my tattoo motor was gone. I had left it in plain sight on the table next to the door. There was no sense trying to hide it – I thought if I left it out in the open it wouldn't look suspicious. But it was gone. I had bought it years ago for a bag of coffee.

I started picking up the scattered little squares of card stock that I'd turned into business cards:

PRISON INK
by Ollie Pencoak
slinging ink and painting cards
since 1990

Slim was carrying on about some colored pencils that he couldn't find. I had bigger problems. Without tattoos, there was no way to come up with the money I owed. My sight went dark for a second. I felt dizzy. I wanted to beat the shit out of that stupid bastard Butch for starting all of this. I wanted to beat the shit out of the COs that had taken my Walkman. I wanted to strangle the prick who had come up with the idea of removing tobacco from the prisons. Mostly though, I just warned my motor back. I was on my hands and knees collecting these cards with my name on them, wishing I could just as easily put in life back together.

$$$$$

"I would like to live during Prohibition," Slim said.
"That doesn't make any damn sense," I said. "Why would you want to live without alcohol?"
"That's why – I'd make my own and be a gangster."
"Do you even know how?"
The rock was quiet. It was nearly dinner and the cell searches had been over for hours. I explained to Slim what little I knew about fermentation and distillation. He listened quietly, asking questions now and then. I felt guilty – which happened every time I got tired of his dreams and interjected some reality. He would get quiet, almost submissive, and I would feel as if I had scolded a child or a shy puppy.

We were brought brown bag dinners of bologna and cheese sandwiches, carrot sticks, and an oatmeal cookie. Someone yelled that the TVs were back on. It was a relief. As I switched channels, I saw Mo pass, his bandaged head a white streak out the corner of my eye. "What happened?" I said.

"I was dumb," he said. "I'd drawn a map to a friend, letting her know where I was. I didn't even think."

Me had a friend from Kalamazoo, he said, a woman named Lorna who wrote him once o had drawn a detailed map of the Michigan Reformatory – the yard, with its concrete benches, the line of phones and the basketball courts, the chapel and the chow hail, the gym and the gun towers, the ribbons of razor wire atop the fences, the octagonal rotunda, even the abandoned backstop from the baseball diamond that hadn't seen action in twenty years – all culminating in a little x on the top bunk in 29.

He had stuck the map in a file folder until he could get some envelopes. The way he described the map, the time and details he'd invested in it, he wanted Lorna to know exactly where he was –literally, of course, but also in a deeper, unspoken way. His map, whether he realized it or not, was a love letter in code. He had spent hours on the details, and the long odds of the two of them ever getting together didn't matter. It was just the idea of her knowing where he was. A sliver of hope in that knowing. The COs, of course, thought of it as escape plans.

"What'd you plead?" Slim asked.

"Stupidity," he said. "I told them the truth."

Slim looked at him with disgust, as if Mo had just said he was a pedophile. He couldn't even consider that the truth was something a person might consider telling. Mo's door opened. "They found me not guilty," he said.

$$$$$

After a week of bag lunches, they let us walk down to the chow hall. The hallways were ankle-deep with trash, the windows spotted with wads of wet toilet paper that had dried to a gray plaster. It was the standard result of a prolonged lockdown. When the porters had tried to clean the mess, they had been pelted with insults and AA batteries, until the staff stopped sending them into the line of fire.

Other than chow, we weren't allowed to go outside for yard until the second week of December. Besides being opened briefly to let us out for chow, the doors were closed at all times. Some legal-beagle inmates, who spent their time in the law library trying to convince themselves the answers were there, were all in an uproar about the prison taking away our constitutional rights without due process. Others said that we had no rights to open cell doors at all, so they hadn't taken anything away. No one was happy, that was for sure.

I was drawing out possible tattoos for Mo, even though he knew I didn't have a motor anymore. "Well, when you get one," he'd said, "I want a flower or heart, something for the friends and family I've lost." It was the day of the last commissary when we could still buy tobacco, and Mo gave me his pouch of Bugler. He didn't smoke.

"I don't know, Mo," I said, as I had already planned on not paying my tobacco bill and was considering doing exactly what Doo-Wop had done. I couldn't tell anyone, of course, but I couldn't refuse Mo's pouch of Bugler either. I figured I'd smoke like a king until the last and after that, I didn't know.

The next day, via messages passed up and down the blocks, the inmates had agreed to protest our lockdown by picking up our chow trays like usual, then walking directly to the window near the exit and handing the untouched food to the dishwasher. It was a civilly disobedient act, but anything out of the norm could be considered inciting a riot, and then all bets were off We'd enter a different dimension of prison life from there. This was no college campus sit-in. This was the real deal. And in a society where the warden was tasked with not losing control, that came with a nearly unlimited amount of power, including deadly force.

The blocks were released half at a time. It was a pretty low-impact protest, yet by the time I picked up my tray, I was nervous. Where generally chow was a hundred men or more sitting four to a table eating, there were maybe a dozen in the entire room. I walked past my usual seat and set the tray on the shelf for the porter to dump it all into the trash. It was a small act but I felt a rush of adrenaline all the same.

There was a space between us all, a chasm separating the men who had eaten their tacos and beans and those of us who hadn't. They had their excuses: They were getting paroled soon. They were too hungry. They couldn't get another misconduct ticket. There are always excuses, but what it really came down to was fear. I did it. Mo did it. Slim and Pete did not, and if the no protesters fit any sort of common profile, it was this: the biggest talkers, the ones who could go on and on about who was full of shit, how crappy the food was, how inhumane the cells were – they were the ones who were afraid. It was hard for me to feel too superior though, knowing that my future included skipping out on my debt with a trip to the hole.

The next day everyone ate lunch and dinner as usual, there were twice as many COs in the chow hall, all packing Tasers, and many looked disappointed that we were behaved. They were no doubt jacked up from the powwow with the warden they had at the start of their shift. The Tasers, bright yellow and black striped like a bumblebee, fit snugly in plastic holders attached to their belts. All of them kept a hand at their hip, ready for action that, at least that day, never came.

Mo and I walked outside the chow hail. A man named Tony caught up with me on the sidewalk. I had never said more than two words to

Tony before, so I knew what it was about. "You owe a lot," he said. "Some people want to know, the fuck you plan to do?" He was from Sweden or Norway – someplace cold like that, had been down for over thirty years. He had an accent and could hardly say a sentence without a few fucks thrown in.

"I'm good," I said. "Next store. Plus, I just got a new motor and a lot of tattoos lined up."

"How about you give them something right now, so you won't flicking lock up? Your TV, maybe."

We walked slowly toward the cellblocks. It was December – cold, but the sun was out, bright and crisp. "No," I said. Mo was walking to my left, his hand on the bandage on his head as if it was suddenly hurting. I could feel him moving away from us. "I don't owe you anything, Tony. I don't even know why you're involved."

"I'm like a fucking bank," he said. "Sometimes a bank will, you know, consolidate loans and make some fucking money on the payment." He twisted a Velcro-banded watch around his wrist, then smiled slightly. "I know you're good. Next store, huh?" He spit on the sidewalk, as if it was the official end to what he had to say, then caught up with a group of guys – nonsmoking thugs, no doubt.

"What's his deal?" Mo asked.

"You're just lucky you don't smoke," I said. "I should have fucking punched him. I'd be out of this whole deal, on my way to the hole."

"It's that easy, huh?"

"Not really," I said. "I'd be in the hole for a while, but they'd probably put me right back here."

"You got the money to pay them?"

"That's all right, man. We've all got secrets. I don't really have seizures either. I just like the Depakote. They give me Tegretol, too, but I sell those. Some guys like to snort them. Soon as I heard they give out meds, I got the idea to fall down and shake like a poisoned rat. I do that every now and then and nobody asks any questions. Sometimes I'll slip half an Alka-Seltzer in my mouth and spit foam everywhere."

We walked up the stairs in I-Block, up to the third floor, then down the hall to the cells. I asked him how badly he had been burned.

"I need a couple more skin grafts. It basically burned off half of my head. We were using naphtha on a Coleman stove and when it went up, it was like the inside of that Lincoln was napalmed. It burned for a long time. You think time in prison is slow, try setting yourself on fire, then see how slow time passes."

Everyone was back in their cells, but Mo and I stood talking through the bars. He said he couldn't explain what it was like in that Lincoln when it all went to hell and his friend was in the back, screaming, and all he could do was flop out onto the parking lot and try to put himself out. Worse than his friend screaming was when the firemen pulled the body out while the paramedics went about stabilizing Mo. What was left was steaming, shrunken, and charred like a log from a doused bonfire.

He had been charged with negligent homicide and about a dozen drug charges and danger to society felonies. He denied responsibility for the death, though. His friend had been aware of the risk. This may have been true, but in the end, it was only an excuse. I didn't try to argue with him, get him to see how he may have been just a little responsible for the trouble he found himself in. Just like everyone else in here, he had a right to be wrong. He would change, or he wouldn't. Some men never do. They spend the rest of their lives denying the truth, protecting the illusions that protect them from their past.

The two of us just stood there awhile. It is hard to explain what standing near Mo felt like to me. He had a kind of knowledge no one really wants to come by honestly, because it involves unimaginable loss. He had literally been to hell and back, and part of him knew it. Someone like that – someone who has had layers burned away to reveal something essential – is worth knowing.

The laundry porters began handing back our clean clothes in our laundry bags. They were whispering to everyone that tomorrow afternoon's yard was going to be a silent protest. We were going to walk around and around the track in a group very slowly. I didn't really understand the point, but we would at least let them know we could push back. We hadn't done anything wrong, yet were being punished as if we had. And all this time, the idiot who *had* done something wrong wasn't even here any longer.

Word got around that about half of the men – Slim and Pete included – weren't going to do anything but stay in their cells during the afternoon yard. I was going, of course. I didn't know how it would play out, but I figured I could be on my way out of here somehow. I picked up my little stack of business cards, reached around the cell, and set them on the fiat, horizontal slats outside Mo's door. "Mo," I said. "Keep these. Maybe I'll see you again."

"I'm sure you will," he said. Though he seemed to know tomorrow would be it for me, he didn't seem to understand that we probably would never see each other again. I'd been around long enough to know better – when someone was gone, they were gone for good.

It hadn't snowed at all in Michigan that winter, except for a few flurries around Thanksgiving. But it snowed that night, all night, as I sat by the window rolling the last of my tobacco. When I thought about it, I would miss rolling cigarettes most of all. Maybe more than the actual smoking. There was something in the ritual of it, the shredding of the long strands into smaller pieces, and that smell – the damp grass and the freshly plowed field – it was soothing and slow, a throwback to a simpler time, with simpler pleasures.

I smoked in relative silence. Slim talked a little bit in his sleep, and I could hear Mo snoring in the next cell. I watched the fat snowflakes fall through the brightness of the lights outside. I smoked the cigarettes as far down as I could, often singeing the ends of my fingers, an easier pain, I thought, than the pain of quitting. I thought that way it would be easier to remember.

$$$$$

Only a hundred of us went out to the yard that day. Usually there were three times that. We all just gathered in a loose group – like those strange flocks of birds that come together and become one – and we walked very slowly around the quarter-mile asphalt track. There was much whispering going on above the soft rustle of our state-issued shoes on the blacktop.

The large yard is an acre of flat ground set outward from the two five-story cellblocks. There were a dozen or so concrete benches on the edge of the track and five chin-up bars, two basketball courts, and opposite those, two dozen phones. There were tables, too, where men played cards and dominoes and were warned via stenciled messages on the tabletops not to sit on the actual table or to stand anywhere around them.

After we'd been walking for ten minutes, two more men with guns appeared on the roof of the blocks. A tall captain in a black, knee-length MDOC coat came out and walked beside the group. "Look," he said, "I know we've got things we need to talk about, and we will, but you guys need to disperse. We'll work something out." No one said anything, though, because no one knew anything. We didn't have a spokesman or a list of demands.

The captain went back into the building and four more men with guns appeared on the roof, one of them with a large-bore shotgun. A new guard on the ground had a bolt of zip-tie handcuffs strapped across his chest like a bandolier. Mo walked next to me silently. All of the guns made me nervous. A long line of COs began spacing themselves on the ground about twenty feet outside the bordering fence, the bright yellow of their Tasers glowing against the drab gray of their uniforms.

And then she was there. The warden, who someone had said was on vacation, had apparently been called in. She was a fifty-something black woman dressed more for spring than winter in an aqua-colored sundress and matching blue pumps. She was a classy lady I'd seen around a few times. Today, though, she had her left arm in a sling. Her fingers stuck out of the end and looked swollen the closer she got to us – like large, spoiling sausages.

Just outside the yard, there was a brick, octagonal chapel with a tall, nondenominational, steeple-like structure on top, and past that, a long, fading white brick wall. Five armed guards now stood on top of that wall.

The warden walked briskly to the group as we passed through the shadow of J-Block. She stood, flanked by four COs, to the side of us. "I'm giving you one warning," she said. "Break up." We kept walking, and when we made it back around to the shadowed area ten minutes later, she began demanding men's prison IDs, and the guys in front reached into their pockets to comply.

Mo elbowed me. "Showtime," he whispered, then popped something white into his mouth. He stepped out of the crowd and fell to the ground, shaking violently on his stomach. Everyone backed away and a CO kneeled down and shifted him onto his back, and I could see the sizzling foam around Mo's lips. Before anyone knew what was happening, before I even knew what I was doing, I took two steps and reached down to the yellow and black stripes at the CO's belt, ripping the Taser right out of his holster.

I leveled it at the warden and squeezed. There was a kick, like that of a handgun, as the tiny explosive launched the sharp probes. I saw the warden freeze, eyes skyward, and drop like a dead tree to the cold ground just before I did the same, stuck by several of those same electric fires in my back. It was like lightning passing throughout my body. It seemed to last forever the way it traveled down my hands, reaching through my fingertips, the current running through me, trying to find its way out.

VICKIE STRINGER: HOW I DID IT

Triple Crown Publications is the first name in "hip-hop lit," a booming genre of raw, gritty urban fiction, sold everywhere from street corners to small African American bookstores to Barnes & Noble. Vickie Stringer started Triple Crown with exactit one asset: the finctionalized story of her life, which she wrote in the federal penitentiary while serving five years for selling a kilo of cocaine to a police informant in Columbus, Ohio. That book, *Let That Be the Reason*, and the follow-up, *Imagine This*, each spent more than a year on the *Essence* paperback bestseller list. As her reputation grew, Stringer started publishing other unknown authors, and then representing them when the big publishing houses came calling. How Stringer went from drug queen to federal prisoner 63752-061 to owner of a $1.8 million company with 36 titles by 25 authors is an amazing story, one that's worthy of Triple Crown Publications.
[As told to Patrick J. Sauer]

I met a guy one summer who was a big Columbus dealer, fell in love, and dropped out of college after my freshman year. I got my first taste of entrepreneurship in those days, managing both a hair salon and an escort service. I found girls by running a weekly ad in *The Columbus Dispatch* seeking models. When I got pregnant, my boyfriend cut out on me, so when my son, Valen, was born I turned to a familiar business that paid well. I excelled at the drug game; I made $30,000 a week. Even out hustling in the streets everyone does business with people they like a trust.

You have to be careful of stereotypes, though. I wasn't from a broken home. I was raised in a middle-class Detroit neighborhood. My mother was a schoolteacher and my father was an electric engineer. I got into crime for kicks, then I quickly got addicted to the lifestyle.

When I found out I was going to be released from prison I felt free, but also like there was nothing waiting for me. I knew I wasn't going to break the law again and lose Valen. I was a 29-year-old felon with no degree, no resume, almost no legal work experience, no money, and no prospects. I wanted my life to have meaning and I had no idea what I was going to do.

Ninety days before I got out of jail, I had an epiphany: God wanted me to tell my story. Six weeks later, I had a manuscript for *Let That Be the Reason*.

I lived in a halfway house and got a job as a bartender at the Columbus airport. After six months, I was able to regain custody of Valen. I've had a lot of success at Triple Crown, but nothing compares with seeing my son again. That was the greatest day of my life.

I was rejected by 26 publishers, so I decided to self-publish. I begged family and friends to lend me $100 apiece and raised enough to print 2,500 copies. I went out and started hustling product again, one book at a time. I was tenacious. I would get up at dawn and start going door-to-door like it was my real job. If you were this guy over here smoking a cigarette, I would walk right up and say, "I wrote a book; would you like to buy it for 10 bucks? My kid needs a haircut." I always had hustling in me, but it was always in a negative way. As soon as I had *Let That Be the Reason*, I turned the hustle into something positive. At the bar, I'd pour my customers a shot of tequila and ask if they wanted to hear my story. In 2002, one of them was in the business and took *Let That Be the Reason* to Upstream Publications, an African American-owned house based in Brooklyn. UpStream responded with a $50,000 offer. When I got the call, I thought it was my brother playing with me.

Let That Be the Reason sold over 100,000 copies. So did my second book, *Imagine This*.

I will never forget the small mom-and-pop African American distributors because they were there for me from day one when all I had was word of mouth. Small-time operations are a lot tougher to work with than the big companies, though, because they take a lot longer to pay. I've started weeding out low-level distributors who work on a consignment basis. Triple Crown is a bill-paying company, so I get real angry sometimes and feel like bringing out my gangsta background, but I don't act that way anymore. Becoming more professional has been one of my biggest challenges in building the company.

INTERVIEW WITH WAHIDA CLARK

Vice talked to the originator of the street lit fiction genre to discuss how she pioneered a nuanced take on the romance novel from within a federal prison.

Wahida Clark is the reigning O.G. of street lit, also called "urban fiction." Best known for her *Thug* and *Payback* series, Clark writes nuanced takes on the schlocky romance novels you see at grocery stores, replacing the cheese with guns, cash, gangs, and drugs. And Clark isn't just fabricating inner-city tall tales; she's writing about what she's lived through.

Born and bred in the streets of Trenton, New Jersey, Clark was involved with the New World, a crew of black separatist bank robbers known for beheading their rivals, and served time as a result. While doing a sentence of 125 months in federal prison for money laundering and wire fraud, Clark began writing fiction while locked up. She wrote her first book, *Thugs and the Women Who Love Them*, using a pen and yellow legal paper in her cell, but was released from prison in 2007 and has published 14 books in the time since, including *Thuggz Valentine*. In the case of *Thuggz Valentine*, Clark remixed the familiar story of Bonnie and Clyde, but tweaked it so it reflects her own experiences while involved with a real crime syndicate.

After opening her own publishing house, Wahida Clark Presents, she put out 70-plus titles from incarcerated authors like CASH, Victor L. Martin (author of *A Hood Legend*), and others. Clark has also signed deals with major publishing houses like Kensington and Hachette, been hand-picked by Birdman to have her books distributed through Cash Money Records, and is now entering the movie and TV game with Wahida Clark films, which currently has two projects in development based on her *Thug Series*. *Vice* gave Clark a call to talk about her rise in the publishing game from within a jail cell, as well as what she's done since being on the outside.

VICE: How did you get into writing?

Wahida Clark: I started writing while serving my ten-and-a-half-year federal prison sentence. When my back was up against the wall, when I discovered that all my money and possessions were gone, when I discovered that it takes money to live in prison, and when it hit me that I have to do something in order to walk out of prison with a cushion, I prayed for guidance and was blessed to recognize and act on the guidance when it came. The guidance was to write street fiction.

My husband was also locked up and our daughters were teenagers, so I had to somehow get my hustle on. My husband wrote a book called *Uncle Yah Yah* and then I saw a clip about Shannon Holmes, who signed his first book deal in prison, and I said I could do this.

What did your husband say when you told him you also wanted to write a book from inside?

At first, my husband didn't respond. I had to holla at him again and again, saying, "Yo, I'm thinking about writing a book. I'm serious. What do you think?" When he finally got back to me, he said what [publishers] are interested in from people in our position is sex, drugs, murder, and crime. I had experience in that world, and what I didn't experience myself in New Jersey, those around me experienced. I wrote about what I knew.

My husband said if I sent him a little sample, he'd give me his advice. I was working in the prison library and studying the craft, and began writing and sending things to him. On top of his encouragement, as inmate who was previously a literary agent gave a creative writing class, and the rest slowly became history. I was blessed that my time in prison was time well spent.

What was it like to sign a book deal while you were incarcerated?

I signed two deals with two major publishing houses while I was serving time – it was crazy and awesome. I was writing those books with paper and ink, too! I hit the *Essence* magazine best sellers list multiple times while incarcerated. It was such an inspiration to so many sisters and brothers on lock that many of them wrote and told me that I was the reason many of them started writing. I would get letters seeking advice, plus receive words of encouragement from authors who are now publishers and are now moving into film. It was a wonderful thing to inspire others. On top of being a four-time *New York Times* Best Seller, it feels like a wonderful accomplishment.

What separates street lit and the *Thug* series from the typical romance novels that middle-ages suburban moms read?

Two different environments produce two different mindsets. They are the same, but they are seen differently. No one can say there isn't violence in romance novels.

What did you do differently with *Thuggz Valentine*?

Thuggz Valentine is the story of a modern-day Bonnie and Clyde – natural born killers who go out in a blaze of glory after taking on the city's police force. The first thing I did differently was write the book in reverse – it opens with the ending. The second was a collaboration with David Weaver, the King of e-book publishing. We had agreed to do an experiment, so I had him publish the e-book version. Needless to say, it worked out well.

Your *Thug* series is now being turned into a film, right? How far into the process are you?

I'm excited. My fans are excited. Since the series is so popular the producers and directors haven't decided which route to go first: a play, a TV series, or a movie.

We are going to do something. In December, we're having a party/talent search/networking event in Atlanta. We are going to find our direction and our stars there.

Do you have any other film projects in the works?

Blood Heist, written by NuariceArt, hasn't been published under Wahida Clark Presents yet, but the film rights were picked up immediately. It's about Angelo and Michael, two brothers joined in the hunt to take the reins on their father's kingdom.

It's a good look to move into film, a natural progression. I'm a storyteller by nature; that's what I do. I am constantly looking for different mediums to tell my stories. Film is just the latest and it also happens to be the biggest art form. There's a lot of crime drama on TV these days, but if I have my way, God willing, I will clean up the whole industry and make something better.

Do you ever think that glamorizes street lit romanticizes or even crime?

We try our best to follow personal principles and literary principles that demand that good triumphs over evil all the time. However, the demand today is for junk food – both physically and mentally.

My husband taught me that it was easier to write books for money than to write books to educate. So of course, we took the road for money, on hopes that it would put us in position to educate. It's a constant grind and hustle. If you are not constantly pushing your business it will remain stagnate. And of course, content is King. Or, in my case, Queen.
[Source: Vice.com]

MIKE ENEMIGO'S EXCLUSIVE INTERVIEW WITH JAILHOUSE PUBLISHING OG AND OUTLAW FILMMAKER SETH FERRANTI

Seth Ferranti rocked the literary world in 2004 when he launched his publishing company, Gorilla Convict Publications, from inside a federal penitentiary, and began penning and publishing raw, uncensored tales about life inside America's prison system, street legends, and other aspects of the criminal underworld. Not since Jack Abbott's *In the Belly of the Beast*, George Jackson's *Soledad Brother*, and Tookie Williams' *Life in Prison* had about prison stories been told from such a true, insider's perspective, without givin even half a fuck about who may or may not like its truth. The Gorilla Convict would go on to become an expert on kingpins from the 80s, like Kenneth "Supreme" McGriff, Fat Cat, Pappy Mason, Rich Porter and others. Seth Ferranti has been one of my mentors since before he even knew I existed, and today I am honored to be interviewing him so we can learn more about his story, including what he's been up to since being freed from prison, and any jewels he's willing to share for other, upcoming incarcerated authors.

Mike: I know you have a lot going on, making real boss moves in the business of storytelling, so I want to thank you for taking the time out to talk with me. I've been following your work now for about 12 years, since 2008 sometime. I'd been flirting with the idea of writing books, and ironically, my celly, who was cleaning out his locker, gave me an old *Black Men* magazine he was going to throw out. When I flipped through it, I saw an interview you'd done about your book *Prison Stories*. I cut out the interview for inspiration, and a couple months later I received my monthly *Smooth* magazine, where I saw a book review on *Street Legends Volume 1*. I immediately ordered both books because you were an example of someone who was doing what I had been thinking about doing. So, to now be interviewing you, having some of my work published on *gorillaconvict.com*, and networking with you in other ways, it's an exciting career moment for me. I'm pointing this out not only to you, but to the upcoming prisoner authors, because I want to show them that dedication and determination will eventually pay off for them. It took 12 years, but now I'm rubbing shoulders with one of the guys I looked to for motivation with my writing career. This is a lesson I want to make sure they understand.

Okay, with that out the way, when did you start going down the road of crime?

Seth: To this day I still don't consider myself a criminal and I never did. I didn't carry a gun, I didn't use violence, I didn't rob anyone. All I did was sell cannabis and LSD, one substance that is basically legal now, and one that is being looked at for its therapeutic value. I always tell people that I'm not a criminal, I'm an outlaw because I broke laws that I thought were wrong. And now finally society has decided that these laws are wrong too. I was just a man before my time. A trendsetter. An OG of the weed game.

So, you start selling drugs, and just like we all do, you eventually get popped. What exactly were you charged with?

I was charged with a Continual Criminal Enterprise. That is a federal kingpin charge. But it was some bullshit. I was a small-time marijuana and LSD activist. Not a big drug dealer by any means, but you know how the feds and law enforcement do when you won't snitch.

How much time did they give you for that?

My sentence in the feds was 304 months. I did 21 years in federal prison for a first-time, nonviolent offense. They call that justice. I call it injustice.

Your story's even been told by *Rolling Stone* magazine and *VICE*. How did that come about?

I sent them lots of letters. It started in a journalism class. I just turned it into a feature on my case in *Rolling Stone*.

So, at 22 years old, even though you were a first-time, non-violent offender, you were sentenced to 25 years in federal prison. That's crazy. How long into your journey did you start thinking about writing books? How did that all come about?

I was a creative person already. I wrote music and had dabbled in poetry as a teen. A modern-day Jim Morrison in my mind. Writing articles and books and then films was the logical progression. I started out doing articles and prison newsletters, sports mostly, but writing for the college correspondence courses that I was taking really helped me to step my game up. Eventually I got a master's degree in prison.

What made you decide to start your own company, Gorilla Convict Publications?

I was mailing out manuscripts of my first book, *Prison Stories*, and got a lot of publishers and agents interested, but they wanted me to change this or that and I didn't want to. I liked the book how it was so I researched self-publishing and put it out myself. This was when Teri Woods and Vickie Stringer were doing their thing with urban novels and I kind of followed their blueprint.

As I've mentioned, you were one of my biggest inspirations and motivators. I remember being in my prison cell and holding a couple of the books you'd written and published from your prison cell, god-knows-where in America. The feeling I got was inspiring. Then, when I read your books, they were written in a raw, informal tone, almost like how we would talk to each other on the compound, and not only did you write the books, you'd published them. For me, this is one of the biggest takeaways from that experience, and it was extremely valuable: *execution*. The difference between you and all these guys who sit around talking about shit all day, or have half-written manuscripts sitting in their lockers, is that you *executed*. You followed through and got your books to market. I felt the need to point this out because it's a major jewel I got from you, and I want our prisoner-authors to understand this. Execution is *key*. Now, I had you to be this example for me. Who did you have? Who provided you with this example?

Jack Henry Abbott, George Jackson, Dannie Red Hogg Martin, Leonard Peltier, Mumia Abu Jamal – these guys were my literary inspirations. They showed me the way, but I was also locked up with an amazing man, writer, and prisoner, Michael Santos. He was my mentor. I learned a lot from him, but most of it was trial and error. I came up with plans and ideas and my wife, Diane, who ran Gorilla Convict while I was locked up, implemented them.

Yeah, but those prisoners were published by actual publishing houses. Established ones. I see your situation as being a little different. Not only did you follow through with completing your books, you bet on yourself and published them, too. This can be intimidating. You mentioned Teri Woods and Vickie Stringer, but they did it while in the free world. What gave you the courage?

I had 25 years in the feds. I was effectively dead to the outside world. I was angry as fuck because of my sentence. I used that anger to do what I did. I refused to be silenced. I reached out to the world and made a career from prison.

Okay, so you first published *Prison Stories*, then you came with *Street Legends*. I can understand getting the idea to do *Prison Stories*, being that you were in prison, but what gave you the idea to do *Street Legends*? I'd never seen a book done like that before.

F.E.D.S. and *Don Diva* magazine came out in the late 90s and were huge in prison. I started writing for them, and I had so much extra material because they were just magazines and had space limitations, I eventually decided to put out books telling these gangster stories.

When I first got locked up in the feds, I was around all these big mafia guys and Colombian cartel guys. I could reach out to my wife and get her to order me books on these guys, but the African American gangsters didn't really get no play. I knew a lot of these dudes or their co-defendants. I was into rap music. I heard the gossip on the pound about these guys and I wanted to write their stories. Not in an exploitive way, but in a way that showed how these guys were targeted and hyped up but the feds and law enforcement. Not to say they were innocent – some of these dudes are bad guys – but some just got caught up in it. I wanted to give the story that the mainstream media didn't cover.

Do you know any of the street legends you'd written about? Did you do time with any of them?

Not all of them, but I was with Supreme who gave me his blessing to write the book. A lot of the other guys, I was with their co-defendants. I tried to get as close to the source as possible. But most of my relationships with these guys were through the mail. Their co-dee's or homeboys that were on the yard with me would vouch for me and they would do the interviews.

How do they feel about your writing?

I would say most liked it because I kept it real. Some guys didn't like it because they had appeals or this or that, but most dudes respected what I wrote because I kept it within the code. I didn't talk about stuff that they weren't convicted of. I didn't speculate or try to attach them to different murders that they may or may not have done.

Okay, a lot of prisoners and aspiring writers are going to read this, so I want to provide them with some type of jewels; some type of guidance. How did you promote your work? I've seen you everywhere. I know you've written for *Don Diva, F.E.D.S., VICE*, etc., how did you connect with these guys? How did you get them to work with you? How did you do things like get interviews in magazines such as *Black Men*, etc.?

I had like 50 magazine subscriptions when I was in. I would look at the masthead and send pitch letters to the editors. I was sending out 100 pitch letters a week. Staff and other prisoners used to think I was crazy mailing so many letters, but it paid off. I was always looking to buy stamps on the yard, not to gamble or for drugs, but to do mass mailings. I would promote my work and build relationships this way. That is the secret to my success. I am relentless.

What about getting bookstores to carry your books, like Wall Periodicals, Black Star, etc.? How'd you get that done?

I created a demand for my books and they came to me. I have always had a good relationship with *Don Diva* and they always promoted my books hard. They would compensate me for my articles with promotion and advertising. I never charged them a cent for any of the many cover stories I wrote for them. The advertising was my main concern. I did the same thing with *VICE* and the other places I wrote for when I was in. Pay me by advertising my work. That's how it was all built.

So, if a prisoner wants to do what you've done, what are the biggest pieces of advice you'd give them?

Be relentless and don't give up and don't listen to other prisoners and staff that try to tell you what you can or cannot do. I did what I wanted.

I was worried about my future. I've been locked up in the hole for investigation over 20 times for my writing. I've written books in the hole. I didn't let the institution intimidate me. I told them 'fuck you', and now I am out reaping the rewards of my hard work while I was in.

Okay, so you were released from prison in Jan 2015. You'd pimped your prison time by using it wisely to educate yourself and build a career. Book-wise, what were the next steps for you? Did you immediately start a new project? Had you stacked up books to drop as soon as you'd be released? Did you start networking, doing appearances? What moves did you make to take your career to the next level?

I've been so busy with journalism and getting into film stuff that I haven't written anymore books since I've been out. 2021 is the year, though. I'm dropping five titles on Gorilla Convict. Some titles by me, and some by other prisoners. Stuff that I've had ready for years, but just now getting around to publishing.

I've been networking and doing appearances like crazy pre-COVID. I just keep going. There is no overnight success. Other people will look at me and say I'm successful, but I'm not where I want to be. I am just beginning.

I hear you on that. Some people consider me successful, but I tell 'em they have no clue, I'm just getting started. Have you ever thought about trying mainstream publisher again?

I just signed two book deals with mainstream publishers. A first for me. But mostly I've been concentrating on the film stuff.

What have been your most successful books?

Prison Stories and *Supreme Team.*

I saw you on *Crime Watch Daily* one day a few years back. I remember it showed you sitting at a huge desk like a boss with stacks of your books, and I think it showed you next to a Rolls Royce. Was that yours? I was extremely excited for you, and again, inspired. How'd you set that up?

It was just a photo shoot with the books, and it wasn't my Rolls Royce. It was a friends. I drive a big truck. A Chevy Z71 off-road. Like I said, not where I want to be, but grinding to get there.

What would you say have been the biggest moves you've made in your writing career? Like, while trying to figure all this out, what did you do, maybe not even knowing how valuable it was going to be, that really made a big difference when it comes to your success?

I think just grinding and continuing to be productive and putting stuff out is the biggest move. Just networking and hooking up with different people. But the best is yet to come.

Okay, so you're out, you're making boss moves, and you get into filmmaking. What made you do this?

It was the next step for me as a writer. I am directing and doing acting now, too. I just love to create. I crave the accolades that come with people liking my work. That is the biggest thing for me, and film has the largest audience, so it was a logical progression.

And your biggest film to date is your documentary *White Boy*, about Detroit's street legend White Boy Rick. I wanna see it so bad. What made you pick Rick, and what is your relationship like with him?

I've been writing articles about the injustice of Rick's case and doing interviews with him through the mail since the mid-2000s. He's out now. Getting his life together. We touch bases every now and then and I hope to work with him on some film projects.

White Boy came about after I was talking to this producer about different ideas for documentaries and White Boy [Rick] came up. The producer found the money for it and we made it. I learned a lot on that production and am grateful for the director, Shawn Rech, who took me under his wing. And I'm especially grateful to Rick who blessed the project. I picked Rick because his case was so fucked up, but also because I had a relationship with him and access to everyone, we needed to interview for the doc.

And you got it picked up by STARZ? How did you pull that off? How'd you make those connections?

The director Shawn Rech had the connections. We enlisted Submarine as a sales agent and they made all the deals for us.

Have you written a book about White Boy Rick, or are you planning to? Because I need to read it, since I can't see the film.

I got a book about Rick, but it will probably never come out. He's out now and is working on his own book deal so I respect his right to get money off his story. Him giving me access and interviews has helped my career a lot and I have lots of others books to put together.

That's official. I respect that. There are rumors that you have more documentaries on the way. Is this true? What are they about? When can we expect them to be available, and where will we be able to see them?

I got three docs in production: *Walk Through Murder*, which focuses on North St. Louis, post-Ferguson, and all the things that are going on currently. It's almost ready. It will be out in 2021. *Dope Gentleman*, which is about the mafia and heroin, and *The Secret History of the LSD Trade*.

And what about the books you have on the way? What can you tell us?

I'm releasing *Prison Stories 2* next year, *Prison Basketball*, a book on the Dirty White Boys prison gang that my friend who's doing life wrote, and a few others on Gorilla Convict. Plus, I'm doing two books with mainstream publishers. One about a guy that got a life sentence, turned gay in prison, got a pardon from Obama, and now is straight on the street, and one about where hip-hop and organized crime meet.

Okay, so let's sum up this amazing story about an amazing storyteller. You went from being sentenced to 25 years in federal prison for being a kingpin to writing books that you published via your own company, Gorilla Convict. You get out of prison, and you're not only still writing books, you're producing documentaries, one that is picked up by STARZ, a major network, and you have many, many more great projects on the way. That's an amazing accomplishment. You're a perfect example of how to use your prison time to create a legit way to make a living. You're free, you're respected and recognized, and you're living the life, all without taking penitentiary chances. You're a perfect example of someone who made a mistake, but learned from it, figured out who you are and what you're truly meant to be, and goes on to live a successful life. I appreciate you for inspiring me and letting me know it can be done, and I appreciate you for talking to me. I'm going to do all I

can to get this story passed all around the Belly of the Beast so other aspiring writers know this shit is real, we ain't playin no games, and if they apply the same commitment, dedication and determination, they, too, can win. Fuck prison, you feel me? We hustle and win legally. There's money to be made. We gettin money.

I've been publishing and getting money from books, but I am not rich or liquid by any means. It's a struggle, but I love my work and have a passion for it. The same with the films. I just put out stuff that I like or that I would want to buy. If other people like it and buy it, that's a plus. But I am getting into the cannabis thing, too, and would like my own brand. We will see.

Any last words, plugs or shout-outs?

Keep striving, go for what you want, and be relentless.

INTERVIEW WITH DUTCH

Iceberg Slim is credited with creating the street lit genre with his 1967 autobiography *Pimp*: *The Story of My Life*, and though he sold over 6 million books before his death in 1992, it was Donald Goines who really ran with the genre. Goines, after learning about Iceberg Slim's book *Pimp* while serving time in prison, penned his semi-autobiographical novel *Whoreson*, which was published in 1972 by Iceberg Slim's publisher, Holloway House. Goines would then go on to write 17 books, all detailing the sex, drugs, murder, and other elements of the Black underworld, before he was brutally murdered on October 21, 1974, in a style much like you'd read in one of his books.

After Goines's murder, with the exception of a few books by Iceberg Slim before his 1992 death, the street lit genre largely remained dormant until around 1999, when Sister Souljah dropped what would become one of the greatest street lit books of all time, *The Coldest Winter Ever*. This reignited the street lit genre, and soon-to-be publishing powerhouse Teri Woods began looking for talent. She would find this talent inside a prison cell in a North Carolina prison, and together they would release one of the greatest street lit series of all time: *Dutch*. Soon, the genre would be crowning a new king: North Carolina prisoner Kwame Teague, aka Dutch.

I recently had the opportunity to tap in with Dutch, from my prison cell in California to his in North Carolina, where we discussed the past, present, and future of the game.

Mike: Dutch, my guy, thanks for agreeing to interview with me, I know you don't do this a lot. Just for those who don't know, introduce yourself, tell us where you're from.

Dutch: I'm Kwame Teague, I go by Dutch. I'm from Newark, New Jersey, but I've been incarcerated in North Carolina since 1994.

What was life like growing up in Newark, New Jersey?

Growing up in Newark, in the 80s, I saw the transition of the Black community, culture and economy change with the explosion of hip-hop. The youth took over the music, fashion, and identity. The community began to change because of the AIDS epidemic, as well as the Democratic party's total embrace of identity politics – a game they've been using on us ever since. Lastly, the crack game broke us down economically. It also gave us the opportunity to rebuild, we just squandered it.

How'd you end up in North Carolina from New Jersey?

I came to North Carolina primarily to get involved in the music scene. I was managing two rappers and I felt we could get a deal easier in North Carolina than up north in New York, New Jersey, or Pennsylvania, because they were already saturated with it. And we did end up getting a deal for my group Brik Flava through Funhouse Records. The record "Bossman" is still on the Internet.

What did you ultimately get locked up for?

Kidnapping and murder.

That's crazy. My prison has its own channel where they show all kinds of educational and informational stuff. I just saw an interview with a guy named David Jassy. David is from Sweden. He came up in the 80s, started rappin', and eventually songwriting. About 10 years ago he came to California to write for Britney Spears, and while at a crosswalk, got in a fight, killing a man. He was sentenced to 15-to-Life. He eventually got to San Quentin where they have all kinds of programs. He came up on a keyboard, where he was ultimately granted permission to facilitate a "hip-hop class." They produced *The San Quentin Mixtape Project*, which got a distribution deal with Roc Nation. One day, he performed his song "Freedom" at a TED event the prison had, and our governor, Gavin Newsom was in the audience. Governor Newson ultimately pardoned David; he was in Dubai, on business, while his interview was conducted over Zoom. I don't know the details of your case, and I don't want to, but it made me think of this — on business for music and getting convicted of murder. But David is out now, doing big things. Point is, it ain't ever over, you feel me?

Naw, it's never over. I'm very hopeful about my future. And I didn't know about David Jassy and *The San Quentin Mixtape Project*, that's a dope story.

So how did you get the name Dutch?

The name Dutch just comes from the title of the book. I named it *Dutch* because I mistakenly thought Dutch was a title of royalty. So, the tagline was: "There Are Princes... There Are Kings... And then there's Dutch." People just started calling me Dutch after that and it stuck.

What got you into writing? How and when did it start?

I got started at an early age, when my older sister Sharon taught me how to write movie scripts. I was attracted to the format — it was so clean and organized. Anyone who has seen a movie script will know what I mean. This was in the 80s.

Who or what inspires you when it comes to writing?

Movies. I love movies. Especially old movies like *Casablanca* and *Maltese Falcon*. I love the witty dialogue. And Donald Goines has been a big inspiration, too. Iceberg Slim was mean, but Donald was a better storyteller.

What gave you the idea to write the *Dutch* series?

The idea basically comes from Newark. The Dutch character, his whole swag, is made up of several major players from Newark that I grew up hearing about.

How did you end up connecting with Teri Woods?

I read about her in a *Vibe* magazine and had my people contact her.

There are a lot of rumors she does foul business. Is this true? Was this your experience?

Without a doubt, Teri and I have had our differences. But no more than what typically goes on in this industry. Whenever your talent is the commodity, the producer/publisher/financer is going to make moves.

Like the old saying goes, "You don't get what you're worth, you get what you negotiate." My second deal was better than my first because I learned my worth and how to negotiate. We were all new and just learning at this time. We're good, though. I'm still in contact with her.

Why do you think *Dutch* was so successful?

I think it was largely based on timing. It was the beginning of the street lit game – aside from Iceberg Slim and Donald Goines, of course – and me, Teri, and Shannon Holmes were able to capitalize on that by being the pioneers.

Do you think that type of success is still possible today?

I think so, but it would take opening up new markets, like Canada, the UK, Germany, etc., where it's not so oversaturated. And probably by appealing to this new generation with audio books, an idea I know you want to take to the next level.

What do you think is the major difference between then and now?

The game then was pre social media and pre music streaming, etc. Now everything is on your phone, and there's so much "right now, at your fingertips" entertainment, it's harder to get people to read. And because the game is so oversaturated, it's harder to make a name now.

I feel you. I've been in the game for 10 years and I'm barely getting a name in the street lit market. I'd been gettin' all my pennies with my how-to and prisoner-info books for prisoners. That's one market that does still read – prisoners – since they don't have access to all the same entertainment and Information options that everyone on the outside has.

Absolutely. There's still some money in these prisons for sure.

So, after Teri, you began publishing your books with DC Book Diva. How'd that come about?

I connected with DC Book Diva – Juanita Short – through a mutual friend. We hit it off immediately because she's so driven, sincere, and she's one of the smartest women I know. And she's gorgeous, too. (Laughs) She is a true diva.

Have you ever tried to get published by a mainstream publishing house that publishes street lit, like St. Martin's Press, who publishes folks like JaQuavis Coleman?

Naw, I never tried to connect with a mainstream publisher because I believe in building our own. I used to preach to other authors all the time that we need to create our own industry, combine our resources, join forces, etc., but our people are so distrustful of each other, and most haven't learned to get past that.

How come you never started your own publishing company?

I just never really had the team for that, to be honest.

I recently saw you did a comic book with Seth Ferranti. How'd you connect with Seth?

Seth and I began writing each other when he was in the feds. I reached out to him and we've been rocking together ever since.

Yeah, Seth is official. I'd even go as far as to say he kinda pioneered street lit journalism, at least as far as books go. I mean, you had magazines like *Don Diva* and *FEDS*, but he took it to the next level with his *Street Legend* books, books about Supreme, Fat Cat, Rich Porter, etc. I know he's who got me into the street lit journalism books. And now he's really doin' boss shit with his *White Boy* documentary on STARZ. Shout out to Seth, for sure.

Yeah, Seth is official. He's doin' his thing.

What do you think about the comic book game?

The comic book/graphic novel game is wide open, but no one has really mastered it yet. I mean, a gangsta-ass comic book has major potential, but it has to have the right appeal – you gotta know how to push it just right. Seth and I are always kickin' ideas, but we haven't initiated anything new yet.

How would you describe your writing style?

I'd say it's more of a straightforward style. I don't do the long, drawn out details. I like to skip the parts that bog down the story. I have a cinematic style.

What do you think are your best books?

I'd have to say *Dynasty 3* and *Dutch 2: Angel's Revenge*. They have the most interesting storylines in my opinion.

What are your top three books written by others?

My favorite writer, hands down, is Al-Saadiq Banks. He brings that Newark shit hard and his stories are realistic. But my favorite three books are *Block Party 3* by Al-Saadiq Banks, *Cheetah* by Missy Jackson, and *Flight* by Tamara John.

That's crazy you mention Al-Saadiq because I be tellin' people the same thing. I write about this in my upcoming book, *Jailhouse Publishing*. When I had online access, I would watch his videos on IG where he would explain his experiences with the writing game – – the struggles he went through, and how he got past it. I tapped in with him and he fucked with me. And just to keep it real, though I had known who he was, of course, I had yet to read one of his books at the time. But he became my favorite street lit author just based on *him*, you feel me? Based on the authenticity I felt from his videos and tappin' in with him. I then bought *Caught 'em Slippin*, and indeed, it didn't disappoint. It was raw. He really writes that "True 2 Life" shit, you feel me? Shout out to Al-Saadiq Banks.

Yeah, Al-Saadiq Banks is the truth for real.

What is something you've learned since writing your first book?

I've learned that not everyone can see your vision, so you have to believe in yourself enough to stay committed.

Fa sho. And give us some game: What's the secret to success, yours or otherwise?

The secret is total commitment to the vision. Stay open-minded and receptive to advice and critique, but be aware enough to see through the hate.

What advice would you give to someone who wants to do what you do?

My advice is to organize, network, reflect, implement. Organize your thoughts until they become concrete plans, then network to move the plan forward, gaining allies and resources. Reflect on your progress, your mistakes, your missed opportunities, and them implement the next phase. Then, starting from organization again, repeat.

What's a typical day like for you?

A typical day for me is, I get up at 4:30 am, shower, collect my thoughts, listen to NPR News, and read the paper. I plot out my day — the calls I need to make, stuff I need to do, etc. Then I go to work as a graphic designer until 11:00 am, and at that time I have lunch, use the phone, and maybe network a little until 12:00, when I go back to work until 3:30. After 3:30 I might use the phone a little more, write, watch the news, then go to bed around 11:00. I wake up the next day and repeat.

There are rumors you're getting into the movie business. Any truth to this?

Movies are my future. The movie *DUTCH* comes out December 24 [2020]. I'm mad hyped to finally see my shit on screen, even though I didn't write the script for this one. I did write the scripts for parts two and three, though. I'm looking for actors and actresses who believe in their talent. Get at me!

What is your ultimate goal with writing; movies?

Movies, and I want to own my own TV network and/or streaming service.

I can see it. The folks iHustle at *Street Money* magazine just hit me today and said they started an Apple TV channel, Roku channel, and

Amazon Fire channel. I gave him your address and he said he sent you a magazine, too. I think you guys will for sure be able to build.

Anyway, good lookin' on the interview. I'ma get this all type up properly and get it all sent out to everybody. And you already know we're going to cook somethin' up. Mike Enemigo, Dutch. Books, movies. What should we tell 'em about that?

Just tell 'em they should be very afraid. (laughs)

LESSONS FROM RICK ROSS

Two days ago, I watched an interview with rapper Rick Ross, where he was promoting his new book *Hurricanes,* a memoir. When he walked onto the stage to sit with TV talk show host Tamron Hall, he was holding a bottle of Belaire Rosé and two wine glasses, which he then sat on the center table during the interview. On the side table, next to Tamron, sat an upright copy of Rick's book – so the cover was showing to the studio audience and TV viewers at all times. He had something else on his hat, a few words, but the editors of the show blurred it out for some reason.

The lesson here is promotion. It may seem obvious that, since Rick was there to promote his book, the cover of the book would be visible during the interview, but what some of you may not know, is that Rick is also the owner of Belaire spirits. See where I'm going with this? As a smart promoter, knowing he was going on national television, even though it was to discuss his book, he also brought along a bottle of his own spirits for all the world to see. I thought this was smart. And who knows what his hat said; it may have been the title of his new album, *Port of Miami 2*, though I'm not certain.

Now, my point to you is, if Rick Ross, a hip-hop superstar who has sold millions of records and has millions of followers on social media has to do this to ensure his products are successful, what would make you think you don't? If Rick Ross cannot just upload his book onto Amazon, then sit back and wait for it to be successful, what would make you, a guy in a prison cell with probably next to nothing in terms of an audience and resources, think you could just upload your book to Amazon and it would be a success?

Obviously, as a prisoner, you are not going to appear on national television anytime soon. However, why wouldn't you use the concept of this strategy to the best of your ability? I wrote my guy King Guru after seeing the interview to respond to a letter I'd received from him, and in it I told him about the Rick interview (hopefully he saw it and will know what what I was talking about firsthand), and that we need to start taking our books with us to the yard, and anywhere else we can get away with taking our books around the prison. Why not? We should certainly take whatever book we're trying to promote at the time to the yard, even if it's just to set it on the table while we work out. People will see it and ask about it, which gives us an opportunity to talk about it, display our expertise, and essentially "sell" it. We can let them check it out right there on the yard, then hand them a flier that tells them how and where they can buy their own copy. This will get people talking around the yard, and also when they go to another yard. To gain more eyes, using this strategy, send a copy of your book to loyal members of your cypher in other prisons who will do the same.

What Rick Ross does, and what he did here, essentially, is incorporate his products, his brand, into his lifestyle. He is not the only rapper who does this. 50 Cent does this extremely well. Anything he's promoting is going to be on his T-shirt and hat. Nipsey Hussle did this with his brand, Mozzy does this, and many others in hop hop do this as well. This is why I say to watch rappers. They are among the best promoters in the game. No cap.

Don't underestimate the power of these "small" moves. They add up! And be sure to literally incorporate your books, and your brand into your lifestyle.

LESSON FROM CATCH AND KILL

The book *Catch and Kill*, by Pulitzer Prize recipient Ronan Farrow, about Matt Lauer and Harvey Weinstein takin booty, etc., dropped yesterday. Since it's fresh, and I like to use real-life, and often real-time examples, I want to point out a couple of jewels.

First is the promo tour Ronan has been on. For the last two weeks or so, this guy has appeared on talk shows everywhere, talking about his book, answering questions about the book and the investigations he did to verify various claims in the book, etc. He's built up a huge amount of buzz. I don't even care about Matt Lauer and Harvey Weinstein or the weird shit they do, but just because Ronan stirred up so much buzz, even I almost want to read his book! Shit; might pick up some game on the various methods he used to pull it all off so successfully.

Point is, I'm willing to bet that, when his book dropped yesterday, he got a shit-load of sales. This is because A) He picked a hot topic many people want to know about, and B) He actively promoted the book; among the ways, by actively going on a promo tour. THIS is how you sell books, people! He didn't just write the book, put it on Amazon, and hope people would just flock to it. He actively pushed it. And Ronan is famous, has a fan base, a platform, connections, resources, and wrote about a hot, press-worthy topic. So if he has to do this in order to be successful, what makes you think you don't?

Now, as a prisoner, you obviously cannot go on a physical promo tour. But what you need to do is make up for what you can't do, with all the things you can do. You need to go on the kind of promo tour you can go on, be it submitting short stories to publishers with a foundation bigger than yours, who are putting together a book of short stories in your genre; writing for mags and blogs; advertising; maybe sending a press release to specific outlets, if the topic is worthy; maybe social media (if you have the resources), etc. You need to try and emulate what he did and how he did it as much as you can from a prison cell, not only using your creativity to write, but also think outside the book for promo opportunities.

The next thing I want to point out is his title – *Catch and Kill*. It's a killer title, literally. A killer title is a must! When I heard someone on the TV say "*Catch and Kill*, the new book," it immediately got my attention. Once I learned *Catch and Kill* was the new book about Matt Lauer and

Harvey Weinstein, I immediately tried to figure out what he meant by the title. After all, Matt didn't "kill" anyone. But when I watched an interview with Ronan, I learned he used the phrase as a metaphor for "buy the story (catch) and bury it (kill)." It made perfect sense to me. And, though I'm not certain it's intended, I also see another meaning. "Catch and kill" means to hunt – to stalk and capture your prey, then take it down. And that's what rape is – it's what rapists do. So, the title fits the story in more ways than one, in my opinion. Sharp...

Ensuring you have a killer, sensational, attention-grabbing title is one of the most important marketing decisions you can make. And, get this; it is also one of the cheapest! Do not drop the ball here.

Reversal: Sometimes, if your book is geared towards prisoners, or if you want to sell your book to prisoners, you may have limits on what you can title your book. My book with King Guru, *How To Hustle & Win: Sex, Money, Murder Edition* has been rejected from prisons on occasion because the title makes the book come off like a how-to book for criminal activity. It's not, and it actually has a very important moral, but the prisons will not read the book, they will just make a decision based on the title. I would love to title a book, *The Prisoner's Guide To Getting Any Bitch, Including The Ones Who Work In Your Prison!* What prisoner wouldn't buy that? But obviously I could never title a book that and expect to be able to get it into prison. No prison in America would allow it.

LESSONS FROM ETHIC

Ethic is the title of the latest, 5-part series by Street Lit queen and *New York Times* Best Selling Author, Ashley Antoinette, wife of JaQuavis Coleman, also a *New York Times* Best Selling Author. They are like the Jay-Z and Beyonce of the urban book game. They each write separately (I think book one in the *Ethic* series is Ashley's 12th solo book), and they've also written several books together; most notably, probably, is their series *The Cartel*.

Ethic is also the first series Ashley published via her new imprint, Ashley Antoinette Inc., where she's doing everything herself. I was fortunate enough to have been able to watch Ashley's rollout of her new series via social media – Instagram and Facebook, and experience how she did it. I've also read books 1-3. This is what I learned.

1. Ethic is a character from Ashley's book *Moth to a Flame*. Apparently, her female readers loved him so much, she decided to elaborate on his character via his own 5-part series. What this means is that Ethic, as a character, is not new. What I've noticed in Ashley's books, as well as her husband's, is that the storylines all cross each other somehow. In one way, shape of form, all of their books connect. In fact, in the beginning of book one, Ashley gives this notice:

"RECOMMENDATION FROM THE AUTHOR

This book is a spin off from my novel, *Moth to a Flame*. If you have not read it, STOP. It is advised that you do so BEFORE beginning this book.

If you have read the *Prada Plan* series and *Luxe* series it will enhance your enjoyment of this book, but they are NOT required before beginning *Ethic*."

Connecting all your books in this way will help them sell each other. As you see here, for the full *Ethic* experience, shed advises her readers to first read *Moth to a Flame*. She also connects her series *Prada Plan* and *Luxe*, though not as strongly. I've not read *Prada Plan* or *Luxe*, but they surely feature *Ethic*, or perhaps one of the other characters in *Ethic*.

If you plan to write fiction, you need to write a series, ideally 3-5 books (though it can be more, as Ashley and JaQuavis's series *The Cartel* currently has 8), so you can hook your readers with the first book (probably that you offer for free or .99 cents, so you offer a risk-or low-free entry), then capitalize on that investment by taking them on as long a ride as possible. And when you decide to start a new series to freshen things up, somehow include the characters from your other books, even if you only make them "minor" characters. All of your books should connect in some way. You want to draw your readers into the world you create, then keep them there as long as possible, making them want to read (BUY!) all your books for the full experience.

And fiction is not the only place you can use this strategy. Look throughout this book and you will see all the places I mention my other books. All my get-money books connect, work together, and enhance each other in some way, each elaborating on a different part of the hustle. *Jailhouse Publishing For Money & fame*, *How To Write Urban Books For Money & Fame*, *Mailbox Money*, *Online Goldmines*, *How To Sell Water To a Whal*e – all of these aspects of hustlin cross each other in some way, allowing me to connect the books. All of my books connect in one way or another, and yours need to as well. This is part of concentrating your forces, which is a major key to success.

2. Ashley put a playlist in the beginning of *Ethic* 2 and 3 (and probably 4 and 5). She writes:

"If you are a member of the Ashley and JaQuavis Reading Club on Facebook, you know that music played a pivotal role in the writing of this book for me. I have attached a playlist of songs that have helped me along this journey. I do suggest that to experience this book in the emotional way that I wrote it, you should listen to the suggested songs as you read along. Don't rush through this one. Savor it. Experience it. If you've been reading my work for a while, you know I like to evoke emotion. I want you to feel this one. If you are looking for something fun and lighthearted, this is not the book for you. This is HEAVY, this is dark, this is love and love comes with pain. To fall in love is to invite inevitable heartbreak. Grab a glass of wine and go there with me. Feel me. Happy reading!

ETHIC II PLAYLIST
H.E.R., Best Part
H.E.R., Changes

Ella Mai, 10,000 Hours
Ella Mai, Found
Ella Mai, Down
Jacquees, Trippin' Remix
Melanie Fiona, Wrong Side of a Love Song
Jagged Edge, Goodbye
Monica, Hurts the Most
Nivea, 25 Reasons
Brandy, Brokenhearted
Cardi B, Thru Your Phone
Cardi B, Money Bag
Blac Youngsta Remix, Booty"

I thought this was a dope idea. I'm not sure if she's connected to these artists and is using it as a way to plug their songs, or not. She's probably just listing the songs, like she said, to help enhance the experience she wants you to have from her books. She uses these songs, which are mentioned throughout the book, to stimulate more of your senses. I attempt to do this by listing songs in my urban books. I place them in the book where I feel the energy of the song matches what's going on in the story at the time. I always had the desire to make mixtapes out of the songs I mention in a story and include them with the sale of the book, so the reader could listen to them later and have a new experience, as now they'd be able to relate the songs to my story. I would also add vocal excerpts from the story to the mixtape, and also sound effects that fit the story. However, I never did it because I lacked the resources and didn't want to complicate my book production process. I never thought about just publishing a playlist, though, which is probably more appropriate anyway, at least until I'm able to properly produce the mixtape "soundtracks" to my books, so I'll probably borrow the playlist idea from Ashley.

3. Even though Ashley is already famous and successful – a *New York Times* Best Selling Author! – for the first book in the *Ethic* series, she most certainly used the 80/20 Publishing strategy I explain in this book. First, the interior design of the book is cheap and unprofessional. The right side of the pages are not justified and there are several other formatting issues throughout the book, like extra spaces between some

paragraphs, and more. I can also tell she didn't use an editor, as there are way too many commas that don't belong. Simply put, it looks like she did it all herself in her new venture to self-publish, and she wanted to get it to market as soon as possible.

Now, as an OCD editor and publisher, the format issues drive me nuts. (I'm glad to see that even THE Ashley Antoinette published a book with such issues, as now I shouldn't feel so bad for my own.) That said, the story was great, and as a reader, the formatting issues didn't bother me – they didn't affect the story, what most readers are concerned with. The story did its job in satisfying me as a reader, making me want to go on to book two. This adds credibility to the 80/20 Publishing theory that story is king.

Now, book two? The design and formatting are official. Maybe she used book one as a learning curve, or maybe she wanted to see if the story would catch before investing too much into it, but book two is official. The back of the cover is more professional, now having additional detail that the first book didn't, like and picture and bio. The font inside the book is better. The formatting of the pages is on point. And someone went through a removed all the excess commas she writes with. The design and quality of book two can hang with any book published by the big houses, and book three looks just like book two.

4. Watching Ashley's *Ethic* rollout was amazing. I don't know the exact amount of time she dropped all 5 books, but I'd say it was about 18 months. Yes, she dropped all 5 in about 18 months, each just a few months after the other.

What she did with book one is hook her core audience, which is mostly women, with an elaboration of Ethic, a man many of her fans love. She specifically designed Ethic to be her fans' "dream man," making them fall in love, then used him to help her seduce her fans. In book one the dedication says:

"I dedicate this book to my fans, but especially to the ladies who have fallen in love with ETHIC. You guys love him so much that I was forced to write a book where he was the focus. I created this character in 2009 and I am so honored that he still resonates with so many women, years later [she published book one in April, 2018]. He is timeless and I hope you enjoy this ride as you continue to fall in love with ETHIC through my words.

Ashley "Ash" Antoinette"

After hooking her fans with book one, she allowed them all to gather in her Facebook group to discuss their love for *Ethic*. (Were any of these fans promotional "plants"? I don't know. She may not need to do that, but you may need to. You can certainly see how planted "fans" talking about certain things and getting the party started could be beneficial, right?) Providing a public forum for *Ethic* fans to mingle is a savvy move. Remember; everybody wants what everybody wants, so the more people who "fall in love" with the character, the more it would snowball.

Like a clever dope dealer, Ashley had her fans fiending after the first hit, literally on her forum begging for more. Right when they could no longer take it, she dropped book two. Then she repeated the process for the next 18 months (or whatever it was), seducing her fans and building momentum for each drop as the series unfolded, her "Ash Army" loyally following her the entire ride.

5. Ashley made the whole *Ethic* experience very personal for her fans. Not only with the letters she wrote to them in her books, but at the end of book three, Ashley gives a notice to her fans that books four and five will be sold exclusively through her store, ashley-antoinette-books.myshopify.com. When *Ethic* four and five dropped she took orders from her fans directly and fulfilled them personally. She would sign each book before sending them out, often updating her progress on social media with pictures, and sometimes apologies for taking so long to get orders out as there were so many. It was all very intimate and hands on, and fans love this.

But this is interesting for another reason, too. Ashley completely cut out all other distributors, including Amazon, opting to do it all herself. Very, very smart, and most certainly profitable. Controlling distribution is a savvy way to market. This may be difficult for you to do as a prisoner because you will have to rely on dedicated assistance from the outside. However, if this is an option for you, you may want to consider it. You should remember, though, that Ashley has a large fanbase already, one that you don't have, and for you, being on Amazon and other online retailers will help you increase visibility.

6. Here's another thing I noticed, quite shockingly: Ashley doesn't have a regular website (nor do most the other street lit superstars!). Her and JaQuavis have ashleyandjaquavis.com, but when you go there, all it has is a picture of them and a place for you to enter your email address to receive updates. This allows them to collect emails, which is very valuable, but other than that, they don't even use personal websites. Instead, they use social media, then link their pages to where their books are sold.

So, the question is, do you, an inmate, really need a website? Can you save this expense and simplify your setup? I have a website. I like it because I own it – it's my own property, not subject to platform changes I can't control, and often don't like. It also allows me to collect emails, and I find it gives me credibility when dealing with people, especially people leery of dealing with prisoners, like family member of prisoners who order books, or companies I contact, trying to work with in some way. They are able to go to one spot and learn all about me, my books, and see that I'm legit. But is it absolutely necessary? Maybe not. If you have the resources and can afford the extra expense, I say do it. But remember, if you want to post all your books on it, and you plan to publish regularly, it will require upkeep. As a prisoner, it might be best to just capture emails, have a bio, a link to your social media pages, if you have them, and a link to your Amazon page where all your books can be purchased.

And that's another thing: most of your important info can be listed on your Amazon Author page. You can post almost anything on it, such as a bio, where you can even list your prison address if you want, a few pics, and even a few videos. You can then link this page to your Facebook and/or Twitter (not sure about Instagram). Then, of course, all your books will show, and can be purchased. Just another reason why you may not need a website, other than to capture emails.

Lastly on this "online profile/store" subject, Google. When anyone wants to go to your website, they will have to type your url into the search engine's search bar. Mine is thecellblock.net. This will take you to my website. But someone could just as easily type in "mike enemigo," and when they do, all my books come up, as well as everything else; articles written about me, places my books are available, reviews – everything. Also, all of my book covers will show – every book with Mike Enemigo on it – and if you want to purchase one, all you gotta do is click on it; it will take you straight to my Amazon page. Keep in mind, however, the bad thing about Google is that you can't control everything that comes up. If somebody writes something bad about you, even if it's not true, a link to the story may appear, and there's really not much you can do about it.

Point is, the need of a website may be shrinking, as evident by the fact that most the major street lit authors don't have one. Though I don't know their exact reasoning, I do know they have a reason. These guys are *New York Times* Best Sellers. I also know that hip hop, what urban falls under, has the savviest of hustlers, often on the forefront of things. Therefore, if you can't get a website, don't stress. It may be easier to go one of these other routes. It may be cheaper, more modern, and a way to simplify your setup, which is one of the major keys.
#JewelsOfTheGame

A LESSON FROM BEST-SELLING AUTHOR AND FINANCIAL GURU

[Robert T. Kiyosaki]

A few years ago, I granted an interview with a newspaper in Singapore. The young female reporter was on time, and the interview got under way immediately. We sat in the lobby of a luxurious hotel, sipping coffee and discussing the purpose of my visit to Singapore. I was to share the platform with Zig Ziglar. He was speaking on motivation, and I was speaking on "The Secrets of the Rich."

"Someday, I would like to be a best-selling author like you," she said. I had seen some of the articles she had written for the paper, and I was impressed. She had a tough, clear style of writing. Her articles held a reader's interest.

"You have a great style," I said in reply. "What holds you back from achieving your dream?"

"My work does not seem to go anywhere," she said quietly. "Everyone says that my novels are excellent, but nothing happens. So, I keep my job with the paper. At least it pays the bills. Do you have any suggestions?"

"Yes, I do," I said brightly. "A friend of mine here in Singapore runs a school that trains people to sell. He runs sells-training courses for many of the top corporations here in Singapore, and I think attending one of his courses would greatly enhance your career."

She stiffened. "Are you saying I should go to school to learn to sell?" I nodded.

"You aren't serious, are you?"

Again, I nodded. "What is wrong with that?" I was now backpedaling. She was offended by something, and now I was wishing I had not said anything. In my attempt to be helpful, I found myself defending my suggestion.

The reporter said to me: "I have a master's degree in English Literature. Why would I go to school to learn to be a salesperson? I am a professional. I went to school to be trained in a profession so I would not have to be a salesperson. I hate salespeople. All they want is money.

So, tell me why I should study sales?" She was packing her briefcase. The interview was over.

On the coffee table sat a copy of an earlier best-selling book I wrote. I picked it up as well as the notes she had jotted down on her legal pad.

"Do you see this?" I said pointing to her notes.

She looked down at her notes. "What?" she said, confused. Again, I pointed deliberately to her notes. On her pad she had written: "Robert Kiyosaki, best-selling author."

"It says best-selling author, not best-writing author," I said quietly. Her eyes widened.

"I am a terrible writer," I said. "You are a great writer. I went to sales school. You have a master's degree. Put them together and you get a 'best-selling author' and a 'best-writing author'."

Anger flared in her eyes. "I'll never stoop so low as to learn how to sell. People like you have no business writing. I am a professionally trained writer and you are a salesman. It is not fair!" she fumed.

SAMPLE MAGAZINE ARTICLE QUERY LETTER

March 19, 2020

Tiffany Chiles
Don Diva Magazine
603 W. 115th Street, #313
New York, NY 10025

Dear Ms. Chiles,

The recidivism rate remains high in the urban community due to most people feeling as if they have only one option to being successful – crime. There is a solution to this problem and I'd like to help shed light on it to your readers.

Over the past few years, I have developed a system in which I call TCB University. The purpose/goal of TCB University is to teach prisoners and street hustlers how to hustle and win *legally*. I believe TCB University will speak directly to your audience, in a language they understand and respect, and will show them alternatives to crime that will allow them .to live the life they desire without going, or going back to, prison.

The 2,000-word article I propose would be a primer on a few ways to hustle and win legally, such as:

- 5 Steps To Owning Your Story
- 5 Steps To Starting Your Own Business, Even With A Record!
- How To Get Rich Selling Information
- How To Legally Protect Your Assets

I've written and published 25 books from my prison cell, all geared toward the prisoner/urban market (see thecellblock.net for more info). I believe I can be an inspirational example to your readers. I have the material to turn around the article within weeks of notification. Enclosed is a small example of my work and a postpaid reply post card.

Thanks for your time. I look forward to working with you.

Sincerely,

Mike Enemigo
POB 1025
Rancho Cordova, CA 95741

info@thecellblock.net

SAMPLE MAGAZINE ARTICLE COVER LETTER

Mike Enemigo
PO Box 1025
Rancho Cordova, CA 95741
info@thecellblock.net

May 5, 2020

Tiffany Chiles
Don Diva Magazine
603 W. 115th Street, #313
New York, NY 10025

Dear Tiffany Chiles:

Enclosed please find my 2,000-word manuscript titled "How To Hustle & Win Legally" to be considered for publication in your magazine. This submission is in response to your request of April 20, 2017 to see the piece, after my query in March.
    "How To Hustle & Win Legally" is an article geared toward the young, urban go-getter looking for ways to make good money legally. It explores ways one can take "street" smarts and use them towards legal business endeavors before it is too late. It also details how prisoners who have a parole date can get out and profit from their intellectual capital so they can make money honestly in an effort to remain free, rather than return to prison like so many in our community do.
    As a prisoner who has no parole date, it has become my passion to learn how to hustle and win legally, and to teach those who still have a chance at freedom all that I've learned so that they can increase their chance at success. My methods are an alternative to what many think is their only option to achieving success – crime – and it is my hope that my article can enlighten your readers of that.

Thank you for your time. I look forward to hearing your thoughts.

Best regards,
Mike Enemigo

SAMPLE OF FINANCIAL ASSISTANCE LETTER

To My Dearest Friend(s):

If you have received this letter it is because I need your help. I am trying to raise the much-needed $2880 for the publishing of my first novel. I am asking for donations for this project. The novel is finished, complete, finally done and sitting on my living room table in an envelope addressed to the printer. The only thing missing is the check to go into it. As my friend, you know that this novel is my dream come true. It is my belief that this novel will bless others and warn them of the awful dangers of the drug game, in addition to reminding us of the power of God. He is a restorer and all of you (my friends) have watched God take me from embarrassment and separation, to RESTORATION. Please find it in your heart to help me by donating $100 to my cause. I will, of course, accept any amount, but I am requesting $100 from each of my friends to reach my eventual goal of $2880.

Please send a check made payable to BOOKMASTERS and mail to the below address.

I believe that I will receive the needed funding for this book. I thank you for all of your support, prayers, comments and encouragement. Soon, I will introduce the world to "Let That Be The Reason".

Sincerely,

Vickie M. Stringer
614-258-8611

Bookmasters
422 S. 18th Street
Columbus, Ohio 43205

EXAMPLE OF A FOREWORD

An O.G. from my city, Sacramento, the Capital of Killa Cali, came up to me one day on the prison yard and introduced himself. During the introduction he said he's a longtime friend of my bruh, Bad Ass Snoop. This is not an uncommon occurrence; people coming up to me, introducing themselves, and even using bruh's name as a way to connect. However, I heard the O.G. out, and next time I got at bruh, I dropped the name to run a check. Few weeks later I got a response from bruh; said O.G. is indeed official – old-school fam from back in the day.

Next time I saw O.G. I told him Snoop sends his love, and If he needed anything from me or my goons, just holla. O.G. then said he knew about my book game and has something he'd like me to fuck with. Well, that's easy, so I told him if he had a book, just get's to me and I got him. But then he said it wasn't his shit he wanted me to fuck with, it was his potna's. I told him I really couldn't fuck with anybody, too busy, but I'd do something for him, then he can do something for his potna. He told me his potna's name is Guru, and we know each other from the streets. I told him I didn't know any Guru, and then I began to see my attempt to help as being a bigger problem than I was interested in dealing with, so I smashed off with some of my young thugs.

A few weeks later I was on the yard with two of my goons, while two more of my goons posted up nonchalantly in the close vicinity. Up walks some tall, light-skinned dude asking if we knew who Mike Enemigo was – the one that does the books. We'd never seen this dude before, and since we done smashed so many pumpkins over the years, for all we knew he was some sort of torpedo seeking vengeance for some schmuck we done knocked down, and he was trying to use us to show him who Mike Enemigo is. So, two of my goons looked at each other, shrugged their shoulders, then looked back at him and told him they have no idea who Mike Enemigo is. As this is done, my two goons close in a bit and position themselves behind ol' boy in case it needed to go bad, ya dig? Dude then looked at me, and after a brief moment I said, "Fuck Mike Enemigo. He finna get it when I see him." Dude paused awkwardly, then threw his hands up and said, "Whoa, whoa; I ain't a part of all that. I'm Just tryna help find him for my folks – Guru."

Guru. I remembered the name from O.G. So, after looking at dude another couple seconds I reached my fist out for a pound and said, "What up, Playboy. I'm Mike."

He smiled and laughed; admired my deviousness.

He began to tell me Guru was on the yard and he has some book business he wanted to discuss. I told him I had my plate full with the books, but to introduce me to Guru anyway. He did.

After meeting Guru I decided we should go for a walk. I wanted to lend him an ear since he seemed pretty passionate and persistent; see what he had to say. So, we began to walk. First thing I wanted to get out the way, however, was why O.G. had said we knew each other from the streets. I told him I didn't know anyone named Guru. He told me Guru is Just his pen name, his name is Wilberto Belardo, from Oak Park.

Ah... Willie, from Oak Park. That rang a bell. He's a fellow hitter out of Sacramento, known for knockin' shit down. We're the same generation. We'd never met; always just missed each other. Nevertheless, I knew who he was, and he knew who I was.

We knew each other. Form the streets.

Guru and I began talking further. Touching base on this and that. He told me about some book ideas he had. I was intent on not picking up anymore writers for The Cell Block. I had what I wanted. However, it didn't take Guru more than five minutes of talking to me before I guaranteed him a book deal for as many books as he wants. Without ever seeing a word he wrote or signing any kind of paperwork, we had a deal, and it was official. I didn't even have to consider it. I knew and know Guru. Even before meeting him. Not only from his reputation from Sac, but also from the energy I received from him the moment we met.

Within minutes I knew Guru was one of us; a member of this secret society of the most authentic muthafuckin' beings alive. We know when we meet. You feel the energy, and you see it in the eyes. You'll understand what I'm talking about once you've read this book.

One of the reasons I started The Cell Block is to give my team an alternative to the street life and a life of crime – a way to get rich and famous, at least by hood standards, without the prison and early-grave chances most of us constantly take in order to achieve our ambitions as Riders. And this is what Guru wanted for himself, so we were on the same page. And though he had his own money and would even be getting out soon, he was not interested in starting his own publishing company; he simply liked what he saw in TCB and was determined to rock with us.

As the common cliches say: Game recognize game, real recognize real. So we made plans. However, things didn't go exactly as we had hoped. Guru did get out, and he went to Florida as we had planned, but before we could do our thang, he was picked up on an old murder that happened before his rather new-found idea of redirecting his energies from crime to writing books.

Damn... Now I was worried. Guru was optimistic; said he was willing to spend all his bread on getting the best lawyer, or lawyers, if necessary. But though I lack faith in the system, I pretended to be confident in an effort to be supportive of someone I consider a friend, whom I've known for a very long time. From the streets.

Guru and I stayed in touch pretty regularly. I consistently encouraged him to work on his books. He assured me that, besides his case, his books were his main priority. He told me he was working on a few of them; *Underworld Zilla*, a series, and some type of "game" guide. Something like that. At this point I wasn't really trippin' on the books in the sense of business, I just wanted my folks to keep his mind focused and positive while going through something as heavy as a murder trial; something I know about firsthand.

A few months went by. Then, one day, a C.O. slid a letter under my door from the Virgin Islands. *What the fuck is this?* I opened it and saw it was from Guru. He said *Underworld Zilla* is done, where do I want it sent; and, oh, yeah, he beat the case, too! Ah, ha, ha, ha! I can't even tell you how happy I was. I told him to send the manuscripts to the Folsom office and I'd put them right in line. He asked me if I was good; if I needed anything. Of course, I told him to send me some pictures and hook me up with a bad native bitch. He did everything I asked, including the things of which we spoke while he was still incarcerated.

Around this time, someone had let me read a book: *How to Hustle and Win*, by Supreme Understanding. I thought it was a good book, full of interesting info, and I would not have been upset had I paid the $15.00 for it. However, it wasn't what I'd expected, or hoped for. Well, hearing from Guru at this time gave me an idea: he needed to write a real *How to Hu$tle and Win*, from a grimier perspective; a Sex, Money, Murder edition. And if I remembered correctly, he even had a few pages of rough draft he'd started along these lines already – the "game" guide.

I got at the native bitch Guru introduced me to and told her the message to give him; that I wanted him to write a real *How to Hu$tle and*

Win: Sex, Money, Murder edition, from a real gunner who has truly done everything of which he speaks. I told him to do it organically and make it authentic.

According to the postmark on the package, he had it done and out within two weeks; said he typed it on an old-school typewriter while blowin' trees and sippin' Scotch. I couldn't fuckin' believe it. I could still smell the smoke on the manuscript, and the perfume from the bitch that mailed it for him.

Guru did exactly as I asked of him; he did it organically and kept it authentic. In an effort to preserve some of this, I'm publishing this book exactly as he typed it, typos and all, straight from an old-school typewriter in the Virgin Islands.
True story.

Money motivated,

M.E.
CEO, The Cell Block

WRITER/AUTHOR RESOURCES

4orPlay Publications, LLC
4100 Esters Rd. #286
Irving, TX 75038

This is an urban publishing company. They publish books like "East Boogie," "Silence is Secrecy," "4orPlay" and more.

They are now also accepting manuscripts for possible publishing. They want you to send the first 7 chapters, which are not to exceed 70 pages, and a synopsis.

Website: 4orPlayPublications.com

APWA
198 College Hill Road
Clinton, NY 13323-1218

The American Prison Writing Archive is an Internet-based, non-profit archive of first-hand testimony to the living and working conditions experienced by incarcerated people, prison employees and prison volunteers. Anyone who lives, works or volunteers inside American prisons or jails can contribute non-fiction essays, based on first-hand experience: 5,000-word limit (15 double-spaced pages); a signed APWA permission-questionnaire must be included in order to post on the APWA. All posted work will be accessible to anyone in the world with Internet access. For more info and to download the permissions-questionnaire, go to www.dhinitiative.org/projects/apwa, or write to the address above.

Ashley Rice Collection
Blue Mountain Arts, Dept. WHIM
P.O. Box 4549
Boulder, CO 80306

This is a greeting card company. Send card material that is light, lively and very original with SASE.

The Blue Book of Grammar and Punctuation

A guide to grammar and punctuation by an educator with experience teaching English to prisoners. It's 110 pages, $14.95, and can be bought from Prison Legal News.

The Blumer Literary Agency
Olivia ("Liv") Blumer
350 Seventh Avenue, Suite 2003
New York, NY 10001

This is a publishing agency. Write/Send SASE for more information. Ask for submission guidelines. Specify what kind of book you are interested in submitting – fiction, non-fiction, etc.

Phone Number: 212-947-3040,
Fax 212-947-0460

California Lifer Newsletter
PO Box 277
Rancho Cordova, CA 95741

CLN is a newsletter published six times per year, with reviews of the latest published and unpublished state and federal cases concerning parole issues and many more topics of interest to prisoners. CLN for prisoners is $30 or (60 First Class Forever Stamps) per year.

Phone Number: (916) 402-3750
Website: lifesupportalliance.org

Children's Book Insider, LLC
901 Columbia Road
Fort Collins, CO 80525

Questions & Information: 970-495-0056

Cimarron Review
205 Morrill Hall
Oklahoma State University
Stillwater, OK 74078

"Cimarron Review is now accepting both electronic and postal submissions. Please read these guidelines before submitting.

We accept submissions year-round in poetry, fiction and art. All postal submissions must be accompanied by an SASE. Please, regardless of whether you're submitting electronically or by the postal mail, include a cover letter with your submission.

Please send 3-6 poems or one piece of fiction. Address all the work to the appropriate editor (fiction or poetry) and mail postal submissions to the above address.

Artists and photographers interested in having their work appear on an upcoming cover of the Cimarron Review should query by E-mail at cimarronreview@okstate.edu. If our editors are interested, we'll reply and request to see more work.

We do NOT accept the following:

• Previously published work (includes work published online).
• E-mailed submissions of any kind.

We no longer accept international reply coupons from writers living outside the United States.

We do not publish theme issues. We are interested in any strong writing of a literary variety, but are not especially partial to fiction in the modern realist tradition and poetry that engages the reader through a distinctive voice – be it lyric, narrative, etc. When submitting fiction, please do not include a summary of your story in the cover letter. Allow the work to stand on its own. We have no set page lengths for any genre, but we seldom publish short-shots or pieces longer than 25 pages. There are, however, exceptions to every rule. Our guiding aesthetic is the quality of the work itself.

For fiction, please number each page.

When submitting electronically, poets should include all poems for submission in a single file.

We do not accept more than one story – even if the stories are very short – in a single submission. Please send only one story at a time.

When sending postal submissions, do not staple the manuscript; paperclips are the preferred fastener.

Electronic submissions should be doc, docx, pdf, or rtf files and should include your contact information in the upper left or right-hand corner of each page.

Response time varies, but we typically respond to submissions within 3-6 months, often much sooner. At times, however due to a backlog, and especially for work submitted in the summer, a response may take longer. If you have not heard from us after six months, please feel free to query by sending an E-mail to cimarronreview@okstate.edu. Please do not query before six months.

Simultaneous submissions are welcomed, but please contact us immediately through postal or E-mail (with the date and genre of your original submission) should your work be accepted elsewhere. Please also withdrawal electronically-submitted stories accepted elsewhere through the online submission manager system. Unless poets wish to withdraw all poems from a submission, they should withdraw individual poems by E-mail or postal mail only.

For publication, Cimarron Review acquires First North American Serial Rights. After publication, rights revert to the author. At this time, Cimarron Review pays its contributors two copies of the issue in which their work appears.

You may contact us through postal nail or at cimarronreview@okstate.edu. Also, please do not submit again to the Cimarron Review until you have heard back from us. We reserve the right to send multiple submissions back to the author with no response."

Copyright Office
101 Independence Ave., S.E.
Washington, DC 20559

Write these guys and request copyright forms and instructions for unpublished works. You can also have your people do this online at copyright.gov at a discount. Be aware that the "Poor Man's Copyright" is a myth. It's not valid in court.

Defiore & Co.
47 E. 19th Street, 3rd Floor
New York, NY 10003

Contact Lauren Gilchrist. Represents nonfiction books and novels. Fiction areas: ethnic, literary, mainstream, mystery, suspense, thriller.

Don Diva

Email submission to: submitdondivamag.com

We only accept submissions from the original author of the articles or a publicist hired by the copyright owner to submit material here. By submitting material, you acknowledge that you are legally entitled to distribute the work and to allow it to be redistributed. (If you are a book publisher or public relations firm with copy to distribute, please include a note to that effect at the top of the article you submit.) We do not pay for articles, and do not accept articles that are primarily advertisements. However, you may place a brief resource box and contact information (but no ads) at the end of your article.

As a condition of submitting your article, you (and any other individual co-authoring) unconditionally and irrevocably waive all claims to compensation for use of the article, and/or any rights with respect to such use you may have under copyright law, the right to publicity, the right to privacy, the law of defamation, and any other common law or statutory claims under the laws of any jurisdiction.

Editing: Don Diva Magazine reserves the right to edit your submission for clarity, style, format, and to enhance search engine placement.

Submission: If you wish to share an article or idea you will need to send it to us via email at submitdondivamag.com and you will need to include the following information in your email for your submission to be considered:

First and Last Name
Email Address
How you would like your name to be displayed (Full name, first name only, nickname, anonymous)
Title of your Article
Article
Disclaimer (below)

Disclaimer: You must include the following disclaimer or we will be unable to consider your material for publication.

"I certify that I am the author or sole owner of the material I am submitting. Don Diva Magazine and/or dondivamag.com or its affiliated publication or websites and its licensees may reproduce, distribute, publish, display, edit, modify, create derivative works and otherwise use the material for any purpose in any form and on any media. I agree to indemnify Don Diva Magazine and/or dondivamag.com or its affiliated publication or websites for all damages and expenses that may be

JAILHOUSE PUBLISHING

incurred in connection with the material."

Email submission to:
submit@dondivamag.com

MANUSCRIPTS/BOOKS
Don Diva is not accepting submissions at this time.

NO SUBMISSION WILL BE RETURNED.

The Editorial Eye
66 Canal Center Plazas, Suite 200
Alexandra, VA 22314

This is a magazine that covers standards and practices for writers and editors.

Get Your Poetry Published
"Be Published Now. Our Services Can Help. Request **FREE** Publishing Kit!"

Website: be-published.com

Hawkeye Editing
PO Box 16406
St. Paul, MN 55116

Editing and typing services. Reasonable rates and rapid response. FREE evaluation of and manuscript, plus FREE proofreading and corrections on a single-page personal letter. Just enclose a SASE for return of your document. For quickest response, their service is also available through CorrLinks.

Hollywood Scriptwriter
PO Box 10277
Burbank, CA 91510

If you want to start writing movie scripts, order this magazine. It's $36 for a 1-year subscription, 6 issues.

Info
PO Box 64
Darien, CT 06820

Looking for a writing coach to help you with your literary works? Write/Send SASE for more information.

INKWELL Magazine
Manhattanville College
2900 Purchase Street
Purchase, NY 10577

Mail Entry Guidelines: Entry fee: $5 for the first poem, $3 for each additional poem. Include your name, address and email in a cover letter or on each poem.

Phone Number: (914) 323-5239
Email: inkwell@mville.edu

Inside Newsletter
ANTI-RECIDIVISM COALITION
1320 E. 7th Street, Suite 260
Los Angeles, CA 90021

This newsletter is one of the better-designed newsletters for sure. They accept writing submissions, too.

K. Carter
PO Box 70092

Henrico, VA 23255

Incarcerated writer? Walkinthoseshoes.com posts inmate essays in Views From The Inside. Also, mentors' authors of all book genres for our 'E-Library'. Mail essays or sample chapters to the above address. Send SASE for more info

LeNoir Publications
350 Bay St, Suite 100-361
San Francisco, CA 94133

This is a company that provides publishing services and specializes in catering to incarcerated individuals. To request a full list of their services, write/send SASE.

Locus
PO Box 13305
Oakland, CA

This is a newspaper that covers the sci-fi writing field. It's $60 for a 1-year subscription; 12 issues per year.

Phone Number: (510) 339-9198
Website: locusmag.com.

Manning Document Processing
PO Box 641
Norwalk, CT 06856

They type, design and prepare manuscripts for self-publishing. Reasonable, accurate and fast.

Manuscripts To Go
16420 Cooley Ranch Rd.
Geyderville, CA 95441

This company will help you with your manuscript(s). Write/Send SASE for more information.

The Marshall Project
156 West 56th St., Suite 701
New York, NY 10010

The background of The Marshall Project is that former New York Times Editor Bill Keller left the Times to start a new nonprofit news organization reporting solely on criminal justice, because he and many of the reporters now at The Marshall Project believed it was a pressing national issue that deserved an exclusive focus.

They launched in 2014, and the majority of their readers tend to be experts, advocates, practitioners, etc., with a direct interest in criminal justice. However, they do get a lot of readers from the general public, primarily because they co-publish many of their articles with publications like The Washington Post, The New York Times, Atlantic, Slate, Vice, etc.

ATTENTION ALL WRITERS!

Want your thoughts to be read in newspapers like The New York Times and The Washington Post? It can happen if you submit your writing to The Marshall Project. This is a call for submissions for The Marshall Project.

"The Marshall Project is a news organization that reports on the criminal justice system, including what happens inside jail and prisons. We have over 10,000 daily readers.

Part of what we do is publish first-person writing and reporting from inside jail and prisons, written by prisoners themselves. We want to give readers a sense of what life is like inside jails and prisons, and we believe that those who are actually inside are the best people to tell us.

If you are interested in writing for us – and reaching an audience of thousands of readers on the outside who want to know what life is like on the inside – here is some information about the type of writing we are looking for.

What we are looking for: Nonfiction writing about a specific aspect of life inside. Try to focus on one specific topic and tell a story about that topic. For example, tell us a story about a friendship you've made while inside; or a story about food or going to mess hall or commissary; or about how you get exercise; or about getting an education or having a job; or how you maintain relationships with family on the outside; or a story of your relationship with staff members; or the experience of solitary confinement or other forms of punishment.

The topic could be almost anything. The most important thing is to choose a very specific part of your experience and to write us a story about it.

What we are NOT looking for: Poetry, fiction, stories about your whole life (rather than a specific topic), essays about anything outside of your direct experience."

Length: 500-2,000 words

Please include your full name, how to contact you, and the url facebook.com/thecellblock.net

Minutes Before Six
2784 Homestead Road #301
Santa Clara, CA 95051

Your voice deserves to be included in the conversation!

Minutes Before Six is a respected online community of imprisoned writers, poets and artists whose mission is to provide contributors a worldwide forum for self-expression. In exchange for your writing or visual art, we offer the unique opportunity to be heard and have your artwork viewed. MB6 reaches on average 35,000 people per month. As a volunteer-based non-profit organization, MB6 can neither sell your work nor afford you more than first-rate exposure and the online publication of select submissions. We ask that you send us your best work.

Website: MinutesBeforeSix.com

Occasion Gallerie
Blue Mountain Arts
P.O. Box 1007
Boulder, CO 80306

Notecard poetry is welcome. Send with SASE.

PEN American Center
588 Broadway, Suite 303
New York, NY 10012

The PEN's Prison Writing Program has three basic areas of concentration:

1. The Handbook For Writers In Prison. This handbook teaches elements of writing fiction, non-fiction, and poetry. It also provides resources for inmates in terms so next steps for their completed works. The Handbook is FREE for all prisoners who write us a letter requesting one.

2. Our annual Prison Writing Program awards contest. PEN awards cash prizes in five categories of writing from prisoners (fiction, essay, memoir, poetry, and drama/screenplay). We receive 1500 entries a year; the contest ends September 1st. We encourage inmates of all writing levels to enter the contest. To enter, simply mail the entry to the address above. No application or form is necessary, though most inmates do send us a short letter telling us a little bit about themselves. Winners lists are available upon request.

3. Our Mentor Program. The Prison Writing Mentorship Program pairs up established writer mentors with incarcerated mentees. Our program requires at least three exchanges of writing between mentees and mentors (that is, three submissions from mentees and three observations/commentaries to the submissions from mentors). To become eligible for the program, an inmate must first enter the annual contest. Winners are offered the opportunity to participate in the mentorship program and, in some instances, writers who do not win an award but show promise are also offered a mentor.

Phoebe Journal

Literary publication that accepts between Sept. 1 - Apr. 15.

P.L.U. MAX
POSSE SOLUTIONS
P.O. Box 900188
Palmdale, CA 93590

This is a legal newsletter that costs $36 a year. Your people can order it by emailing them at possesolutions@gmail.com. POSSE SOLUTIONS is founded and ran by Nick Woodall, a paralegal and consultant who had LWOP, and after 30 years in CA prisons filed his own clemency petition which was granted.

The Poetry Wall; Cathedral of St. John the Divine
1047 Amsterdam Ave.
New York, NY 10025

They accept poetry of all kinds for display, and invites people to correspond with inmates whose poetry is on display.

Poete Maudit
PO 216
Farmersville, CA 93223

Mission statement: Providing an outlet for aspiring authors to have their voices heard. At Poete Maudit Publishing we're dedicated to serving the incarcerated writing community. We offer a wide range of services including traditional publishing, self-publishing assistance, typing, and editing. For more info, send SASE to the address above.

We also run an online writers' workshop. Every month we select two essays and two poems written by our prison correspondents and post them on our website. A congratulatory letter is sent to the winners. To participate, send a short essay (250-500 words), piece of creative writing, or poem to: Larry Coonradt; Postal Annex 40485 Murrieta; Hot Springs Rd., Suite B4; PMB 201; Murrieta, CA 92563.

Website: poetemaudit.net

Poets and Writers, INC
90 Broad St., Suite 2100
New York, NY 10004

An organization that publishes many books on writing, as well as a bi-monthly magazine. Write to receive a catalog.

The Poet's Workshop
C/O Sarah Lindahl
St Louis County Jail
4334 Haines Rd
Duluth, MN 55811

Publishes monthly magazine including poetry by prisoners. FREE to prisoners who submit poetry that is published.

Poetry Society of America
15 Gramercy Park
New York, New York 10003

Writer's competition.

Phone Number: (212) 254-9628

The Prison Journal
6041 Watch Chain Way
Columbia, MD 21044

Prison Journalism Project
SUBMISSION GUIDELINES

The Prison Journalism Project publication was started to share your stories about dealing with the coronavirus from inside and around the criminal justice system.
We heard reports that some people had not been able to get a hold of even a bar of soap to maintain

minimum sanitary practices. We heard that shelter-in-place orders have prevented you from seeing your loved ones, isolating you even more than you already are. We also know that the spike in unemployment has impacted families and their ability to care for their loved ones inside. There are reports of some states releasing older inmates, but re-entering society in a moment like this presents tremendous challenges. Of course, there are also triumphs in adversity – babies being born, families growing closer, and the essential work some of you do, risking your own health for the safety of others. Some of these stories are coming out, but not enough. Every experience is unique, complex and nuanced. We wanted to make sure that your experiences were also remembered when future generations look back on the history of this period.

We have also now expanded the scope of the publication because it was evident that you had a lot more to share with the world about your experience with incarceration. We are accepting stories across all topics that touch you beyond the pandemic. Some of you might have thoughts about the George Floyd killing or your own experience with police brutality. Some of you might have something to say about prison conditions or criminal justice reform. Of course, we are still very much interested in your experiences amid the pandemic. But you should feel free to submit stories about topics that you care about and want the world to know.

The Prison Journalism Project was established in 2019 to highlight the voices of the men, women and youth behind bars as well as those of their loved ones. Our goal is to help establish fresh reputations as journalists and writers and help people become thought leaders in criminal justice issues. We think what you have to say is tremendously important.

Please note that any facts in your piece must be information you gathered firsthand, not speculation or information that you've obtained second or thirdhand (that is, information that someone has passed onto you about someone else). We cannot accept stories about your individual cases, nor can we accept stories that are accusatory about a specific person, group or institution because of our limitations in verifying the facts. Any data that is mentioned must also be attributed. We reserve the right to exclude portions of your work that don't conform to this policy.

WHO: We invite anyone who touches the criminal justice system to submit your work. We welcome first-time writers as well as experienced writers. You can be currently or previously incarcerated, a family member, a friend, a volunteer, a prison staff member, an attorney, etc. When you submit, we will ask for your full name and contact information, so we can verify who you are. We prefer to publish full name bylines because they give your story more weight and integrity. However, if you would like to publish with your first name only or a pen name, please state your reason when you submit, and we will honor that. Please note that we do not use titles (Mr., Ms., Dr. etc.) in bylines.

WHAT: We understand that self-expression of experiences can take many forms, so we have established categories for a broad range of genres: journalism, essay, memoir, fiction/poetry, visual stories and audio stories.

Please make sure that your stories have a header with your full name, contact information, date, wordcount, genre and suggested title/headline for your piece. If you would like to publish by first name only or a pen name, please attach a note at the bottom of your submission with your reason.

If you are submitting a written piece, we invite you to include an accompanying photo, graphic or a suggestion of one. We also invite you to provide a 2-3 sentence bio that we can attach to your piece that will inform the reader about who you are, where you're from, and anything else that you might like the reader to know. If you are currently or formerly incarcerated, you may include information about your sentence, but you are not required to do so. If you do not submit a bio, we will add a sentence with the date that we received your piece.

If you are sending a written work electronically, please submit stories in an attachment as a Word or Google doc. Filenames should include your last name (example: PJPsubmissionSmith.doc).

By submitting your work, you will be granting us permission to edit/condense your work and publish it on our site on a non-exclusive basis. This means that you will retain the rights to your work and can publish it elsewhere as well. Sometimes, we will take a screenshot of a part of your letter and use it in lieu of an accompanying photo. We think it's a nice way to help readers connect with the writer. We will make sure that any personal information is blacked out, but if you prefer that we not publish a photo of your letter, please note that.

We will strive to publish at least an excerpt of every submission as long as they meet the parameters below. Please read through to the end of this document before you submit your work.

WHEN: We are accepting stories on a rolling basis.

WHERE: E-mail: prisonjourn@gmail.com

Jpay: prisonjourn@psu.edu

Postal mail: Prison Journalism Project
2093 Philadelphia Pike #1054
Claymont, DE 19703

JOURNALISM: This category includes any articles that tell people about things that actually happened. A journalistic work requires you to gather information through reporting and research. Facts, including data, must be attributed and verifiable, and the story must be fairly presented. Stories should be less than 1,500 words. Here are a few examples:

- Explanatory: this could be an article about strategies for maintaining sanitary conditions in your cell or a how–to/tips piece for surviving isolation.
- Q&A: this could be a question and answer style interview story about how someone you know is dealing with the pandemic. You can provide a short introduction of the person you are interviewing and follow with a list of questions and condensed answers.
- Essay: this could be an article written in the first person about your personal experience with a focus on facts. How has your day-to-day life changed? How have prison rules changed? What other developments have impacted you and the people you know? We would also like to hear about access to medical care or about the future of educational, therapeutic, or religious programming.

MEMOIR: This category includes stories about your personal experiences. Compared to the journalistic essay, a memoir gives you more creative freedom in how you express yourself and allows you to reminisce more deeply about your past, present and future. Stories should be no more than 1,500 words. Here are a few sample prompts:

- How is this pandemic affecting your family or your relationship with your loved one? If you have lost someone, consider sending us an eulogy.
- How has this pandemic changed the way you view your life? How has it changed the way you view other people in your life?
- What do you want people to know about what you are experiencing or thinking? Write it as a letter. Start your piece by addressing it to "Dear Friends."
- As the pandemic changes how we connect to each other in the world, what can people learn from you about social isolation, solidarity, or scarcity?

If you don't consider yourself to be a writer, but would like to tell your story to someone, please submit your request with a short summary of what you would like to share and your contact information. We will accommodate those requests to the best of our ability.

FICTION/POETRY: We will accept short stories and poems. Work should be 1,500 words or less. Please submit no more than 2-3 poems.

VISUAL STORIES: This category can include:

- a photo essay: a series of 5-8 photos focused on a theme with a detailed caption of 2-3 sentences for each photo that explains it and what you're trying to convey with it. This can also be one photo with a 4-5 sentence caption.
- a comic or short graphic story: a fictional or non-fiction story that you are telling in comic strip format. No more than two pages.
- art: a sketch or a painting with a brief explanation of your intention behind it.

AUDIO STORIES: Record yourself discussing any of the subjects referenced above. Record others (with their explicit permission!) doing the same. Your recorded stories might match any of the genres detailed above (journalism, memoir, fiction/poetry). Recordings should be no longer than two minutes in length. You can choose to edit your work from a longer recording. Or you can plan out your piece ahead of time, so it doesn't exceed the maximum.

Prison legal news
Editor
Prison Legal News
P.O. Box 1151
Lake Worth, FL 3346

Prison Legal News Writer's Guidelines

PLN's target audience consists of prisoners and their families, lawyers and political activists. We publish news and law articles pertaining to imprisonment. We also publish book reviews, but no fiction, poetry or commentary. Law articles are done only by assignment, so you must query first if you wish to write this type of article for us.

You must include a completed, signed copy of our writer contract (enclosed–copy on reverse side of guidelines for your records) when making submissions. If possible, send submissions or query letters via email to: articlesprisonlegalnews.org, but remember to send us the completed contract through the regular mail unless you are only sending a query letter. Do not send Mac files. If you do not have email access, send submissions or queries directly to our office:

Editor
Prison Legal News
P.O. Box 1151

Lake Worth, FL 3346

Please submit two typed copies of your article or an original with one carbon copy. Those who have no typewriter access should submit one legibly printed hand-written copy. PLN does not return manuscripts.

Manuscripts should conform to the following guidelines:

- Typewritten on 8-1/2" x 11" white bond paper with one-inch margins on all sides.

- Text should be left justified, not full justified.

- Do not use hyphenation.

- Typewriters: 10 characters/inch in courier or regency font. Computers: 12 pt font, Times New Roman or Arial.

- The article's title should appear at the top of the first page only. Do not use all capitals. The byline, if any, should be on the next line.

- Use single spacing and indent paragraphs. Do not skip a line between paragraphs.

- Do not underline anything. Use bold print or italics to emphasize a particular word.

- If the article is based on other published sources, list them at the end of the article as follows: Source: Publication A, Publication B. Report C. Please provide copies of the material relied on in your article.

- If the article refers to a previous PLN article, reference it in brackets. Example: [See: Title of Article, PLN, May, 2000].

- Use the following terminology:

Prisoner *not* inmate
Guard not *correctional* officer
prison or jail *not* correctional facility

This does not apply to terms that appear within a quote or in the name of a facility.

We pay ten dollars for articles under 1500 words and forty dollars for feature articles over 1500 words. Payment is made when the article is accepted for publication in PLN.

PLN reserves the right to edit on modify all article submissions, though we will not do extensive rewriting or editing without consulting the author. Let us know when you make your submission if your article has been published, or will be published, in other forums.

Prisoner Express
127 Anabell Taylor Hall, Cornell University
Ithaca, NY 14853

These guys offer free Screenplay, Poetry, and Journal courses.

JAILHOUSE PUBLISHING

Professional Press
P.O. Box 4371
Chapel Hill, NC 27515

This company provides you with an opportunity to publish your book(s) at an affordable price. Send a SASE for their FREE brochure containing details.

Phone Number: 800-277-8960

Website: profpres.com

Rolling Stone - LETTERS
1290 Avenue of the Americas
New York, NY 10104-0298

Letters become the property of Rolling Stone and may be edited for publication.

Sagewriters
Box 215
Swarthmore, PA 19081

SageWriters is a community of free and imprisoned writers, artists, musicians, filmmakers, playwrights and activists working together to give an artistic voice to movements for justice, healing, reawakening compassion in our elected officials, creating a community love ethic, supporting effective re-entry programs, ending prisons as we know them and developing community-based Houses of Healing.

Phone Number: 610-328-6101
Website: SAGEWRITERS.com

Sanders, Louise S
PO Box 361402
Decatur, GA 30036

They type manuscripts and papers. They also format paragraphs and chapters, edit grammar, punctuation, etc. Send SASE for FREE price list.

Sentinel Writing Competitions
Sentinel Poetry Movement
Unit 136
113 - 115 George Lane
South Woodford, London E18 1AB
United Kingdom

Writer's competition.

Sinister Wisdom, INC.
P.O. Box 3252
Berkeley, CA 94703

Publishes work by lesbians only – prose, poetry, essays, graphics, and book reviews. FREE to women in prison.

Skin&Ink Letters
219 Route 4 East, Suite 211
Paramus, NJ 07652

Send letters, photos, drawings, etc., to this tattoo magazine. Must include return postage if you want you shit back.

Slipstream Poetry Contest
Dept. W-1
PO Box 2071
Niagara Falls, New York 14301

Writer's competition. The annual Slipstream poetry contest offers a $1,000 prize plus 50 professionally-printed copies of your book.

Guidelines:
Send up to 40 pages of poetry: any style, format, or theme (or no theme), and a $20 check, bank draft, or money order for reading fee. Due to recent increases in the cost of mail, manuscripts will no longer be returned. Send only copies of your poems, not originals.

SMOOTH Fiction, c/o SMOOTH
P.O. Box 809
New York, NY 10013

Website: fiction@smoothmag.com

SMOOTH magazine accepts short fiction submissions to be published in their magazine.

SMOOTH-Talk
P.O. Box 809
New York, NY 10013

Feeling like nobody cares? Here's your chance to speak your mind and let your voice be heard – even if nobody's listening. Send your letters, photos, drawings, x-rays, etc.

State V. Us Magazine
PO 29291
Baltimore, MD 21213

State V. Us is an online and print publication that spotlights high-profile cases; corruption in prisons, the police departments and other branches of the government; wrongful convictions; true stories of men and women in prison; and success stories of formerly incarcerated individuals. If you have a story to tell, email them, or write to the address above. They also sell advertising space if you have a product to promote.

State V. Us was nominated for the 2018 and 2019 Titan Awards for Magazine of the Year. The print magazine is high-quality, full color, and each issue is $10.99, or you can subscribe to the next 4 issues for $35.00. It comes out quarterly.

Website: StateVsUsMag.com
Facebook: StateVsUsMagazine
IG: StateVsUs
Twitter: StateVsUs
#StateVsUsMag

Teachers and Writers Corroborative
520 8th Ave., suite 2020
New York, NY 10018

This organization publishes a number of books on writing, which are filled with ideas and exercises. Write to request a catalog.

Website: twc.org.

The Threepenny Review
PO Box 9131
Berkeley, CA 94709

1. At present The Threepenny Review is paying $400 per story or article, $200 per poem or Table Talk piece. This payment buys first serial rights in our print and digital editions, and the copyright then reverts to the author immediately upon publication.

2. We do not consider submissions that arrive via email. Everything must be sent either through the regular mail or via our designated online upload system (see www.threepennyreview.com). All mailed manuscripts must include an SASE; those that arrive without as SASE will not receive a reply. Mailed submissions should be sent to 'The Editor's at the above address.

3. We do not print material that has previously been published elsewhere, and we do NOT consider simultaneous submissions. We do our best to offer a quick turnaround time, so please allow us the privilege of sole consideration during that relatively brief period; writers who do not honor this request will not be published in the magazine.

4. Response time for unsolicited manuscripts ranges from one week to two months. Please do not submit more than a single story or article, or more than five poems, until you have heard back from us about your previous submission.

5. All articles should be double-spaced (except poetry, which can be single-spaced or double-spaced)! Critical articles should be about 1500 to 3000 words, stories and memoirs 4000 words or less, and poetry 100 lines or less. Exceptions are possible.

6. Critical articles that deal with books, films, theater performances, art exhibits, etc. should cite these occasions at the front of the article, using the following format:

Book Title
by Author's Name.
Publisher, Year Published, Price (cloth) (paper).

Remember that The Threepenny Review is a quarterly and national (and in some respects international publication), therefore, each 'review' should actually be an essay, broader than the specific event it covers and of interest to people who cannot see the event.

7. Writers will be consulted on all significant editing done on their articles, and will have the opportunity to proofread galleys for typographical errors.

8. It is recommended that those submitting work for the first time to The Threepenny Review take a look at a sample copy beforehand. Sample copies are available from the publisher for $12.00.

9. We do not read manuscripts in the second half of the year (July through

December), so please do not submit work during those six months. Anything sent them will be discarded unread. The only two ways to submit work to us are through the mail and via our online system."

Voices.con Newsletter
PO Box 361
King City, CA 93930

The Voices.Con Newsletter is written exclusively by term-to-life prisoners, unless otherwise noted, focusing on issues of primary concern to those serving a long-tern incarceration: The newsletter is published monthly at the VoicesDotCon.org website. This information has been designed to be of potential benefit in any jurisdiction having term-to-life prisoners and is made available to any other supportive family and friends as well. No persons affiliated with the Voices.Con newsletter are lawyers. Information provided herein is not intended as a substitute for proper legal advice. All questions or comments on information contained herein should be directed to Janet@VoicesDotCon.org.

Suggested Guidelines for Submissions:

1. We have only one agenda; advocating on behalf of the term-to-life prisoner and distributing information that will further this cause, enabling the term-to-life prisoner to effectively advocate on his or her own behalf.

2. You may write an essay/article on any related subject or issue of concern to the term-to-life prisoner population.
3. We prefer that all submissions be between 250 and 500 words. Please clearly print or type all submitted material.
4. We also accept and encourage all submissions of topical artwork. Please include a SASE with any submissions of artwork or written material where a return has been requested.

Website: VoicesDotCon.org
Email: Publisher@VoicesDotCon.org

Walk In Those Shoes
c/o Kimberly Carter
POB 70092
Henrico, VA 23255

The United States is the most incarcerated country on the planet. Housed in our prisons are some people who have committed heinous crimes. Also, hundreds there are the mentally ill; the innocent; those not yet charged; the addicted; the young and reckless; those raised in poverty by addicted parents; those whose only role models were drug dealers; those who had court appointed legal representation with a backlog of cases; those caught up in mandatory minimums; those whose parents were incarcerated before them; and those who were charged as young adults who, two and three decades later, are no longer the people they were when they entered. They've grown up and fully matured. They've changed their lives for the better, but they are serving life sentences and will never be given another chance.

We can do better. Walk In Those Shoes is about compassion and opening the door to creative solutions. While supporting creative writing and reading, we can also shed light on issues that could be improved. Acknowledging there is work to be done is the starting point for change, and giving those on the inside a platform to start the discussion not only benefits them, but also readers. Raising awareness goes hand in hand with literacy here.

It's through struggle we find our strength and although some will visit the site and get angry about the crimes represented here, it's the hope more will see past that to the potential and also gain an understanding of what can go wrong when the system doesn't work as it should.

Our Purpose...

Compassion and mercy are a great place to start repairing our prison 'system'. Walk In Those Shoes is here to promote empathy through the writing and experiences of those caught up in it.

There is an entire world behind walls and inside courtrooms that is too often misunderstood and never experienced. Things can go wrong and when they do, families pay the price, sometimes for generations.

A talented, motivated attorney is a bright light and can be an advocate. An unethical attorney can ruin countless lives during the course of a career.

A fair-minded judge can see through drama – a courtroom is more than half drama – and find the truth. A racist judge can ruin countless lives during a career.

A fair sentence and treatment can get a life on track. An overzealous prosecutor with no interest in truth can ruin countless lives during a career.

A prison that's designed to allow growth, through structure, rules and opportunities can give children a better version of their parents. A prison run by the 'good ole boys club', with little training and a loathing for those that reside there can ruin countless lives along with their families during their existence.

Change starts with awareness, and Walk In Those Shoes aims to encourage incarcerated writers to share their experiences while achieving literary goals.

When possible, Walk In Those Shoes will advocate for those suffering injustice.

Contact Us...

If you are currently or formerly incarcerated, are a family member of someone who is incarcerated, or care about mass incarceration in this country, we'd love to hear your thoughts.

Views From The Inside is exclusively for the writing of those in prison. Submissions most likely to be posted are those that are thought provoking and make us feel. What is most
often rejected is work that is polarizing and confrontational. Our goal is to communicate the issues in a way that lends itself to producing positive change and revealing the limitless potential behind bars.

We often post writing that helps the reader get a picture of life behind bars, everything from getting laundry done, to loneliness, to relations with staff and cell mates. Submissions
that share stories of life prior to incarceration are also considered, if they help to reflect the heart of the person who is incarcerated, or describe how they may have gotten on a path
to prison.

Please do not submit previously published material. Submissions are always accepted and cannot be returned. We consider a submission permission to edit and post. Length is very flexible, although 1,500 words or less is a typical post. Handwritten submissions are accepted.

Poetry is considered.

We also work with a handful of writers in achieving their goal of book publishing. There are always several book projects going on at one time with very limited resources, so if time is of the essence this would not be a good option.

We are building a 'library' of books written from behind bars. Write me or send me a sample of your work at the above address.

As stated above, we occasionally work with book authors of all genres in all aspects of completing their work. If you would like assistance making your story a reality, feel free to submit a chapter to the above address. We will get back to you as soon as possible if we can assist you. We hope to encourage writers to achieve their goals.

Word Out Books
PO 2689
Eugene, OR 97402

Word Out Books, an imprint of Winding Hall Publishers, is based on a straightforward principle:

Writers deserve to be heard. We make it possible for writers of all genres, and from all backgrounds and circumstances, to become published authors.

When your book is published by Word Out Books, it is not "self-published" – it is published by a real publishing company under the Word Out imprint.

By charging fair, transparent fees up front, Word Out Books allows authors whose works might otherwise never be published to see their books in print and made available to the world.

How It Works

Our range of services includes publishing your manuscript in book form and making it available for sale in print and e-book on Amazon and other online outlets, as well as editing and cover design services. When you submit your original manuscript by mail or email, an editor will read your manuscript and contact you with the services we offer based on your submission. Some services, such as typing a manuscript that was submitted handwritten, or scanning a typed manuscript, will be required in order for us to publish your book. Other services, such as copy editing and premium book cover design, are optional. We also offer typing, editing and book cover design as individually priced services.

Services and Fees

Required Services and Fees: In order to publish your book, we must have payment up front for all required and selected optional services. We accept installment payments, but will not begin work on your project until all payment is received.

Required services include: Publishing Service - $335

Our Publishing Service includes the following:

1. Registering your work with the United States Copyright Office. (You keep all copyright ownership of your work. Word Out Books is granted exclusive publication rights.)
2. Book cover with text only (no images)
3. ISBN – Every book sold commercially must have an International Standard Book Number assigned to it. Each edition and version of a book – for examples, an e-book and a paperback edition of the same book – must have its own ISBN. Single ISBNs cost $125, but our publishing company buys at volume discounts to save you money. We will assign ISBNs to the print (paperback) and ebook versions of your book.
4. Formatting and setup of your book in both paperback and ebook versions.
5. Setup and management of

sales on Amazon.com, the largest bookseller in the world, and other online outlets.

6. One free copy of your book shipped to your address.

7. Marketing for your book through social media, plus outstanding customer support.

Typing or Scanning Services: Unless your manuscript is submitted via email, it will either need to be typed (if handwritten) or scanned (if submitted typed). You will need to pay either the typing or scanning per-page fees (not both):

Typing - $2.50 per page:

We understand that not every author has access to word processing or typing equipment. Word Out Books is happy to accept handwritten manuscripts, provided they can easily be read. If we cannot read your handwriting, we may ask that you re-submit the manuscript printed by hand in block, capital letters. Please write clearly. If we can't read it, we can't publish it!

Scanning - $1.00 per page:

All typed manuscript pages submitted as a–hard copy (not by email) will need to be scanned into our computer system. Pages should be free of any stray marks, smudges or handwritten notes as these will not scan properly. If the scanned document results in too many errors, there will be an extra $1/page charge to manually correct errors, which must be paid before publication starts.

Optional Services and Fees: The following services are optional and are charged in addition to the required fees listed above. Professional editing and an eye-catching cover will make your work much more desirable to the reading public.

Editing

All books, even works by best-selling authors published by the largest publishing houses, require editing to be marketable. You can choose which level of editing you want for your work. Editing fees are added to the per-page typing or scanning rates above.

Proofreading Edit – $2 per submitted typed of handwritten page: Corrects basic punctuation, spelling, and capitalization errors.

Copy Edit – $4 per submitted typed or hand–written page: In addition to basic editing, our Copy-Editing Service corrects grammar and syntax mistakes, notes inconsistencies, and provides other suggestions to improve the quality of writing. You can review our editing suggestions and accept or reject them prior to publication. We strongly urge you to consider copy editing if you plan to sell your book to the public.

Book Cover Design

Color, Text and Simple Graphic $75
Premium Full Graphic $125

Royalties

Word Out Books will set the price at which your book is sold ("list price"). Royalties are based on a percentage of the book's selling price and will vary, depending upon the length of the book, whether it is a print or ebook, and other factors. Royalties are paid quarterly. You will receive a royalty statement showing how many copies were sold and the rate at which your royalties were calculated. We will pay royalties by check to the name and address specified by you.

How To Get Started

1. Send us a copy of your manuscript.
2. Include any additional comments, questions or information you'd like us to have.

VERY IMPORTANT: Please be sure you do not send us the only copy of your manuscript! Manuscripts cannot be returned, regardless of whether we ultimately publish them!

What We Will Do

Once we have received your manuscript, we will contact you regarding the publication services we are able to offer you and enclose a form for you to complete with the services you are requesting. Rarely, we must decline to publish a manuscript, usually because it violates one of our publication policies.

Word Out Books does not publish the following:

- Books that advocate the commission of crimes or incitement to commit crimes

- Books that could be considered libelous

- Books designed to allow a person convicted of a crime to profit from that crime

- Other books which, in our exclusive editorial judgement, violate the ethical principles of our company

- Invoicing

When we accept your manuscript for publication, we will send you an invoice requesting payment for the services you have chosen. Payment may be made by check, bank draft, or money order. We do not accept credit card payment or cash.

We will not begin work until all requested services have been paid. After publication work has begun, fees are non–refundable. If you wish to cancel publication or other services you've ordered, please contact us within 10 business days of payment, so that we can process your refund.

Please Note: If we do not receive your payment or a request for additional time for payment within 90 days of our receipt of your manuscript, we will assume the project is a no–go and will destroy the manuscript without further obligation to the author. We cannot keep unpaid manuscripts indefinitely. Again, please do not send us the only
copy of your work!

Please let us know if you have any questions regarding our services or fees. We're always happy to answer your questions. We want to help you get your word out to the world with Word Our Books!

Website: WordOutBooks.com

Email: Editor@WordOutBooks.com

Wow Me Web Designs
PO 7879
Flint, MI 48507

Hello Everyone,
I've been getting hundreds of letters and I want to apologize if you did not get a response in a timely manner. I have been very busy and could not handle all of the orders on my own. In July, 2018 I hired two web designers and two graphic designers to help me with the heavy work load. My new employees are just as skilled as I am and I have entrusted them to produce high quality work and service on behalf of my company. I hope the following helps with any questions you have about our services. Thank you. Jazzie, at Wow Me Web Design

ONE PAGE WEBSITE - $109.99

Our one-page websites are for businesses that just want to get their name out and are working with a small budget. Direct your clients to your website to learn more about your business, what products or services you sell, make an online donation/payment, or contact you with questions.

This package includes:

- Basic Company Logo
- Contact Information
- Payments/Donations Button
- Image Banner/Slider
- Social Media Links
- List of Services
- 3 Images

THREE PAGE WEBSITES - $299.99

Our three-page websites will give you all the same functions as above, but we put your services and contact information on its own separate page. In addition, you get 3 blogs, 8 photos,

1 video, and add your social media feed.

This package includes:

- Basic Company Logo
- Contact Information
- 3 Blogs
- Social Media Feed Image Banner/Slider Social Media Links
- 8 Photos For Gallery Payments/Donations Button
- List of Services 6 Images
- 1 Video

The above packages are great for: Authors/Books, Stores with 3 products or less, Personal Sites, Donation Sites, Small Businesses, Consulting, Landing Page, Blogs, Informational Sites, Artist, Small Non-Profit, Marketing, Activist, Resource Site, Small Law Office, Small Medical Practices

PREMIUM WEBSITE PACKAGES – $549.99 (Payment Plan Accepted)

Our premium websites are for non-profits and businesses with a wide range of products and services.

This package includes: (Choose Your 10 Pages)

- Home
- About
- Contact

- Payments
- Donate
- Events
- 3 Blog
- Sermons
- 7 Video Gallery
- 10 Photo Gallery
- Services
- Resources
- Testimonials
- Shop (3 Product Limit)
- Music mp3
- Informational Page
- Coupon Page

Includes Add-Ons:

- Basic Company Logo
- Contact Information
- Social Media Feed
- Image Banner/Slider
- Social Media Links
- Customer Chat Box
- List of Services
- 10 Images
- Email Capturer Box

E–COMMERCE / ONLINE STORE PACKAGES (Payment Plan Accepted)

Our full ecommerce sites start at $749.99. Get everything included in the premium package, with an addition to 35 products/pages installed and shipping and credit/debit card processing.

ADD-ONS

- Business Email Address, $12.99/year
- Extra Pages, $49.99
- Social Media Account Setup, $29.99
- Custom Logo, $79.99 Flyers, $69.99
- Banners, $69.99
- Business Cards, $39.99
- Brochure Tri-Fold, $79.99

- Online Chat Box, $79.99

- Small 3-5 Product Store, $149.99
- Email Capture Box, $59.99

- Large Posters, $79.99
- Bookmarks, $14.99
- Postcards, $69.99
- Google Business Number, $19.99
- Google Business Page Setup, $29.99
- Book Covers Basic, $69.99

- Book Covers Custom, $149.99
- Domain Names, $10.99/year

- Website Hosting, $10.99/month
- Ecommerce Website Hosting, $24.99/month (or pay by the year)
- Google Analytics – Track your website interactions, $79.99

- Google Adsense Setup – Make money selling ad space on your website from Google.
- Get 10,000 views on your website a month and Google will pay you $500-$800/month. $129.99/year
- Live Video or Audio Website Feed. Set up Facebook, Podcast, or YouTube. $79.99
- Social Media Management – Monthly service. Cancel anytime. Add friends, get messages mailed or emailed to you weekly. $39.99/month
- 30 Second Advertising Commercials, $79.99
- SEO: Starting at $499/month. Request personal quote.

COMMON QUESTIONS

What is social media feed? Anything you post on social media such as Facebook will also appear on your website.

How do I make payments? Pay by check, money order, paypal, or our website.

When will I receive my login information? All login and account information will be mailed or emailed to you after payment is received in full.

Can I update my website? Yes. After your website is paid in full, you will receive instruction on how to keep it updated.

What are your update fees? If you prefer for us to keep your website updated (change wording, videos, pictures, etc.), fees range from $35-$400/month. Maintenance and Security updates are free.

How long to complete graphic work? All graphic work can take 1-3 days to complete, such as flyers, business cards, and brochures.

Can I get a picture of my site or graphic work? Yes. Please send a SASE for a color copy.

Will my website or graphic work be customized? Yes. All of our work is customized and tailored to fit the customer's vision.

What if I already have a logo? Please email your logo to contact@wowmewebdesigns.com.

What if I've already purchased a domain and/or hosting? We only use GoDaddy, but if you have a hosting or domain account, please mail or email us the company's name, web address, with your user name and password and we will build your site using that account.

Are your websites mobile ready? Yes. All our sites are mobile ready with up-to-date browser standards.

Down payment options? If your website or graphic is over $500, you may pay 50 percent down and the remaining balance after completion.

Do you print graphics? No, we are a design company, but we do have a printing company that we partner with for special orders. We offer 500 printed fliers for $30. Please send request with SASE.

When will you start my project? As soon as your payment is received. Do you do special requests? Yes. Please send request with SASE.

Can you add to our site later? Yes. You can add different plugins and extra pages at any time.
How long will my site take? Estimated completion times are 2-3 days for a 1-page site; 3-5 days for a 3-page site; 2-3 weeks for a 10-page site; 4-8 weeks for an ecommerce site.

Website: wowmewebdesigns.com

Email/Corrlinks:
contact@wowmewebdesigns.com
Phone: 347-618-9116

Writers' Digest
4700 E. Galbraith Rd
Cincinnati, OH 45236

This magazine covers everything in regards to helping you write and or get published. It's $19.96 for a 1-year subscription, 6 issues per year. To contact Writer's Digest editorial, please e-mail: writersdigest@fwmedia.com

(Note: Due to the high volume of e-mails received, we are unable to answer all questions or requests.)

For query submissions, please e-mail: wdsubmissions@fwmedia.com; (Note: Allow 8-12 weeks for a response.)

For questions regarding Writer's Digest Competitions, contact Writer's Digest Competitions at (715) 445-4612 x13430.

For questions about our monthly Your Story Contest, please email YourStoryContest@fwmedia.com.

Phone Number: (513) 531-2222
Website: writersdigest.com.

Writer's Guild of America - East
555 West 57th St., Suite 1230
New York, NY 10019

This is an organization of professional writers and agents.

Website: wgaeast.org.

Writer's Guild of America - West
7000 West 3rd St.
Los Angeles, CA 90048

This is an organization of professional writers and agents.

MIKE ENEMIGO PRESENTS

THE CELL BLOCK

BOOK SUMMARIES

MIKE ENEMIGO is the new prison/street art sensation who has written and published several books. He is inspired by emotion; hope; pain; dreams and nightmares. He physically lives somewhere in a California prison cell where he works relentlessly creating his next piece. His mind and soul are elsewhere; seeing, studying, learning, and drawing inspiration to tear down suppressive walls and inspire the culture by pushing artistic boundaries.

THE CELL BLOCK is an independent multimedia company with the objective of accurately conveying the prison/street experience with the credibility and honesty that only one who has lived it can deliver, through literature and other arts, and to entertain and enlighten while doing so. Everything published by The Cell Block has been created by a prisoner, while in a prison cell.

THE BEST RESOURCE DIRECTORY FOR PRISONERS, $17.95 & $5.00 S/H: This book has over 1,450 resources for prisoners! Includes: Pen-Pal Companies! Non-Nude Photo Sellers! Free Books and Other Publications! Legal Assistance! Prisoner Advocates! Prisoner Assistants! Correspondence Education! Money-Making Opportunities! Resources for Prison Writers, Poets, Artists! And much, much more! Anything you can think of doing from your prison cell, this book contains the resources to do it!

A GUIDE TO RELAPSE PREVENTION FOR PRISONERS, $15.00 & $5.00 S/H: This book provides the information and guidance that can make a real difference in the preparation of a comprehensive relapse prevention plan. Discover how to meet the parole board's expectation using these proven and practical principles. Included is a blank template and sample relapse prevention plan to assist in your preparation.

CONSPIRACY THEORY, $12.00 & $4.00 S/H: Kokain is an upcoming rapper trying to make a name for himself in the Sacramento, CA underground scene, and Nicki is his girlfriend. One night, in October, Nicki's brother, along with her brother's best friend, go to rob a house of its $100,000 marijuana crop. It goes wrong; shots are fired and a man is killed. Later, as investigators begin closing in on Nicki's brother and his friend, they, along with the help of a few others, create a way to make Kokain take the fall .... The conspiracy begins.

THEE ENEMY OF THE STATE (SPECIAL EDITION), $9.99 & $4.00 S/H: Experience the inspirational journey of a kid who was introduced to the art of rapping in 1993, struggled between his dream of becoming a professional rapper and the reality of the streets, and was finally offered a recording deal in 1999, only to be arrested minutes later and eventually sentenced to life in prison for murder... However, despite his harsh reality, he dedicated himself to hip-hop once again, and with resilience and determination, he sets out to prove he may just be one of the dopest rhyme writers/spitters ever .... At this point, it becomes deeper than rap .... Welcome to a preview of the greatest story you never heard.

LOST ANGELS: $15.00 & $5.00: David Rodrigo was a child who belonged to no world; rejected for his mixed heritage by most of his family and raised by an outcast uncle in the mean streets of East L.A. Chance cast him into a far darker and more devious pit of intrigue that stretched from the barest gutters to the halls of power in the great city. Now, to survive the clash of lethal forces arrayed about him, and to protect those he loves, he has only two allies; his quick wits, and the flashing blade that earned young David the street name, Viper.

LOYALTY AND BETRAYAL DELUXE EDITION, $19.99 & $7.00 S/H: Chunky was an associate of and soldier for the notorious Mexican Mafia – La Eme. That is, of course, until he was betrayed by those, he was most loyal to. Then he vowed to become their worst enemy. And though they've attempted to kill him numerous times, he still to this day is running around making a mockery of their organization .... This is the story of how it all began.

MONEY IZ THE MOTIVE: SPECIAL 2-IN-1 EDITION, $19.99 & $7.00 S/H: Like most kids growing up in the hood, Kano has a dream of going from rags to riches. But when his plan to get fast money by robbing the local "mom and pop" shop goes wrong, he quickly finds himself sentenced to serious prison time. Follow Kano as he is schooled to the ways of the game by some of the most respected OGs whoever did it; then is set free and given the resources to put his schooling into action and build the ultimate hood empire...

DEVILS & DEMONS: PART 1, $15.00 & $5.00 S/H: When Talton leaves the West Coast to set up shop in Florida he meets the female version of himself: A drug dealing murderess with psychological issues. A whirlwind of sex, money and murder inevitably ensues and Talton finds himself on the run from the law with nowhere to turn to. When his team from home finds out he's in trouble, they get on a plane heading south...

DEVILS & DEMONS: PART 2, $15.00 & $5.00 S/H:
The Game is bitter-sweet for Talton, aka Gangsta. The same West Coast Clique who came to his aid ended up putting bullets into the chest of the woman he had fallen in love with. After leaving his ride or die in a puddle of her own blood, Talton finds himself on a flight back to Oak Park, the neighborhood where it all started...

DEVILS & DEMONS: PART 3, $15.00 & $5.00 S/H:
Talton is on the road to retribution for the murder of the love of his life. Dante and his crew of killers are on a path of no return. This urban classic is based on real-life West Coast underworld politics. See what happens when a group of YG's find themselves in the midst of real underworld demons...

DEVILS & DEMONS: PART 4, $15.00 & $5.00 S/H:
After waking up from a coma, Alize has locked herself away from the rest of the world. When her sister Brittany and their friend finally take her on a girl's night out, she meets Luck – a drug dealing womanizer.

THE ART & POWER OF LETTER WRITING FOR PRISONERS: DELUXE EDITION $19.99 & $7.00 S/H: When locked inside a prison cell, being able to write well is the most powerful skill you can have! Learn how to increase your power by writing high-quality personal and formal letters! Includes letter templates, pen-pal website strategies, punctuation guide and more!

THE PRISON MANUAL: $24.99 & $7.00 S/H: The Prison Manual is your all-in-one book on how to not only survive the rough terrain of the American prison system, but use it to your advantage so you can THRIVE from it! How to Use Your Prison Time to YOUR Advantage; How to Write Letters that Will Give You Maximum Effectiveness; Workout and Physical Health Secrets that Will Keep You as FIT as Possible; The Psychological impact of incarceration and How to Maintain Your MAXIMUM Level of Mental Health; Prison Art Techniques; Fulfilling Food Recipes; Parole Preparation Strategies and much, MUCH more!

GET OUT, STAY OUT!, $16.95 & $5.00 S/H: This book should be in the hands of everyone in a prison cell. It reveals a challenging but clear course for overcoming the obstacles that stand between prisoners and their freedom. For those behind bars, one goal outshines all others: GETTING OUT! After being released, that goal then shifts to STAYING OUT! This book will help prisoners do both. It has been masterfully constructed into five parts that will help prisoners maximize focus while they strive to accomplish whichever goal is at hand.

MOB$TAR MONEY, $12.00 & $4.00 S/H: After Trey's mother is sent to prison for 75 years to life, he and his little brother are moved from their home in Sacramento, California, to his grandmother's house in Stockton, California where he is forced to find his way in life and become a man on his own in the city's grimy streets. One day, on his way home from the local corner store, Trey has a rough encounter with the neighborhood bully. Luckily, that's when Tyson, a member of the MOBTAR, a local "get money" gang comes to his aid. The two kids quickly become friends, and it doesn't take long before Trey is embraced into the notorious MOB$TAR money gang, which opens the door to an adventure full of sex, money, murder and mayhem that will change his life forever... You will never guess how this story ends!

BLOCK MONEY, $12.00 & $4.00 S/H: Beast, a young thug from the grimy streets of central Stockton, California lives The Block; breathes The Block; and has committed himself to bleed The Block for all it's worth until his very last breath. Then, one day, he meets Nadia; a stripper at the local club who piques his curiosity with her beauty, quick-witted intellect and rider qualities. The problem? She has a man – Esco – a local kingpin with money and power. It doesn't take long, however, before a devious plot is hatched to pull off a heist worth an indeterminable amount of money. Following the acts of treachery, deception and betrayal are twists and turns and a bloody war that will leave you speechless!

HOW TO HUSTLE AND WIN: SEX, MONEY, MURDER EDITION $15.00 & $5.00 S/H: How To Hu$tle and Win: Sex, Money, Murder edition is the grittiest, underground self-help manual for the 21st century street entrepreneur in print. Never has there been such a book written for today's gangsters, goons and go-getters. This self-help handbook is an absolute must-have for anyone who is actively connected to the streets.

RAW LAW: YOUR RIGHTS, & HOW TO SUE WHEN THEY ARE VIOLATED! $15.00 & $5.00 S/H: Raw Law For Prisoners is a clear and concise guide for prisoners and their advocates to understanding civil rights laws guaranteed to prisoners under the US Constitution, and how to successfully file a lawsuit when those rights have been violated! From initial complaint to trial, this book will take you through the entire process, step by step, in simple, easy-to-understand terms. Also included are several examples where prisoners have sued prison officials successfully, resulting in changes of unjust rules and regulations and recourse for rights violations, oftentimes resulting in rewards of thousands, even millions of dollars in damages! If you feel your rights have been violated, don't lash out at guards, which is usually ineffective and only makes matters worse. Instead, defend yourself successfully by using the legal system, and getting the power of the courts on your side!

HOW TO WRITE URBAN BOOKS FOR MONEY & FAME: $16.95 & $5.00 S/H: Inside this book you will learn the true story of how Mike Enemigo and King Guru have received money and fame from inside their prison cells by writing urban books; the secrets to writing hood classics so you, too, can be caked up and famous; proper punctuation using hood examples; and resources you can use to achieve your money motivated ambitions! If you're a prisoner who want to write urban novels for money and fame, this must-have manual will give you all the game!

PRETTY GIRLS LOVE BAD BOYS: AN INMATE'S GUIDE TO GETTING GIRLS: $15.00 & $5.00 S/H: Tired of the same, boring, cliché pen pal books that don't tell you what you really need to know? If so, this book is for you! Anything you need to know on the art of long and short distance seduction is included within these pages! Not only does it give you the science of attracting pen pals from websites, it also includes psychological profiles and instructions on how to seduce any woman you set your sights on! Includes interviews of women who have fallen in love with prisoners, bios for pen pal ads, pre-written love letters, romantic poems, love-song lyrics, jokes and much, much more! This book is the ultimate guide – a must-have for any prisoner who refuses to let prison walls affect their MAC'n.

THE LADIES WHO LOVE PRISONERS, $15.00 & $5.00 S/H: New Special Report reveals the secrets of real women who have fallen in love with prisoners, regardless of crime, sentence, or location. This info will give you a HUGE advantage in getting girls from prison.

GET OUT, GET RICH: HOW TO GET PAID LEGALLY WHEN YOU GET OUT OF PRISON!, $16.95 & $5.00 S/H: Many of you are incarcerated for a money-motivated crime. But w/ today's tech & opportunities, not only is the crime-for-money risk/reward ratio not strategically wise, it's not even necessary. You can earn much more money by partaking in anyone of the easy, legal hustles explained in this book, regardless of your record. Help yourself earn an honest income so you can not only make a lot of money, but say good-bye to penitentiary chances and prison forever!

(Note: Many things in this book can even he done from inside prison.) (ALSO PUBLISHED AS HOOD MILLIONAIRE: HOW TO HUSTLE AND WIN LEGALLY!)

THE MILLIONAIRE PRISONER: PART 1, $16.95 & $5.00 S/H

THE MILLIONAIRE PRISONER: PART 2, $16.95 & $5.00 S/H

THE MILLIONAIRE PRISONER: SPECIAL 2-IN-1 EDITION, $24.99 & $7.00 S/H: Why wait until you get out of prison to achieve your dreams? Here's a blueprint that you can use to become successful! The Millionaire Prisoner is your complete reference to overcoming any obstacle in prison. You won't be able to put it down! With this book you will discover the secrets to: Making money from your cell! Obtain FREE money for correspondence courses! Become an expert on any topic! Develop the habits of the rich! Network with celebrities! Set up your own website! Market your products, ideas and services! Successfully use prison pen pal websites! All of this and much, much more! This book has enabled thousands of prisoners to succeed and it will show you the way also!

THE MILLIONAIRE PRISONER 3: SUCCESS UNIVERSITY, $16.95 & $5 S/H: Why wait until you get out of prison to achieve your dreams? Here's a new-look blueprint that you can use to be successful! The Millionaire Prisoner 3 contains advanced strategies to overcoming any obstacle in prison. You won't be able to put it down!

THE CEO MANUAL: HOW TO START A BUSINESS WHEN YOU GET OUT OF PRISON, $16.95 & $5.00 S/H: $16.95 & $5 S/H: This new book will teach you the simplest way to start your own business when you get out of prison. Includes: Start-up Steps! The Secrets to Pulling Money from Investors! How to Manage People Effectively! How To Legally Protect Your Assets from "them"! Hundreds of resources to get you started, including a list of 'loan friendly" banks! (ALSO PUBLISHED AS CEO MANUAL: START A BUSINESS, BE A BOSS!)

THE MONEY MANUAL: UNDERGROUND CASH SECRETS EXPOSED! 16.95 & $5.00 S/H: Becoming a millionaire is equal parts what you make, and what you don't spend – AKA save. All Millionaires and Billionaires have mastered the art of not only making money, but keeping the money they make (remember Donald Trump's tax maneuvers?), as well as establishing credit so that they are loaned money by banks and trusted with money from investors: AKA OPM -- other people's money. And did you know there are millionaires and billionaires just waiting to GIVE money away? It's true! These are all very-little known secrets 'they" don't want YOU to know about, but that I'm exposing in my new book!

OJ'S LIFE BEHIND BARS, $15.00 & $5 S/H: In 1994, Heisman Trophy winner and NFL superstar OJ Simpson was arrested for the brutal murder of his ex-wife Nicole Brown-Simpson and her friend Ron Goldman. In 1995, after the "trial of the century," he was acquitted of both murders, though most of the world believes he did it. In 2007 OJ was again arrested, but this time in Las Vegas, for armed robbery and kidnapping. On October 3, 2008 he was found guilty sentenced to 33 years and was sent to Lovelock Correctional Facility, in Lovelock, Nevada. There he met inmate-author Vernon Nelson. Vernon was granted a true, insider's perspective into the mind and life of one of the country's most notorious men; one that has never provided…until now.

BMF, $18.99 & $5 S/H: The Black Mafia Family was a drug organization headed by brothers Demetrius "Big Meech" Flenory and Terry "Southwest T" Flenory. Rising up from the shadows of Detroit's underbelly, they created a cross-country cocaine network, becoming two of the wealthiest, most dangerously sophisticated drug traffickers the United States has ever seen.

BLACK DYNASTY, $15.00 & $5 S/H: After their parents are murdered in cold blood, the Black siblings are left to fend for themselves in the unforgiving streets. But when the oldest brother, Lorenzo, is introduced to his deceased father's drug connection, he is given the opportunity of a lifetime to put his family back on top.

AOB, $15.00 & $5 S/H: Growing up in the Bay Area, Manny Fresh the Best had a front-row seat to some of the coldest players to ever do it. And you already know, A.O.B. is the name of the Game! So, When Manny Fresh slides through Stockton one day and sees Rosa, a stupid-bad Mexican chick with a whole lotta 'talent' behind her walking down the street tryna get some money, he knew immediately what he had to do: Put it In My Pocket!

PIMPOLOGY: THE 7 ISMS OF THE GAME, $15.00 & $5 S/H: It's been said that if you knew better, you'd do better. So, in the spirit of dropping jewels upon the rare few who truly want to know how to win, this collection of exclusive Game has been compiled. And though a lot of so-called players claim to know how the Pimp Game is supposed to go, none have revealed the real. . . Until now!

JAILHOUSE PUBLISHING FOR MONEY, POWER & FAME: $24.99 & $7 S/H: In 2010, after flirting with the idea for two years, Mike Enemigo started writing his first book. In 2014, he officially launched his publishing company, The Cell Block, with the release of five books. Of course, with no mentor(s), how-to guides, or any real resources, he was met with failure after failure as he tried to navigate the treacherous goal of publishing books from his prison cell. However, he was determined to make it. He was determined to figure it out and he refused to quit. In Mike's new book, Jailhouse Publishing for Money, Power, and Fame, he breaks down all his jailhouse publishing secrets and strategies, so you can do all he's done, but without the trials and tribulations he's had to go through...

KITTY KAT, ADULT ENTERTAINMENT RESOURCE BOOK, $24.99 & $7.00 S/H: This book is jam packed with hundreds of sexy non nude photos including photo spreads. The book contains the complete info on sexy photo sellers, hot magazines, page turning bookstore, sections on strip clubs, porn stars, alluring models, thought provoking stories and must-see movies.

PRISON LEGAL GUIDE, $24.99 & $7.00 S/H: The laws of the U.S. Judicial system are complex, complicated, and always growing and changing. Many prisoners spend days on end digging through its intricacies. Pile on top of the legal code the rules and regulations of a correctional facility, and you can see how high the deck is being stacked against you. Correct legal information is the key to your survival when you have run afoul of the system (or it is running afoul of you). Whether you are an accomplished jailhouse lawyer helping newbies learn the ropes, an old head fighting bare-knuckle for your rights in the courts, or a hustler just looking to beat the latest write-up – this book has something for you!

PRISON HEALTH HANDBOOK, $19.99 & $7.00 S/H: The Prison Health Handbook is your one-stop go-to source for information on how to maintain your best health while inside the American prison system. Filled with information, tips, and secrets from doctors, gurus, and other experts, this book will educate you on such things as proper workout and exercise regimens; yoga benefits for prisoners; how to meditate effectively; pain management tips; sensible dieting solutions; nutritional knowledge; an understanding of various cancers, diabetes, hepatitis, and other diseases all too common in prison; how to effectively deal with mental health issues such as stress, PTSD, anxiety, and depression; a list of things your doctors DON'T want YOU to know; and much, much more!

All books are available on Amazon and thecellblock.net website. Prices may differ between Amazon and our website.

You can also order by sending a money order or institutional check to:

The Cell Block
PO Box 1025
Rancho Cordova, CA 95741

Made in the USA
Columbia, SC
17 February 2023